An Independent Profession

Editors: E. Osborne Ayscue, Jr. and Leslie B. Rindoks

Cover Photo by Kurt Rindoks
Author Photo (Howard Covington) by Joseph Rodriguez
Additional Acknowledgments & Permissions, page 208
Book Design, Leslie Rindoks

The publisher would like to thank Shelia Bumgarner, Robinson-Spangler Room, PLCMC; Maria David, photo librarian at *The Charlotte Observer*; and Kim Andersen Cumber at the North Carolina State Archives for their valuable assistance in locating and providing many of the images in this publication.

ISBN 978-0-9838936-1-5
Library of Congress Control Number: 2011943665
Printed in China

An Independent Profession

A Centennial History of The Mecklenburg County Bar

by
Marion A. Ellis
and
Howard E. Covington, Jr.

with a foreword by
E. Osborne Ayscue, Jr.

LORIMER
PRESS

Davidson, North Carolina
2012

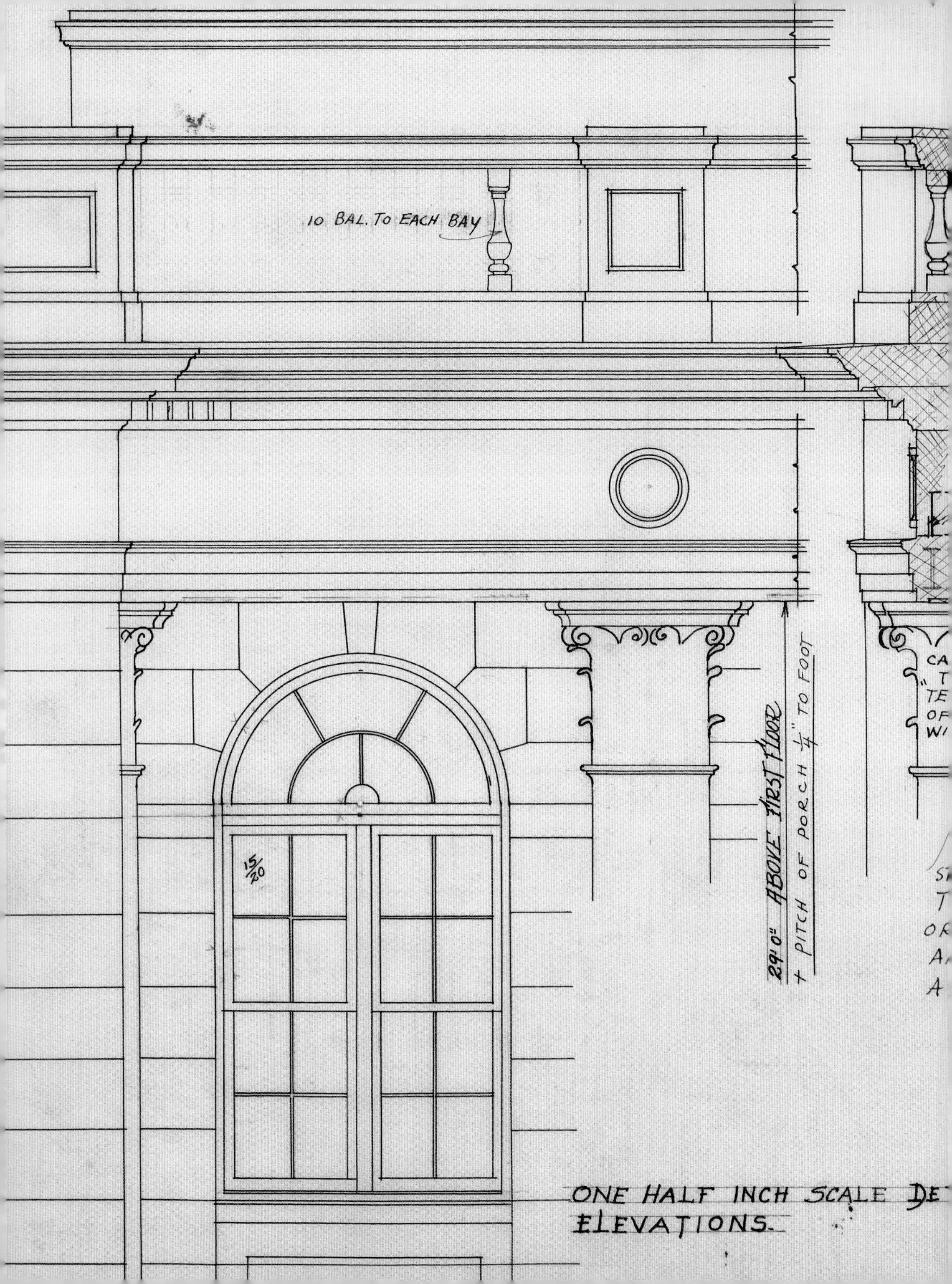
10 BAL. TO EACH BAY
15/20
29'0" ABOVE FIRST FLOOR
+ PITCH OF PORCH 1/4" TO FOOT
ONE HALF INCH SCALE DE
ELEVATIONS.

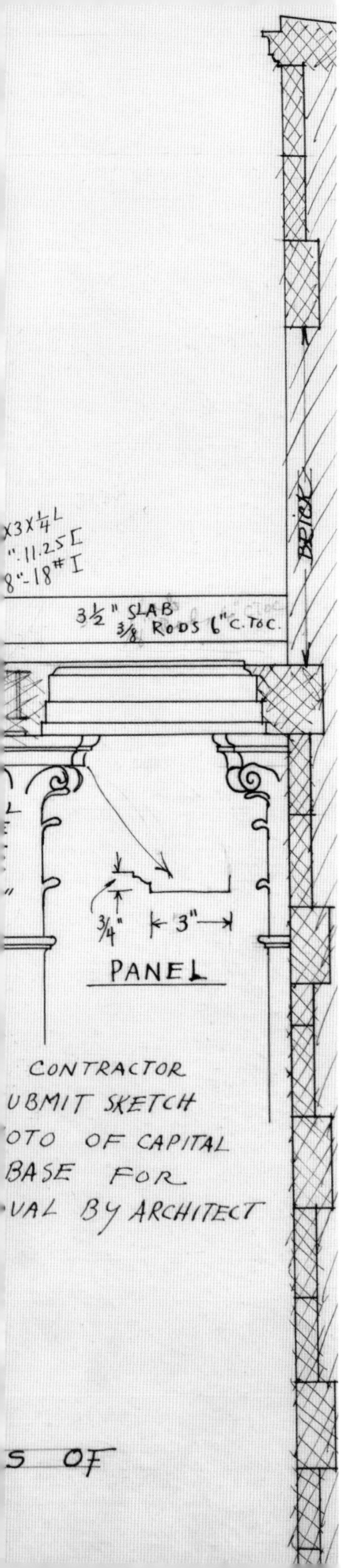

COURTHOUSE ELEVATION BY LOUIS ASBURY

We build on foundations we did not lay.
We warm ourselves at fires we did not light.
We sit in the shade of trees we did not plant.
We drink from wells we did not dig.
Our lives are full of gifts from persons we did not know.

– OLD MAASAI PROVERB

In grateful recognition of the professional legacy
we have inherited from those who have gone before us.

THE MECKLENBURG COUNTY BAR, 2012

TABLE OF CONTENTS

A Compleat MAP of NORTH-CA

LINA *from an actual Survey*. By Captn. Collet Governor of Fort Johnston —— Engraved by I. Bayly.

Hezekiah Alexander statue at the Rock House, Charlotte

Foreword

In 1769, Princeton graduate Waightstill Avery arrived in Charlotte, the county seat of colonial North Carolina's Mecklenburg County, at the urging of his kinsman, Hezekiah Alexander, to set up the community's first law practice.

He found a village of fewer than two hundred citizens located at a small rural crossroad at the intersection of two old Native American trading paths. The new log courthouse on the northeast corner of that crossroad, an edifice that established its identity as a town worthy to be called a county seat, sat on ten-foot high pilings to accommodate a public marketplace underneath. Its sole second-floor room served as courtroom and community meeting place.

From an eighteenth century frontier village that British General Lord Cornwallis had described as a "hornet's nest" after his army's encounter with the local militia and that General George Washington, after a post-war 1791 visit, described in his diary as "a trifling place," by the end of the twentieth century, Charlotte and Mecklenburg County had emerged as a shining symbol of the New South.

Evolving from its early roots in an agrarian economy, through its rise and subsequent decline as the source of most of the nation's gold supply, the home of the nation's first branch Mint, and its later rise and decline as a textile manufacturing center, in the twenty-first century, Charlotte has become an international center of trade and commerce. Its airport, the ninth busiest in the nation, provides non-stop service to most major cities and an assortment of foreign destinations. An energy-producing center, it is the home of the nation's largest publicly-owned electric power company. It has become the nation's second largest banking center and the home of its largest bank.

Charlotte's open society and vibrant economy have attracted people from all over the country, many of them young lawyers. The farms and woodlands that comprised most of the county until well past the middle of the twentieth century are gone. Today an urban and suburban community stretches from one end of the county to the other and indeed spills over into adjoining counties and into nearby South Carolina. The population of the county, increasingly multi-ethnic, is steadily approaching the one million mark, its contiguous trading area approaching two million.

Once a rural backwater, Charlotte is now home to several universities. Its new downtown arts campus includes three museums – one devoted to traditional art, including a nationally recognized collection of arts and crafts, one to a private collection of modern art, one to African American art – and the newest of the community's more than a half dozen performing arts venues. Its downtown is the home of a National Football League team and a National Basketball Association team and, with a tip of the hat to a homegrown sport, the NASCAR Hall of Fame.

A broad religious community has produced leaders ranging from evangelist Billy Graham to free-thinking and sometimes controversial Bishop John Shelby Spong and one of the first seven women who challenged the status quo and forced the ordination of women as priests in the Episcopal Church. In addition to a multitude of Protestant churches, some dating back to colonial times, it now counts among its major religious institutions a Greek Orthodox cathedral, well over a dozen Roman Catholic churches and Shalom Park, an iconic institution that provides on one campus a home for each of the three major branches of Judaism. In recent years, new houses of worship, reflecting a growing mix of other cultures, have appeared.

Charlotte has provided a home for writers and journalists ranging from W. J. Cash, whose seminal work, *The Mind of the South*, defined a region struggling to throw off the yoke of its history, to Harry Golden, whose *Carolina Israelite*, pricked the conscience of the community in the civil rights era. It provided a start to that twentieth century nomad observer of American life, North Carolina native and broadcaster Charles Kuralt.

From its earliest days, the local bar has produced far more than its share of leaders, both in the profession and in the life of community, the state and the nation. Perhaps equally important is the leadership Charlotte-Mecklenburg has provided in the community's moral discourse. From a pre-Civil War slave-holding society, it emerged in the 1970s civil rights era as a model for the nation in dealing with the desegregation of its schools through the process of the law. A bar whose first voluntary professional organization excluded the town's two African American lawyers, in the twentieth century it provided a home for North Carolina's first racially integrated law firm, one that has in the modern era produced more local, state and national leaders, both in the legal profession and in public service, than any other law firm in the community.

From a collegial organization with few formal functions, the local bar has grown into a national model of self-regulation and a creative source of service to the wider community. It is perhaps a symbol of what the community has become and the role that lawyers have played in its history that, as this work was in the editing stage, one of its members became the first Latino judge to be confirmed to the Fourth Circuit Court of Appeals and its current mayor, an African American native of Charlotte, a lawyer, played a major role in attracting to the city the 2012 Democratic National Convention.

The year 2012 will also mark the one hundredth anniversary of the creation of the first formal organization of local lawyers, who had for the preceding 143 years functioned as a collegial group without the benefit of any organizational structure. That anniversary has given rise to the publication of this history, the story of a local bar that began with one lone lawyer in a colonial backwater and has grown into a community of professionals whose numbers now approach 4,500 members.

Three decades into the nineteenth century, French scholar-author Alexis de Tocqueville came to the New World to examine our unique national experiment. He commented at length on the singular role of an independent legal profession in creating and guiding a democratic society that had eschewed traditional aristocracy based on heredity and inherited wealth and rank. The Mecklenburg County bar has played a major role in helping to shape the community's history. In turn, it has been shaped by that history.

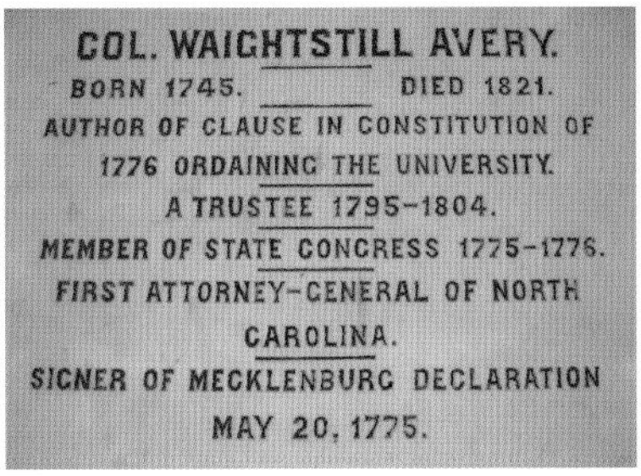
COL. WAIGHTSTILL AVERY.
BORN 1745. DIED 1821.
AUTHOR OF CLAUSE IN CONSTITUTION OF
1776 ORDAINING THE UNIVERSITY.
A TRUSTEE 1795-1804.
MEMBER OF STATE CONGRESS 1775-1776.
FIRST ATTORNEY-GENERAL OF NORTH
CAROLINA.
SIGNER OF MECKLENBURG DECLARATION
MAY 20, 1775.

Authors Marion A. Ellis and Howard E. Covington have produced a fascinating historical account of the role an independent legal profession has played in this community and in the wider world since Waightstill Avery hung out his shingle to practice law at that frontier crossroad two hundred and forty-three years ago.

E. Osborne Ayscue, Jr.
January 1, 2012

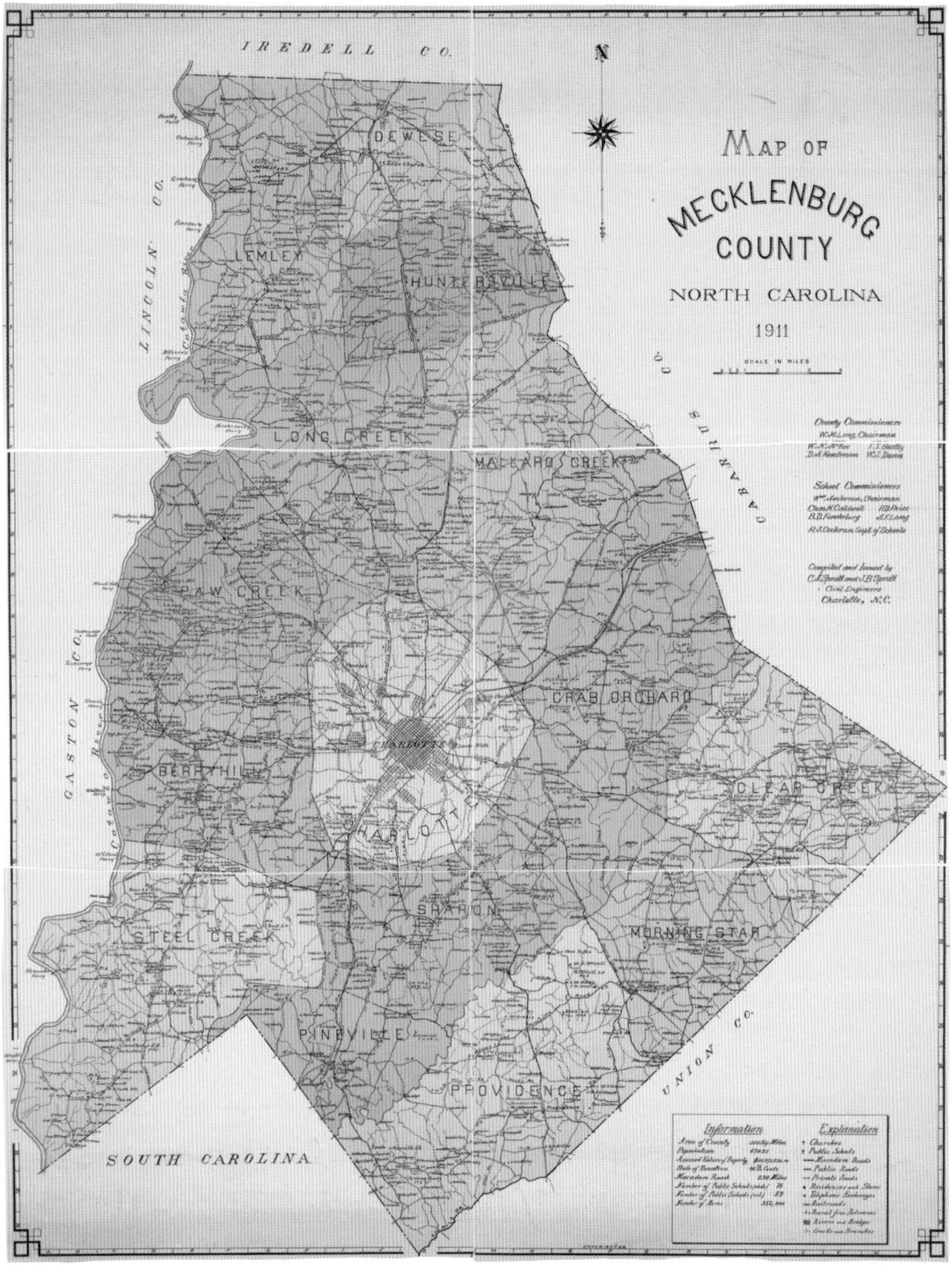

MAP OF
MECKLENBURG
COUNTY
NORTH CAROLINA
1911
SCALE IN MILES
N
IREDELL CO.
LINCOLN CO.
CABARRUS CO.
GASTON CO.
UNION CO.
SOUTH CAROLINA
DEWESE
LEMLEY
HUNTERSVILLE
LONG CREEK
MALLARD CREEK
PAW CREEK
CRAB ORCHARD
CHARLOTTE
BERRYHILL
CLEAR CREEK
SHARON
STEEL CREEK
MORNING STAR
PINEVILLE
PROVIDENCE
County Commissioners
W. M. Long, Chairman
D. A. Henderson
Wm. J. Dunn
School Commissioners
Chas. H. Caldwell
R. J. Cochran, Supt. of Schools
Compiled and Issued by
C. A. Spratt and J. B. Spratt
Civil Engineers
Charlotte, N.C.
Information
Area of County
Population 67031
Assessed Values of Property
Rate of Taxation
Macadam Road 230 Miles
Number of Public Schools (white) 76
Number of Public Schools (col.) 59
Number of Acres 352,000
Explanation
Churches
Public Schools
Macadam Roads
Public Roads
Private Roads
Residences and Stores
Telephone Exchanges
Railroads
Rivers and Bridges
Creeks and Branches

CHAPTER 1
A MODEST BEGINNING

When the Mecklenburg Bar Association, the first formal organization of local lawyers, was created in 1912, perhaps the most noteworthy activity of the group's sixty-two members was an annual mid-winter banquet, where lawyers, judges and court officials, all of whom knew one another well, got together for a good meal and to poke fun at one another. The Association published a few local rules to help manage the court docket, but membership was voluntary. Those who paid the $2 annual dues received a printed court calendar set by a committee of its members.

Indeed, in the collegial group of professionals who made up the local legal community, little else was needed. For most of them, a professional career was the legacy that came with the place in society to which they had been born. Many were themselves the sons of lawyers. Most of them practiced in the same office building. They saw one another almost daily. The creation of the Bar Association formalized a loose association of lawyers that in the mid-1880s had established a law library, supported by its members. A little more than a decade before, a group of predecessors had adopted "rules" that were no more than a schedule of suggested fees for lawyers' services.

The center of the county's legal community was Charlotte, a city that at the dawn of the twentieth century had slowly begun to shake loose from its agrarian past to become a growing center of manufacturing and commerce. It was said that ambitious entrepreneurs in rural communities of the Carolinas could find in Charlotte, the hub of a growing textile industry, everything they needed to equip and open the new mills. These mills created wage-paying jobs along the route of railways laid in the 1850s, one that ran from Richmond to Atlanta, cutting across piedmont North Carolina through Charlotte and on into South Carolina and Georgia, the other an east-west route.

[EDITOR'S NOTE: *Throughout this work, "Bar" denotes the formal governing organization, while "bar" refers collectively to those then engaged in the practice of law.*]

In the intervening years, the railroads pulled Charlotte from obscurity, and by the first decade of the new century the city enjoyed exuberant vitality as a commercial center for an entire region. Charlotte raced past the old port city of Wilmington to become the largest city in the state, and by 1920 its population would reach a then-astonishing 42,000 residents. A little more than a generation earlier, the city's major thoroughfare, Tryon Street, had been virtually impassable when it rained, and the city had a population of fewer than a thousand. Now there were office buildings on Tryon Street, including the state's first steel-framed skyscraper at "the Square," the very cross-road of streets, now called Trade and Tryon, that had been the center of the town from its beginning.

Electric power had arrived in 1904. James B. Duke's Southern Power Company had begun to harness the Catawba River, named for the Native American tribe that once inhabited the region. Its headwaters rise on the slopes of the highest mountains east of the Mississippi River and flow to the Atlantic Ocean. That company, called Duke Power Company throughout most of the twentieth century, produced power from hydroelectric plants along the Catawba.

Along with the entire state of North Carolina, Charlotte-Mecklenburg was changing, and the leaders in the local bar saw the need to respond to those changes. The creation in 1899 of the North Carolina Bar Association, led into existence by Charlotte lawyers, undoubtedly inspired the Mecklenburg lawyers to turn their existing confederation of local lawyers that had for years supported a common law library into a bar association of their own. Its founding came at a time when the profession was on the cusp of change. Americans now sought more accountability from their institutions, both public and private. The Sherman Antitrust Act and the creation of the Interstate Commerce Commission were among the early manifestations of that era of reform. The legal profession needed to follow suit. The press of business also may have motivated the creation of a formal organization. Mecklenburg needed more regular court sessions, and the Association set additional terms of court as an early goal. Its calendar committee, which would run the courts for over half a century, began to control the progress of cases through the court.

The legal profession, too, was changing. From the earliest days, a law license could be obtained with relative ease unless the applicant was a known scoundrel. The requirements were loose; often, with the right sponsors, they were honored more in the breach than in the observance. Candidates for the bar were required to "read" or study law for two years, but the type of instruction they were to receive was left undefined. Most of the senior members of the Mecklenburg bar had learned the law, "read law," while working with one of their elders before standing for an examination before members of the state's highest court. Some of the newer members had attended organized "law schools," but only a handful of those schools, schools like Harvard, Columbia, and Yale, warranted that title. The law school at the University of North Carolina offered two years of instruction under teachers who owed their faculty positions to their years of practice and, occasionally, their service in the state judiciary. Some law students began their studies there as undergraduates. Until the 1920s, only a high school education was necessary for admission to the UNC School of Law. Even then, law students could sit for the bar examination after two years of legal training. A third year was added to the law school curriculum and its faculty began to consist of professors trained in legal academia, but not until the late 1920s did most law students begin to return for the third year.

A law license could be obtained with relative ease unless the applicant was a known scoundrel.

The formation of the North Carolina Bar Association in 1899 and its subsequent adoption the next year of a code of legal ethics addressed the need for a closer examination of how lawyers were trained, how they were licensed and how they conducted themselves professionally. This early code of ethics put North Carolina ahead of its time. Though the American Bar Association had been organized in 1878, it did not adopt such a code until 1908.

PLATT D. WALKER

In 1912, Mecklenburg had its share of extraordinary lawyers. Both Platt D. Walker and Armistead Burwell, law partners, had served on the state's highest court. Heriot Clarkson and his law partner, Charles H. Duls, had helped bring now defunct Elizabeth College to the city. Clarkson had been appointed solicitor (state court prosecutor) in

1904 by Governor Charles B. Aycock. In 1905, Clarkson, Charles W. Tillett, Sr. and George Wilson, along with E. T. Cansler, Sr., had led an Anti-Saloon League campaign that succeeded in eliminating legal whiskey from the community. Clarkson, an active Episcopalian and passionate member of the temperance movement, continued as a leader in the statewide prohibition campaign that succeeded in 1908, when voters approved a measure to ban the sale and manufacture of alcohol in the state. He would later serve on the state Supreme Court for twenty years until his death in 1942. Colonel Thomas LeRoy Kirkpatrick, active in city affairs, was a champion for good roads in the state. Tillett and Walker had figured prominently in the creation of the North Carolina Bar Association, and the latter had been its first president.

HERIOT CLARKSON, STATE COURT PROSECUTOR AND PASSIONATE MEMBER OF THE TEMPERANCE MOVEMENT, CAMPAIGNED SUCCESSFULLY FOR PROHIBITION.

Like a majority of lawyers around the nation, most of the county's lawyers practiced alone in what would now be seen as an uncomplicated world. Their days were filled with drafting wills and deeds, drawing contracts and bills of sale, pursuing claims on behalf of their clients in court or representing their opponents and prosecuting or defending those charged with crime. Experienced trial lawyers like E. T. Cansler might enjoy retainers from the railroads and insurance companies, but the practice of most lawyers was focused on individual clients. A typical lawyer's schedule left time for participation in politics and civic affairs, a role his fellow citizens expected of him.

Charlotte's first Federal Courthouse was located in the 1891 post office building at the corner of West Trade and Mint Streets, next door to the United States Mint, but it would be years before the federal court would become a focal point for local law practice. In 1912, the common ground for attorneys was the county's impressive 1897 courthouse on South Tryon Street, its fourth. Most of the lawyers' offices were in adjacent buildings. Not until 1914 would Julia McGehee Alexander, the city's first female lawyer, open an office in the Latta Arcade, directly across from the courthouse. Other women lawyers would not be far behind.

The growing number of two- and three-member law firms was a sign of things to come. These often involved an older lawyer who took on a younger lawyer to help ease his workload. In exchange, the newcomer learned from the older lawyer's experience and got a start in developing a clientele of his own. Long-term partnerships were unusual, however, as older lawyers went onto the bench, died or left to seek other opportunities.

Fathers also took in their sons. E. T. Cansler and his sons, E. T., Jr. and John, were a significant presence in the Bar for nearly a century. The elder Cansler began his law practice in the late 1880s, and then in 1892 joined Platt D. Walker after Walker's partner, Armistead Burwell, went to the state Supreme Court. When Burwell returned to Charlotte in 1895, the firm was Burwell, Walker & Cansler until seven years later, when Walker was elected to the Supreme Court. A link to that past, John S. Cansler was still in active practice at his death in 1978. A classic dignified Southern gentleman, his luncheon address to newly-licensed lawyers, explaining what their colleagues at the bar would expect of them, was a tradition that had lasted well into the second half of the twentieth century.

The new local Bar Association was to bring more order and dignity to the courts and the profession, to enhance its stature in the community. In its first year, it opposed a decision by the county board of commissioners to hold criminal proceedings in the new county jail. It argued that taking the court to the prisoner, rather than having the accused stand before the bench, would diminish the dignity of the proceedings. Moreover, it pointed out, such a procedure would demoralize the average citizen if,

U.S. Court House and Post Office, completed in 1891. The U.S. District Court for the Western District of North Carolina met here until 1913.

THE COUNTY'S FOURTH COURTHOUSE, ON SOUTH TRYON STREET, BUILT IN 1897

when called to appear as a witness, his testimony was to be taken in the jail.

Over the intervening years, this voluntary 1912 organization, since formalized by statewide legislation to include every licensed lawyer, grew into one whose numbers exceeded those of the bars of several of the fifty states. Underneath it all, however, remained the principles that had guided those sixty-two lawyers who created the 1912 Mecklenburg Bar Association.

"This association is formed," the organizers wrote, "to cultivate the science of jurisprudence, to promote reform in the law, to facilitate the administration of justice and the trial of causes, to elevate the standard of integrity, honor, and courtesy in the legal profession, to encourage thorough and liberal education and to cherish the spirit of brotherhood among the members thereof."

Charles Fagan's bronze statue of Captain Jack, at the intersection of East Fourth Street and Kings Drive

CHAPTER 2

A Rich History

In 1879, when eleven lawyers in the community pooled their resources and organized a badly needed law library, the informal predecessor of the 1912 Mecklenburg Bar Association, Charlotte no longer deserved George Washington's dismissive description as "a trifling place." Then again, in 1879 it was not yet a center of commerce. It was still an overgrown country market town, a county seat where agriculture and farm supplies accounted for most of the trade.

The first session of court in the county was held on February 26, 1763 in the rural home of Thomas Spratt, located on what is now Crescent Avenue. Within five years thereafter, local citizens had built a log courthouse to cement the village's claim to be the county seat. It was to serve the county for forty-two years.

There was a rich local history, and the members of the Mecklenburg bar held fast to that history. It was a threat to life and limb to dispute the events that were said to have taken place on May 20, 1775 in the county's 1768 log courthouse. Legend has it that on that date the people of the town of Charlotte, which they had named for King George III's wife, Princess Charlotte of Mecklenburg, had renounced their allegiance to the Crown and declared their independence. By May 31st, eleven days later, other sessions at the courthouse had produced the Mecklenburg Resolves, a written set of radical resolutions that themselves however fell short of declaring independence. A copy of these Resolves was carried to the Continental Congress then meeting in Philadelphia by a courier, local tavern owner Captain James Jack.

In his pouch was said also to have been a copy of the May 20th Declaration of Independence. Although exhaustive efforts to prove the existence of this Declaration would provoke debate for over two hundred years, the community still clings to the tradition that its citizens produced the nation's first declaration of independence from the Crown.

Site of the first court held in Mecklenburg County, February 26, 1763 home of Thomas Spratt

The intersection of those two old trading paths where the 1768 courthouse stood is still known as Independence Square. Over the years, three presidents of the United States, William Howard Taft in 1909, Woodrow Wilson in 1916 and Gerald Ford in 1975, and one former vice-president, Adlai E. Stevenson of Illinois in 1898, have addressed local May 20 gatherings. Further celebrating the local legend, sculptor Charles Fagan's 2010 bronze statue of Captain Jack, mounted on a horse at full gallop headed in the direction of Philadelphia, stands east of downtown Charlotte at the intersection of East Fourth Street and Kings Drive.

Among those participating in fomenting separation from England was a young lawyer with the colorful name of Waightstill Avery, then one of the region's best-known men of the law, who had come to Charlotte in 1769. A graduate of Princeton who had studied law in Maryland before coming to the Carolinas, he was by 1775 one of five lawyers practicing in Charlotte. Before the Revolutionary War, he had served as the colony's Attorney General. By then, the village had a population of two hundred and it was to become a leader in transforming North Carolina from a colony into one of the original thirteen states of a new nation. Avery's knowledge of the law was such, and his library so complete, that an early state Supreme Court justice rested his written opinion on a point of law that Avery asserted could be found in a volume in his library. A young lawyer named Andrew Jackson, born in the Waxhaw community, often met Avery in court. Jackson once took exception to Avery's repeated reliance for legal precedent on the writings of British common-law authority Francis Bacon. Jackson, who had studied law in Salisbury before being admitted to practice in 1787, is said to have removed a copy of Bacon's treatise from Avery's saddlebags and replaced it with a side of pork. After Avery criticized Jackson in court for his levity, the two met in a duel, one which ended by each firing harmlessly into the air.

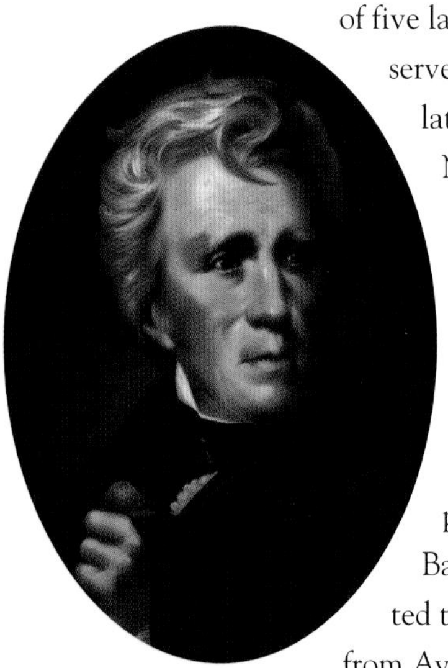

ANDREW JACKSON, BORN IN THE WASHAW (WAXHAW) COMMUNITY, PRACTICED LAW IN NC AND SERVED AS THE 12TH PRESIDENT OF THE UNITED STATES.

Mecklenburg laid claim to a number of men who made their mark in the state's formative years. Among them was Colonel William Richardson Davie, who studied under Spruce Macay, the Salisbury lawyer who had also trained Jackson. Davie was born in England, grew up in the Waxhaw community, and as an adolescent, studied at Queen's Museum, later Liberty Hall, in Charlotte. During the Revolutionary War, the Colonel commanded a troop of cavalry that harassed the British as they moved through the Carolinas. In 1780, after recovering from wounds suffered in early engagements, Davie and his men, who were vastly outnumbered by the approaching British under

WILLIAM RICHARDSON DAVIE, ONE OF THE MOST IMPRESSIVE NORTH CAROLINIANS OF HIS TIME, HELPED ESTABLISH THE UNIVERSITY OF NORTH CAROLINA AT CHAPEL HILL.

Lord Charles Cornwallis, repulsed three attacks at Charlotte before they retreated to safety. It was this series of engagements that gave rise to Cornwallis' description of Charlotte as a "hornet's nest." After the war, Davie traveled the legal circuit, helped write the state's first Constitution, introduced the legislation that created the University of North Carolina in Chapel Hill, the nation's first state university, and in 1798 was elected Governor by the General Assembly. Avery, for whom Avery County is named, also participated in drafting that first Constitution.

By 1800, there were about thirty lawyers admitted to practice before the court in Mecklenburg County, but only a third of that number lived in Charlotte. In 1810, the simple original log courthouse was replaced by a second courthouse, built of brick, with a hipped roof and a cupola. Also located on the Square, it remained in use until 1845. Superior Court sessions were held only twice a year, and so the hall was more frequently used for public meetings and as a platform for political speeches. A county court, presided over by a panel of magistrates, met quarterly.

For the first half of the nineteenth century, Charlotte remained a western outpost, removed and disconnected from most of the state. It was a modest settlement that

A REPLICA OF MECKLENBURG COUNTY'S FIRST COURTHOUSE

primarily served the needs of farmers in the surrounding area. Dr. J. B. Alexander, one of the county's early historians, reported in his 1902 *History of Mecklenburg County* that the establishments in early nineteenth century Charlotte provided only basic provisions – salt, whiskey, molasses, sugar and cheese – and that everything else necessary for daily life was produced on the farm. Even table cutlery was used only by "the most fashionable and wealthy." Most people ate with their fingers. According to Alexander, "Every good citizen was expected to cultivate a farm, raise his own cows, hogs and chickens."

Sorting out legal matters could be confusing. The superior court clerk, the county clerk and the register of deeds kept records in their homes, which were out in the country. That remained the case until the state legislature required these officials to maintain the records at the courthouse. As a result, according to a description of the 1825 era published a half-century later, the upper story of the courthouse was "cut up into offices, thereby spoiling the only good ballroom in town."

By 1840, Charlotte's population was 849, with about 19,000 more citizens spread throughout the rest of the county. The main streets of the town boasted twelve stores, one bank agent, three taverns, a tannery, a printing office, one weekly newspaper, two academies, one common school, two ministers, six lawyers, six doctors, four miners and fifty mechanics.

> If Osborne could not win an acquittal, it was generally understood that his client was guilty beyond any doubt.

The best local lawyer of that era was reputed to be James W. Osborne. Alexander wrote that if Osborne could not win an acquittal, it was generally understood that his client was guilty beyond any doubt. Charlotte's Joseph Wilson was the state's prosecutor in a district that reached westward from Charlotte to the mountains. "He discharged his duties," Alexander related, "when the country was swarming with law-breakers." Punishment was harsh and swift, often carried out on the courthouse steps on the day of conviction. The guilty could be subjected to the pillory or administered up to thirty-nine lashes, with a second round of similar punishment allowed in another ten days. Disfiguration was also practiced. The penalty for manslaughter was branding on the face or hand with the letters "M" and "S." The branding iron was held in place for as long as it took the condemned, or his attorney, to repeat the words "God Save the State" three times.

The county's third courthouse, built in 1845 to serve a growing community, faced Trade Street one block west of the Square, near the corner of what is now West Trade and Church Streets. An imposing two-story structure, its tall brick columns, faced with whitewashed wood, supported a high roofline. The first floor was occupied by offices.

COMPLETED IN 1845, THE COUNTY'S THIRD COURTHOUSE STOOD ON THE NORTHEAST CORNER OF TRADE AND CHURCH STREETS. NOTE THE WATER TOWER, OR STANDPIPE, IMMEDIATELY BEHIND THE BUILDING. THIS TOWER MADE POSSIBLE THE FIRST RUNNING WATER FACILITIES IN CHARLOTTE.

Under the front portico, a matched set of wide, curving staircases rose to the second floor and the entrances to the courtroom and the grand jury room. A nearby building behind the courthouse ultimately housed most of the town's lawyers.

Outsiders during that era, however, still considered Charlotte a rural backwater. A prominent 1848 visitor, Admiral Charles Wilkes, characterized Charlotte as a disgusting place, insulated from the world and possessed of drunkards. It took him more than two days of travel over rough roads to reach Charlotte from Columbia, South Carolina. What he found was a community with streets so thoroughly clogged with mud that crossing from one side to the other was possible only at the Square, and then only with difficulty.

Wilkes had come to the city to settle the estate of his brother-in-law and arrived just before his relative's land was auctioned off in a scheme to benefit a group of local landowners, one of whom claimed to be his brother-in-law's agent. He upset their plans, and remained long enough to take a measure of the local judiciary in a county court presided over by five judges. Wilkes took his place among the spectators, who were required to stand throughout the proceedings on a brick floor; seats were provided only for the judges, clerk, lawyers and the jury. He was sure that the chief judge was drunk. "There were three lawyers within the bar acting in the case and others sitting around, most of them employed picking their teeth." As the case proceeded, he described the lawyers as loud and boisterous, noting that "oaths were freely given and returned."

"There was no understanding what the ruling of the Judge's was, and the lawyers claimed for one construction and the others for an opposite. The jury took up the case and discussed it among themselves with many expletives and denunciations of the court and counsel. One counsel essayed to speak and he was met by a downright interruption that he lied. By this time all was uproar and there was no one to control the proceedings."

It was, he concluded, a town devoid of any virtue. "In Charlotte, the inhabitants have no amusement whatever except that of bibing whiskey and getting drunk," he wrote in his autobiography. And a favorite place was the courthouse. Lawsuits were common and filed on the slightest provocation, since one had to have a case on file to become a spectator in court. With a case on file, "this permits them to have a drunken frolick and, as they expressed it, a 'good time.'"

"As a whole it may be classed as a town of no account, altho' it assumes to be the originator of the Declaration of Independence and glories in the name of the 'Hornet's Nest'." Wilkes related that by all accounts the community had more "enlightenment" before the Revolution than it did more than a half century later.

Wilkes left, fearful of ever having to return. In the course of settling the business that brought him into this backcountry, he discovered the records of the register of deeds were under the care of a clerk who also ran an apothecary shop. Even though the courthouse was equipped with a fire-proof safe, all the books recording property transactions were in the back of the shop "with jars of varnish and much combustible material that in case of any accident would have destroyed the whole Records."

"I believe that the North Carolinians have an abiding respect for the Laws & all the officials of the courts," he wrote, "but there is so much ignorance and want of energy that almost all the public duties they are charged with are neglected or so badly performed that it amounts to the same thing as if no law existed."

A HORNET'S NEST, HEARKENING BACK TO CHARLOTTE'S REVOLUTIONARY WAR HISTORY, IS NOW THE LOGO OF THE CHARLOTTE-MECKLENBURG HISTORIC LANDMARKS COMMISSION.

It was not until mid-century that Charlotte became truly connected to the outside world. A railroad first reached Charlotte from Columbia in 1852, after eighteen of the county's leading merchants and professional men, including four attorneys, organized a campaign to bring it to the city. By 1856, the east-west rail line was open as far as Goldsboro in eastern North Carolina over a route that ran through Greensboro and Raleigh.

Charlotte never figured in any battles or skirmishes during the Civil War. Indeed, the railroads brought about the town's two closest connections to that war. From 1862 to 1865 the Confederate Navy Yard, ironworks relocated inland from Norfolk to the site in 2011 of the East Trade Street city bus terminal, produced projectiles, torpedoes and propeller shafts for Confederate gunboats and shipped them by rail to seaports. And it was the rail line from Greensboro that brought Confederate President Jefferson Davis to the city in April 1865. Davis and his long train of followers, representing the defeated government of the Confederate States of America, fled south after the fall of Richmond. He arrived in Charlotte just in time to receive word of the assassination of President Abraham Lincoln.

Jefferson Davis and his party remained in Charlotte for much of a week. Davis stayed in a house at the corner of South Tryon and Fourth streets that was owned by William Phifer, who had come to Charlotte from Massachusetts. It was the only refuge offered to him by nervous Charlotteans, worried about retribution for those who offered aid to the fleeing officials. Throughout the week, Davis conducted cabinet meetings in the offices of a bank. The leading lawyer in the group was George Davis of

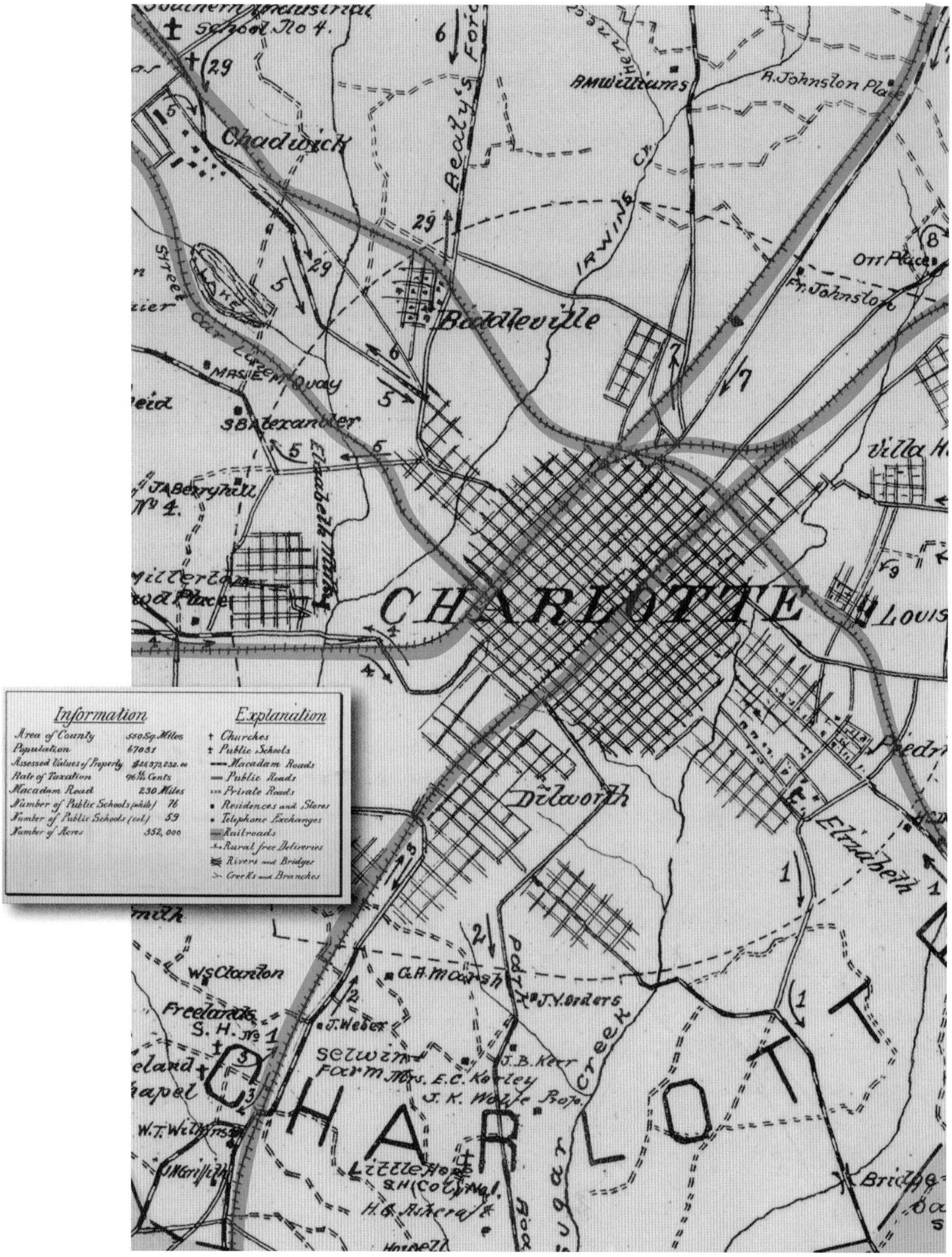

DETAIL FROM 1911 MECKLENBURG COUNTY MAP

The Great Seal of the Confederacy

Wilmington, the Attorney General of the Confederacy. "The Government of the Confederate States is no longer potent for good," he told the president. "It is already virtually destroyed."

North Carolina's Confederate governor, Zebulon Baird Vance, later to become a Charlotte lawyer, was on hand for part of the continuing debate over whether to sustain the fiction of a functioning government. President Davis tried to persuade Vance to join with him and head west, where the President believed a fragment of his government could be sustained. Others convinced Vance that he would be needed more in North Carolina during the coming weeks and months of deep uncertainty, and Davis' party left without him.

For years thereafter, the vault of the 1845 courthouse contained the official seal of the government of the Confederate States of America, left behind by the fleeing Confederate officials.

In the months following the war, as many as 6,000 Union troops would occupy the city, as Charlotte adjusted to changes that upset the social order and thrust newcomers, both white and black, into their midst. More than thirty years after the Union occupation, the historian J. B. Alexander was still fuming about the post-war days. He was especially intolerant of Mayor Ed Bizzell, who he claimed was from the North and was married to a "Negro." Confederate Brigadier General Rufus Barringer, a lawyer, allied himself with the Republicans, telling his friends it was in the best interest of the South to accept the Reconstruction Acts of 1867. His realignment, and apparent defection, did not hurt his prestige. Mecklenburg Democrats elected him to represent the county at the state constitutional convention in 1875.

Monument honoring the signers of the Mecklenburg Declaration of Independence

CHAPTER 3

The Post Civil War Era

The postwar period brought a new generation of lawyers to the local legal community. With them came a new era, and their influence spread gradually throughout the state. This pattern, the arrival of a new generation of lawyers, was to be repeated after both World War I and World War II.

In addition to Zebulon Vance and General Barringer, a number of other men returning from service in the Confederate Army joined the practice of law in Charlotte. For the remainder of their lives, they were known by the military titles they had earned during the war. They included General Robert D. Johnston, Colonel John E. Brown, Major Clement Dowd, Colonel W. W. Fleming, Colonel Hamilton C. Jones, Colonel Edwin A. Osborne, Major William A. Owens, Captain William M. Shipp and Captain George F. Bason.

Vance was perhaps the best known of the attorneys who settled in Charlotte. The state's popular wartime governor chose the city after his release from federal custody, even though his hometown was farther west, near Asheville. He joined a law practice with the aging James Osborne. Vance was elected to the United States Senate in 1870 but was refused a seat because of his service to the Confederacy. He was re-elected Governor of the state in 1876, and, after receiving a pardon, was later appointed to the Senate, where he served until his death in 1894. Among Vance's more celebrated trials was his unsuccessful *pro bono* defense of Confederate veteran Tom Dula, whose hanging is memorialized in the Kingston Trio's 1958 hit recording, "Hang Down Your Head, Tom Dooley."

Compared to the years before the war, the bar was more cohesive and organized though there would be no formal organization for another forty-two years. Vance was one of those who in 1869 signed a document purporting to be rules of the "Bar of Charlotte." The "rules" the ten signers, most of them men who had seen service in the war, agreed to was a schedule of fees. A deed for property valued at less than $500 was to bring $5, the same price as "oral advice." If a client wanted one of them to write his opinion on a matter of law, the fee was $10. Appearance in criminal cases cost $5 for a misdemeanor and $20 for larceny. The drawing of a will cost $10. Collecting debts brought a commission of between 5 percent and 12.5 percent, depending on the amount due and whether it was local or "foreign."

Zebulon Baird Vance, North Carolina's Confederate governor and one of Charlotte's most well known attorneys.

Signers of the document, copies of which still exist, included Vance, Osborne, Hamilton C. Jones, II, who served two terms in the state Senate and was appointed United States Attorney by President Grover Cleveland, and W. P. Bynum, who became a justice of the state Supreme Court in the early 1870s. The life of another signer, Colonel Edwin A. Osborne, took a different course. He became an ordained deacon in the Episcopal Church, served as the first superintendent of Thompson Orphanage, whose 1889 chapel still stands between East Third and East Fourth Streets, and as a chaplain in the Spanish-American War.

The Law Library Association of Charlotte was formally chartered by a private law of the 1885 session of the General Assembly. This first association of independent attorneys, allied to advance the better performance of the profession, is considered the forerunner of the 1912 Mecklenburg Bar Association. Members were given one share of stock valued at $200. Some who had contributed books received stock in exchange. The collection was housed in the old building behind the 1845 West Trade Street courthouse, at the corner of West Fifth and Church Streets, where most of the lawyers then had their offices.

George E. Wilson was the first president of the Law Library Association, and the secretary was a young Heriot Clarkson. Only twenty-two, Clarkson was a South Carolina native who, through a position in the offices of Jones and General Johnston and a nine-month stint at the law school at the University at Chapel Hill, was admitted to the Bar in 1884. The other members of that Association at its founding were Johnston and Jones, W. H. Bailey, Armistead Burwell, T. R. Robertson, Platt D. Walker, John E. Brown, George E. Wilson, Calvin E. Grier, Francis I. Osborne, W. C. Maxwell, T. M. Pitman, H. W. Harris, W. W. Fleming and E. K. P. Osborne. The organizers would subsequently bring into their group others who would distinguish themselves in the years ahead.

Three of the original members, Walker, Burwell and Clarkson, would later serve on the North Carolina Supreme Court. Before his appointment to the Court, Walker

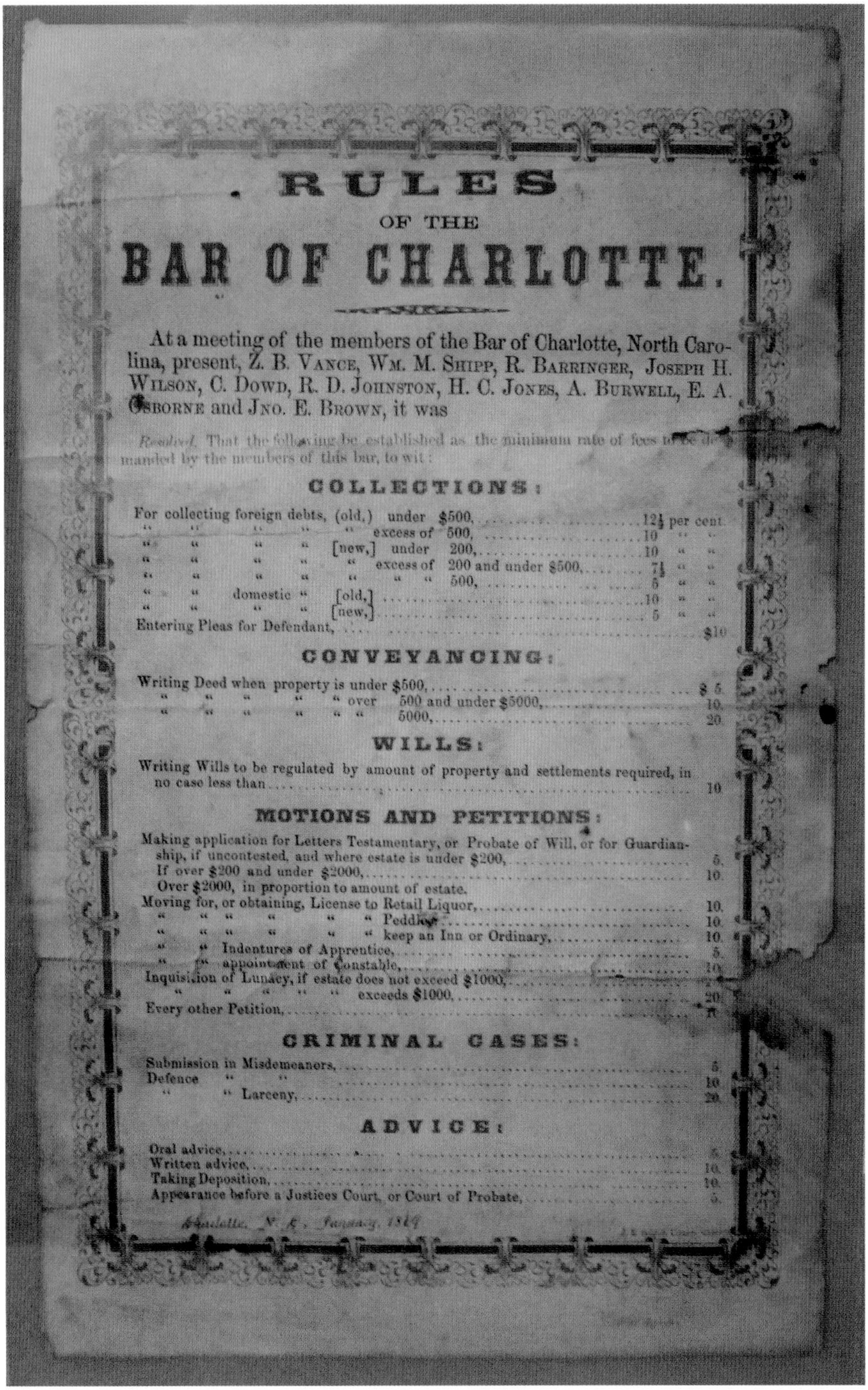

RULES
OF THE
BAR OF CHARLOTTE.

At a meeting of the members of the Bar of Charlotte, North Carolina, present, Z. B. Vance, Wm. M. Shipp, R. Barringer, Joseph H. Wilson, C. Dowd, R. D. Johnston, H. C. Jones, A. Burwell, E. A. Osborne and Jno. E. Brown, it was

Resolved, That the following be established as the minimum rate of fees to be demanded by the members of this bar, to wit:

COLLECTIONS:

For collecting foreign debts, (old,) under $500,	12½ per cent
" " " " " excess of 500,	10 " "
" " " " [new,] under 200,	10 " "
" " " " " excess of 200 and under $500,	7½ " "
" " " " " " " 500,	5 " "
" " domestic " [old,]	10 " "
" " " " [new,]	5 " "
Entering Pleas for Defendant,	$10

CONVEYANCING:

Writing Deed when property is under $500,	$ 5
" " " " " over 500 and under $5000,	10
" " " " " " 5000,	20

WILLS:

Writing Wills to be regulated by amount of property and settlements required, in no case less than	10

MOTIONS AND PETITIONS:

Making application for Letters Testamentary, or Probate of Will, or for Guardianship, if uncontested, and where estate is under $200,	5.
If over $200 and under $2000,	10
Over $2000, in proportion to amount of estate.	
Moving for, or obtaining, License to Retail Liquor,	10.
" " " " " " Peddler,	10.
" " " " " " keep an Inn or Ordinary,	10.
" " Indentures of Apprentice,	5.
" " appointment of Constable,	10.
Inquisition of Lunacy, if estate does not exceed $1000,	[illegible]
" " " " " exceeds $1000,	20.
Every other Petition,	[illegible]

CRIMINAL CASES:

Submission in Misdemeanors,	5.
Defence " "	10.
" " Larceny,	20.

ADVICE:

Oral advice,	5.
Written advice,	10.
Taking Deposition,	10.
Appearance before a Justices Court, or Court of Probate,	5.

Charlotte, N. C., January, 1869

1869 Rules of the Bar of Charlotte

would become the first president of the North Carolina Bar Association. Francis Osborne would become Attorney General of North Carolina and then a federal district judge.

In a 1945 presentation at a local bar meeting, James A. Bell referred to these years as "the pre-modern-convenience period," describing life in the old lawyers' building as follows: "The offices were heated by open grates; the water [from] a bowl and pitcher on the inside, and other facilities on the outside a few hundred feet to the rear; one janitor and man-of-all-work for all the lawyers in the building; one telephone in the library on the second floor for the entire law building and answered, if at all, by any lawyer who happened to be in the library.

"No stenographers, no typewriters – all correspondence, pleadings and legal documents were written out in long hand by the lawyer *in propria persona*. This accounts largely for the lawyer language of 'aforesaid' and 'as hereinafter said', etc., so common to this day."

The Law Library Association was as close as the attorneys in Charlotte came to a common bond. The city's doctors had formed a medical association in 1848, but, as was the case throughout most of the profession, Charlotte lawyers practiced on their own without formal organization. A few of the older lawyers took on younger partners, but these arrangements usually did not last long, and the names on the shingles changed often. Grier and Burwell were together for only a year or two before Burwell was named to the state Supreme Court. By the time Burwell returned to Charlotte after losing to a Republican in the elections of 1892, Grier had died at the age of forty-three. Following Johnston's departure for Alabama, where he became president of a bank, Jones brought in a younger man, Charles W. Tillett. By that time, Heriot Clarkson had embarked on a new partnership with Charles H. Duls, a man closer to his age, beginning a firm that ultimately became Parker, Poe, Adams & Bernstein, LLP.

While the Law Library Association had no official standing in the judicial system, it began to take on duties that affected the handling of cases before the courts that met in the county. A member of the Association was put in charge of the scheduling of cases to be heard and, from time to time, it spoke to matters affecting the profession. The management of the court calendar did require some effort, as the criminal courts in Charlotte in the latter part of the nineteenth century were part of a judicial district that reached from the state's largest city, Wilmington, all the way to Charlotte.

In 1896, work began on a grand monument to civic success, a new courthouse, Charlotte's fourth, on South Tryon Street at East Third Street on the site of an early school, Queen's Museum. When work on the courthouse had begun, the builders discovered a link to the remote past. Buried there were the remains of British soldiers killed in a Revolutionary War battle. The building, apparently first fully occupied in 1897, was described as a "Victorian version of a European capitol building," a flattery some considered pretentious. It sat on an open plaza populated with large trees. Built at a cost of $50,000, it was designed by Frank P. Milburn, a Charlotte architect. A prominent portico in the center of the building supported an open balcony on the second floor that looked out upon the plaza and the traffic on South Tryon. A tall dome, reminiscent of the one atop the United States Capitol, crowned the building of buff-colored brick and stone. Inside, the floors were marble and the second level included two courtrooms with tall, wide windows. County offices occupied the first floor and the basement. Confiscated liquor was stored in an upstairs room, but after it began disappearing, court officers took to pouring out the "evidence" once it had served its purpose in court.

Shortly after the building opened, a granite obelisk honoring those claimed to be signers of the Mecklenburg Declaration of Independence was dedicated on May 20, 1898. Eight young women, all of them descendants of the signers, pulled the ropes to release a drape covering the monument.

This building, on the northwest corner of Tryon and Sixth Streets, was the temporary location of Charlotte's city hall while the city's first "real" city hall was under construction.

The lawyers had remained clustered together in the building adjacent to the 1845 courthouse after the county erected the new courthouse. Its tenants eventually relocating their offices and the law library to the Piedmont Building, built in the 200 block of South Tryon Street in 1898 and considered to be the first modern commercial building in North Carolina. Then in 1908, the Law Library Association opened its own building, the Law Building, on South Tryon Street. By this time, Charlotte had more than forty lawyers. Some of the partnerships of that era became the foundation for leading local firms a century later.

As it began the twentieth century, Charlotte was a busy place. The new courthouse and the new city hall that opened in 1891 were symbols of the promise that local boosters saw in the city. A local hotel brochure called Charlotte the "industrial centre of the New South." Certainly the booming textile industry had raised the city's prospects. The first cotton mill had opened in 1881. When the new courthouse opened, there were five more mills operating in Charlotte. Three times that number, employing 6,000 workers, were in business by 1900. Nearly three hundred mills had sprung up within a radius of a hundred miles. The city's newest hotel was the Selwyn, whose foundation was made from the bricks that had once been part of the 1845 West Trade Street courthouse. It was a hotel fit for traveling men, conventions and important social events. Not long after it opened, construction commenced on the Realty Building, later renamed the Independence Building, at the intersection of Trade and Tryon. At twelve stories, it was the city's first "skyscraper." It survived until 1981, when it was demolished to make way for a new building.

The city's trolley cars, no longer pulled by horses, ran on electricity. A new modern residential suburb called Dilworth, was served by a trolley line. Homes had traded oil lamps for electric lights. Businessmen with offices in

Charlotte's "new" City Hall, built in 1891, on the corner of Fifth and North Tryon Streets.

the new Realty Building began to use typewriters.

Historian J. D. Alexander lamented in his 1902 writings that not all change was for the good. He complained the community no longer tolerated physical punishment for criminal offenses. He yearned for the return of the lash and the cutting off of ears of offenders, and he was not opposed to lynching when the occasion called for it. "The penitentiary has been substituted for these forms of punishment, and has proved less effective than the old fashioned way of applying the lash to the bare back, as in ante-bellum times," Alexander wrote. "Since our people have become somewhat Yankeeized, there is considerable opposition to capital punishment or hanging; but the common people are disposed – in flagrant cases – to take the law into their own hands and mete out justice swiftly."

> "Since our people have become somewhat Yankeeized, there is considerable opposition to capital punishment or hanging."
>
> —J. D. Alexander
> *History of Mecklenburg County*

By this time, however, the legal profession had outgrown the traditions of an earlier age and was responding to change in the world around it. On February 10, 1899, Charles W. Tillett and a few other lawyers from Charlotte were in Raleigh for a meeting at the Supreme Court that drew sixty-five lawyers from across the state. The subject was the formation of a statewide bar organization. The gathering was the work of J. Crawford Biggs of the law school at the University in Chapel Hill.

By the time the evening session was concluded, Charlotte lawyer Platt D. Walker had been elected president of the new North Carolina Bar Association. Walker, a native of Wilmington, had arrived in Charlotte in 1876 after his mentor, William L. Steel of Rockingham, had been elected to Congress. Also politically active, Waker ran, unsuccessfully, in the Democratic Party primary for Attorney General in 1884, and then retired from politics for nearly twenty years. In 1902, he was elected to the state Supreme Court and he remained on the bench until his death in 1923. Over the years, eighteen lawyers from the Mecklenburg bar were to serve as presidents of what was to become one of the nation's most progressive statewide voluntary bar organizations.

The North Carolina Bar Association succeeded where an earlier effort to organize the state's lawyers had failed. At the 1899 meeting in Raleigh, those who had been involved in the earlier effort to organize a similar group voted to dissolve their association and turned over the books, ledgers and $80 from its bank account to Walker. In July of that year, Walker presided over the first meeting of the North Carolina Bar Association, held at the Atlantic Hotel in Morehead City. Working with him at that meeting was Tillett, who was a member of the committee on permanent organization.

When the sessions concluded, membership in the Association was recorded as 269, although approximately 900 lawyers were licensed in the state. In the first issue of the *North Carolina Law Journal*, a publication that Tillett urged the Association to create, he urged that it was the duty of every lawyer in the state to join and support the new organization. His plea ignored the fact that this voluntary organization would not be open to African American lawyers for more than fifty years.

The impetus for the creation of the North Carolina Bar Association was a concern among leaders in the profession over the meager requirements for becoming a lawyer and the lack of ways to discipline those who abused the trust of their clients and their responsibilities to the court. According to historian J. Edwin Hendricks, Walker's July 1899 inaugural speech called on attorneys to set high standards of professionalism and to strive to meet high ideals of "honesty, justice, liberality and service."

Charles Duls, elected in 1912 as the Mecklenburg County Bar's first president.

Some of the same noble sentiments motivated the Mecklenburg County lawyers when they gathered in 1912 to organize the local bar. Meeting on the afternoon of January 30, 1912, the Charlotte lawyers organized the Mecklenburg Bar Association, which took over the work of the existing Law Library Association. According to a report in *The Charlotte Observer*, "It was deemed wise to include all attorneys who are not interested in the Charlotte Law Library Association." Those at the meeting did not make too much of their work that day. When it came to nominating officers, the lawyers called upon nominees to express themselves on opinions of the day, such as the question of women's suffrage. E. T. Cansler, Sr. gave a lengthy speech – the newspaper called it "lurid" – on the lack of utility of a vice-president in an organization such as was being put together. Cansler then withdrew his name from nomination, insisting to his fellow lawyers that he was not doing so out of fear of losing the election. He did suggest that if a vice-president was deemed necessary, he believed it should be someone from outside the Law Building. Thomas LeRoy Kirkpatrick, who would later figure in the genesis of another local legend, was then unanimously elected. Charles Duls was elected president and was immediately asked to see what he could do about getting a special term of court to relieve a backlog of cases.

Among the Association's first acts was to adopt a local rule that prohibited an attorney from taking a default judgment when he knew his opponent was represented by counsel without first giving notice of doing so. That local rule, which survives to this day, formalized a practice of courtesy that prevented a lawyer from taking advantage of an oversight by a fellow lawyer.

A few surviving Civil War veterans were among the Association's organizers. Calvin E. Grier had enlisted at the age of fifteen. When the war ended, he was nineteen, a captain, and adjutant of Scales' Brigade. He had sustained seven battle wounds and was twice shot through. Perhaps the best known of the local veterans was General Barringer, whose eldest brother, a congressman, had "desked" with a fellow member from Illinois named Abraham Lincoln. Barringer was known as a conciliator who avoided litigation. Hanging on the wall in his office was the painting of two farmers quarreling over a cow. One tugged at its tail and the other pulled on its head while a lawyer sat coolly by its side taking all the milk.

The new local Association put on a firm footing the support of the law library, which no longer had to depend on the financial support of its limited membership and could draw on the money collected as dues from the Association's members. The law library remained most convenient for those in the Law Building and was available to any member, although when the Association's bylaws were adopted at a meeting a few weeks later, the members agreed to restrict the Association to whites only.

At the time, there were only two local African American lawyers. John T. Sanders had read law under a white lawyer for a short time and had been admitted to the practice of law in 1906, two years after the county's first African American lawyer, John Sinclair Leary, Sr., died. Working in Sanders' office at 227 East Trade Street at that time was another attorney, H. H. Cardwell. Both appeared to have been primarily engaged in business and not in a general law practice, but they were listed in the city directory as attorneys-at-law. Almost a quarter century would pass before another African American would begin a law practice offering full representation to clients in Charlotte, and full membership in the local Bar would come only in 1955.

President Woodrow Wilson and other dignitaries on his visit to Charlotte, May, 1916

CHAPTER 4

KEEPING PACE WITH GROWTH

The nation celebrated its Declaration of Independence on July 4, but in 1916 Charlotte was prouder still of its own Declaration of Independence. It was only right, then, that the annual May 20 celebration of the signing of the Mecklenburg Declaration would inspire the city and its dignitaries to produce an event with all the fanfare and pomp that could be mustered. None other than President Woodrow Wilson and his wife were scheduled to attend.

Organizers produced a parade complete with 2,500 marching soldiers, martial bands, dozens of floats displaying the bounty of farm and factory, a phalanx of new Ford automobiles, assembled only the day before at the company's Charlotte plant, and a contingent of two hundred Boy Scouts. An estimated hundred thousand people – most of whom had arrived aboard special trains from throughout the Carolinas – stood shoulder-to-shoulder to view the parade that followed a serpentine route through the city's streets and required nearly an hour to pass the reviewing stand. The festivities also included a military ball the night before the President's arrival. A mock battle was to be staged on the outskirts of town while the President paid a visit to Davidson College, which he had attended before transferring to Princeton when his father became its president. At the center of it all, the man who would welcome President Wilson before his noon speech to a crowd estimated at 35,000 gathered on the lawn of the Presbyterian College for Women, was Mayor Thomas LeRoy Kirkpatrick.

Kirkpatrick was a busy man with a promising legal and civic career. He had read law under Heriot Clarkson and Charles Duls, then studied for a year at the law school at the University in Chapel Hill before passing the bar in 1900 at age twenty-three. In 1907, he had helped organize the Business Men's Municipal League, which eagerly adopted the city's new slogan, "Watch Charlotte Grow." He was subsequently elected an alderman and finally, in 1915, the mayor of Charlotte. Kirkpatrick had acquired the rank of colonel after Governor Locke Craig appointed him Judge Advocate

General of the North Carolina National Guard. From that day on, he would be known as "Colonel Kirkpatrick." He was known, too, for his colorful red vest.

When the President's railroad car, the "National," arrived in Charlotte at 10:15 A.M., Kirkpatrick met the President and his party at the station and took his place along with Mrs. Kirkpatrick in an automobile immediately behind those carrying the President and Mrs. Wilson, two presidential aides and a six-man Secret Service detachment. Shortly after noon, when the last unit of the parade had passed in review, Kirkpatrick rose to introduce Governor Locke Craig, who, in turn, was to introduce the president.

MAYOR THOMAS LEROY KIRKPATRICK WHOSE REPUTATION WAS UNFAIRLY TARNISHED BY FIRST LADY EDITH WILSON

What followed became, like the century-old tradition that gave rise to the celebration itself, a saga whose factual basis is shrouded in controversy. The glorious memories that Kirkpatrick enjoyed from that day were dashed twenty-three years later when the First Lady's book, *My Memoir*, was published. From that day on, Kirkpatrick would be known in local legend as the man who had reputedly upstaged the President, inconvenienced his wife and allowed the distressing heat of the day to take its toll on the Marine Corps band that had been shuttled to Charlotte especially for the occasion.

Mrs. Wilson portrayed Kirkpatrick as a vain, puffing-proud country orator who was not even properly dressed. She said that he appeared wearing an oversized frock coat that he must have borrowed from "a giant." According to her, the mayor took his place behind the podium to make his introduction and, as he "warmed to his subject," he went on and on, much to the distress of the First Lady and others, suffering the "blazing afternoon sun," who were seated on a platform that she said provided no relief from the heat.

If Kirkpatrick's remarks were indeed full of ruffles and flourishes, he came by his patriotic enthusiasm honestly. His great-great-grandfather had fought in the Revolutionary War battle of Kings Mountain, where the British had suffered a key defeat. When he was a teenager, Kirkpatrick had joined the Queen City National Guard and he later volunteered for service during the Spanish-American War. In Mrs. Wilson's recollection of his performance, as Kirkpatrick pressed on with his lively speech, members of the Marine Band, who were dressed in winter-weight red uniform coats, began passing out under the heat of the sun, and members of the Boy Scouts went to their aid.

"The speaker would look at their prostrate forms," she wrote, "but with a debonair flair of his coattails, attack another page of the typed matter before him. Hardly had the band received first aid when women all around me began to faint, and the Scouts, with perspiration pouring down their boyish faces, came to tender their services." She reported that Kirkpatrick finally reached the end of his speech after speaking for nearly an hour. "My husband's address was calm and mercifully short."

The First Lady's account might have remained buried in her memoir, to be repeated as gospel only among members of the Mecklenburg Bar, were it not for President Gerald Ford, who revived Mrs. Wilson's account when he spoke in Charlotte on May 20, 1975, the 200th anniversary of the Mecklenburg Declaration of Independence. "I must admit I was a little apprehensive about coming to the 'Hornet's Nest,'" the President said before he began his address, "after I heard what happened to President Wilson on May 20, 1916, fifty-nine years ago."

While Mrs. Wilson's story made for a good read, according to the exhaustive coverage of the day's events by *The Charlotte Observer*, it appears to be without foundation. Mrs. Wilson probably endured many long-winded speakers in 1916 – it was an election year – but the disaster she reported in her book apparently did not happen in Charlotte. If the newspaper's detailed account of each minute of the President's nine and one-half hours in Charlotte is to believed, the colonel's "introduction" lasted at most a few minutes, not the fifty she reported. It was a balmy day and, while the sun was warm, the organizers had been anticipating rain and there was a canopy to protect those seated on the platform. The newspaper account also did not mention hearty Marines needing help from the Boy Scouts. Moreover, the president was reported to have begun his speech at 12:34 P.M. and concluded at 12:52 P.M. "Mercifully short" amounted to an address of eighteen minutes. That Kirkpatrick pounded on the podium, rattling the glasses and a pitcher of ice water that Mrs. Wilson put there, was not reflected in the newspaper account.

PRESIDENT AND FIRST LADY WILSON UNDER THE CANOPY HUNG AT THE CHARLOTTE STAGE IN ANTICIPATION OF INCLEMENT WEATHER.

The reporters were, however, impressed with the words of the President, who spoke in measured phrases in a voice that seldom rose above a level required for polite conversation. At the time, Europe was torn by war, and Wilson told the Charlotte crowd that he hoped that tentative peace negotiations would prevent further bloodshed. The President raised the prospect that European leaders would look to the United

States as an example of how people of different cultures and backgrounds could form a common union.

That, of course, was not to be. A year later, America would enter the war, and Kirkpatrick, along with millions of others, would volunteer for service in Europe. The President wrote to the Colonel to say that he was needed in Charlotte, where, on July 13, 1917, the city received word that it would be the site of a major army training camp.

Camp Greene, named for Revolutionary War General Nathanael Greene, became the training arena for fifty thousand soldiers. Much of it was on a farm owned by Sydenham Alexander, a former state senator and congressman and the father of Julia Alexander, the city's first female attorney. By the end of summer, the army's contractors had built an encampment on Charlotte's western edge that was equal in size and population to the city itself. Over the next two years, the 2,600-acre camp would provide a $4.7 million boost to the local economy. It would also launch a new burst of growth and development by introducing men from all across the land to Charlotte. Massachusetts National Guardsmen were bivouacked in sight of cotton mills that were already drawing business away from the New England textile industry. Soldiers from Montana saw African Americans for the first time. While it was believed at the outset that African Americans would not be stationed at camps in the South, Camp Greene

COLONEL MACOMB AND STAFF AT CAMP GREENE

ended up with a large contingent under the command of black officers.

Charlotte had competed with five other cities, including Fayetteville and Wilmington, for the location of the training camp. The army wanted open land, and lots of it, as well as a sober environment. Local boosters found the land, although they had to double the acreage at the last minute. A group of Charlotte lawyers had already helped to take care of the latter requirement by leading a successful 1905 crusade to close the local saloons.

The army's arrival threatened and even overwhelmed many of Charlotte's residents. Charles Tillett wrote articles for *The Charlotte Observer* to ease the fears of city residents, who were anxious about the soldiers who filled the stores, cafés and restaurants. "The democracy of the soldier life captivates me," Tillett wrote. "I love to be about the camp about the time the boys are getting their dinner; to look at them take their somewhat crude utensils and each receive his portion of food, and then after the meal is over, wash his own dishes. It makes no difference who he is or where he came from, he obeys the regulations with uncomplaining spirit. What could be finer than that?"

In fact, Camp Greene did what the Charlotte Chamber of Commerce had been trying to do since the turn of the century: it made Charlotte grow. The military not only infused the local economy with cash from the soldiers' pay, but it also enticed newcomers – many of them men who passed through Camp Greene – to return and settle in what appeared to be a prosperous commercial and retail center.

By 1919, when the thirty or so men who were members of the Mecklenburg Bar returned from their own military service, they found a city that was the largest in the state, with a population of nearly fifty thousand. As the city's banks prospered, builders put up new homes in the suburbs. The 1920s became a decade of growth.

Along with the new business came those to serve its needs. The 1920 city directory listed more than sixty lawyers, most of whom maintained their offices in the Law Building on South Tryon Street. Twenty-four of them were in partnerships of two or three lawyers; the rest were solo practitioners. Two firms – Clarkson, Taliaferro & Clarkson and Pharr, Bell & Sparrow – included three lawyers each.

The composition of the bar was also changing. Among the new attorneys in the city were four women, Julia Alexander, Margaret Berry Street, Willie Mae Stratford and Carrie Lee McLean. Women lawyers were rare; only seventeen women had been admitted to the bar in North Carolina between 1900 and 1920. Tabitha Anne Holton of Jamestown in Guilford County was the lone woman to have been licensed in the nineteenth century. When she applied for admission in 1878, only five states, none of them in the South, had admitted women lawyers. After the justices of the state Supreme Court, who administered the bar examination, denied her the opportunity to sit for the examination, she returned with her lawyer, Albion Tourgée of Greensboro, to press her case. Tourgée argued that the male gender used in the state law regarding licensing of lawyers was merely a technicality. He also pointed out that the Court had granted licenses to African Americans and further that the Court surely would not deny a license to a lawyer, even a woman, who had been admitted to the bar elsewhere in the United States. Having heard these arguments, Chief Justice William Nathan Harrell Smith questioned Holton and approved her application. She received her license on March 6, 1878 and practiced for eight years in Yancey County before dying of tuberculosis in 1886.

In 1920, Charlotte had a disproportionate share of the women in the profession in North Carolina. There were three in Asheville and one each in Greensboro, Fayetteville, and Winston-Salem, but none in Raleigh or Wilmington, two of the most important political cities of the day. The first woman to practice in Charlotte had been Julia Alexander. From an old, established family in north Mecklenburg, she had studied law at the Universities of Michigan and North Carolina before passing her bar

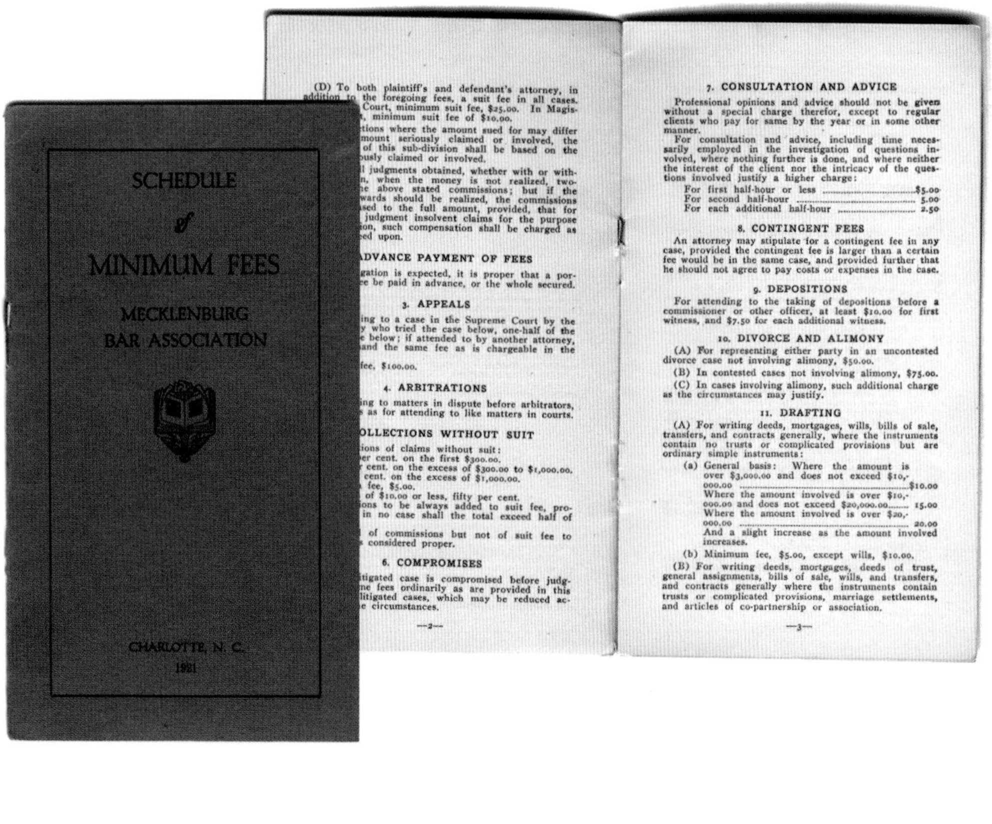

examination in 1914. She joined the North Carolina Bar Association the following year and opened her office in the Bryant Building. She was followed by Margaret Street, who in 1915 was the first woman to earn a degree from the law school at the University of North Carolina. Street passed the bar examination that year and moved to Charlotte in 1917. She became active in the movement to improve the state's roads, working with her sister, Harriet Morehead Berry of Chapel Hill. Leadership in that movement often put her in competition with Charlotte's leading roads advocate, Thomas Kirkpatrick, who advocated as a military necessity a road from Wilmington through Charlotte to Asheville.

Julia Alexander, first female lawyer to argue a case before the state Supreme Court.

Willie Mae Stratford read law with several Charlotte lawyers before she took the bar examination in 1919. Associate Supreme Court Justice Platt D. Walker declared her examination paper was "the best [he] had ever read." She, too, had an independent practice before marrying William T. Shore, another Charlotte lawyer. She continued to work in her husband's law office, leaving in about 1920 to raise a family. In 1930, she wrote, "I am helping to rear some boys who ought to make good lawyers and good men."

Carrie McLean was born in Lincolnton and came to Charlotte to teach in the public schools. She also enrolled in business courses and eventually found a job as a secretary for Stuart W. Cramer, a textile executive, and later for John H. Mayes, also in the textile business. She taught typing and shorthand at the Presbyterian College for Women (now Queens University of Charlotte) and read law under Thaddeus A. Adams to prepare for the bar examination. She was licensed in 1918 but did not begin her practice immediately. Instead, she worked as a stenographer in the firm of Tillett and Thomas C. Guthrie before setting out on her own. During her career, she earned a high rating from Martindale-Hubbell and was often engaged to write briefs in civil cases for other local lawyers.

Unlike most of her female colleagues, who avoided litigation, Julia Alexander did not shy away from the courtroom. She was the first woman to argue a case before a jury and to win a case in Superior Court. In 1918, she also was the first woman to argue a case before the state Supreme Court, an appeal involving the ownership rights in an alleyway in which she represented her father. The typesetter for the *North Carolina Reports*, apparently assuming in that era that she was a man, recorded her name as Julian M. Alexander. The practice of law became a platform for

Alexander to pursue her interest in civic affairs. In 1919, she was instrumental in the organization of the North Carolina Federation of Business and Professional Women's Clubs, and in 1920 she ran unsuccessfully for mayor of Charlotte. She was elected to the North Carolina House of Representatives in 1925, the second woman to serve there. Lillian Exum Clement Stafford, an Asheville attorney, elected in 1920 by a vote of 10,368 to 41, had been the first woman in the entire South to serve in a legislative body.

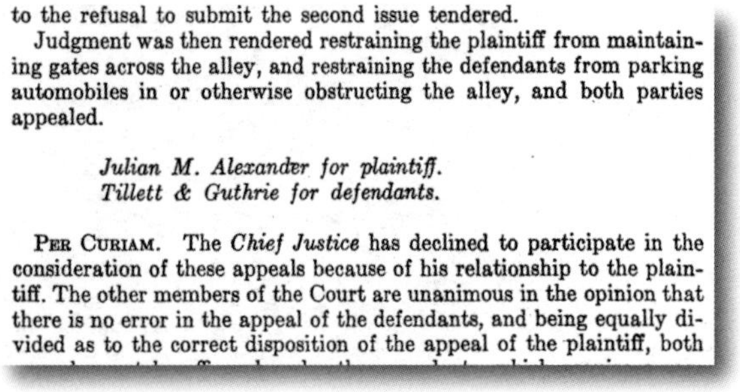
to the refusal to submit the second issue tendered.

Judgment was then rendered restraining the plaintiff from maintaining gates across the alley, and restraining the defendants from parking automobiles in or otherwise obstructing the alley, and both parties appealed.

Julian M. Alexander for plaintiff.
Tillett & Guthrie for defendants.

PER CURIAM. The *Chief Justice* has declined to participate in the consideration of these appeals because of his relationship to the plaintiff. The other members of the Court are unanimous in the opinion that there is no error in the appeal of the defendants, and being equally divided as to the correct disposition of the appeal of the plaintiff, both

EXCERPT FROM N.C. SUPREME COURT OPINION FILED MAY 8, 1918. NOTE MISSPELLING OF JULIA ALEXANDER'S NAME, ERRING IN FAVOR OF THE MALE GENDER.

Despite Julia Alexander's trail-blazing career, breaking barriers and overturning social conventions, she was no liberal. She sided with a decidedly conservative crowd in the General Assembly. The 1925 legislature opened in early January with Charlotte lawyer Edgar W. Pharr as speaker of the House. Alexander was chosen secretary of the Democratic caucus in the House. Pharr promised a session of "progress with moderation," which reflected the reserved approach of the new governor, Angus McLean, who had been elected in 1924 with a pledge to bring to Raleigh a more measured government than the state had experienced under his predecessor, Cameron Morrison.

Morrison, a Charlotte lawyer, had won a bruising campaign for the Democratic nomination in 1920 and in the fall defeated John J. Parker, the Republican candidate, who then practiced in Greensboro. Morrison's term had been marked by a dizzying expenditure of public funds. The legislature approved two bond projects – the first for fifty million dollars and a second for fifteen million – to pay for paved roads linking all of the county seats. Construction also began on a paved thoroughfare – Route 10 as it was called – that eventually connected the Outer Banks at Manns Harbor to Murphy in far-western Cherokee County. In the process, Kirkpatrick got the money for his Wilmington-to-Asheville road. In addition, bond money paid for an array of new buildings at the state's universities. The expansion of infrastructure, from roadways to shipping terminals on the coast, further linked Charlotte to an ever-expanding modern world.

Although Morrison began his practice in Richmond County, three counties to the east, Charlotte claimed him as its own. Since 1904, he had practiced law in the city in partnership with Henry C. Dockery. In 1916, he was considered a contender for the Democratic nomination, but he demurred until 1918, when he declared his candidacy. He won the support of the party's conservative leadership, led by United States Senator Furnifold Simmons, but his campaign stopped short after his wife died unexpectedly in November 1919. The loss was profound, and Morrison fell into a deep depression that lasted for months. A relative asked Heriot Clarkson to go to see his old friend. Some years later, Clarkson's son, Judge Francis O. Clarkson, Sr., related that his father made the requested visit. When he returned home, he told his family that Morrison agreed to go on if Heriot Clarkson would manage his campaign. Clarkson did more than that. He managed the campaign and then went to Raleigh in 1921 to help the new governor transform his plans into legislative action. In 1923, Morrison appointed Clarkson to the Supreme Court to fill the seat vacated by the death of Charlottean Platt D. Walker.

The 1925 General Assembly that seated Julia Alexander would be most remembered for a contentious debate over evolution. Governor Morrison had given the anti-evolutionists an early victory when he orchestrated a ban by the State Board of Education of two high school textbooks that included the teaching of the theory of evolution. Speaking at the dedication of a church education building in Charlotte, Morrison said that, as Governor, "I looked over the textbooks and found this theory of Darwin. You know, Darwin's theory on the descent of man is just a sideshow of this evolution question, and I found that these books had monkeys and men all mixed up in there together. This fool theory, I told the state Board of Education, must be thrown out."

GOVERNOR CAMERON MORRISON WITH HIS DAUGHTER ANGELIA

Early in the 1925 session, Representative David Scott Poole of Hoke County introduced a resolution asserting that it "was injurious to the welfare of the people of North Carolina" for any tax-paid teacher to "teach or permit to be taught as a fact, either Darwinism, or any other evolutionary hypothesis that links man in any blood relationship with any lower form of life." The resolution cleared the House committee and headed to the floor, where the galleries were packed with observers. The debate was vigorous and righteous, but not without its humorous side as well. Future United States Senator Sam J. Ervin, Jr., then a member of the House, said on the floor: "I know nothing about evolution; neither do I care anything about it. To be very frank with you, gentlemen of the House, I don't see but one good feature in this thing, and that is that it will gratify the monkeys to know they are absolved from all responsibility for the conduct of the human race."

The resolution failed to clear the House, despite the determined support of Julia Alexander and others. A little more than a year later, the issue was still very much alive, thanks in part to *The Fundamentalist*, a periodical published by Alexander. She wrote in the inaugural issue, "This paper will always stand for the fundamentals of the Christian faith, and for the fundamentals of American government." In early May 1926, just weeks before the Democratic primaries, where Alexander was running for re-election, a meeting of religious fundamentalists gathered under the name The Committee of 100 in an effort to keep alive the anti-evolution movement.

The campaign against Darwinism, which had spread into a battle over intellectual freedom at the University of North Carolina, was too much for Charles W. Tillett, Jr., an outspoken defender of University president Harry W. Chase and of his alma mater. He and other University graduates, including fellow Charlotte attorneys William T. Shore and R. M. Boyd, attended the Committee of 100 meeting and, through a parliamentary gaffe on the part of the organizers, were granted standing. Later in the day, Tillett's group outmaneuvered the sponsors of a resolution aimed at all public schools, including the University, that would have allowed only those who believed in the entirety of the Bible to teach. The proponents' argument fell apart after Shore rose to ask what the committee proposed to do about those who fell outside this narrow boundary, "How," he asked, "about a Jew, or a Catholic or men of no expressed religious affiliation?" The sponsors stumbled in their answers and the meeting broke into considerable confusion. Feelings ran high; one outraged Baptist minister challenged one speaker to step outside and settle their differences "in a manful way."

Several weeks after the meeting, one of the organizers of the Committee of 100, Zebulon V. Turlington of Mooresville, was asked why the session adjourned in confusion. According to Robert W. Winston in his biography of legendary University of North Carolina philosophy professor Horace Williams, who had taught Tillett and others and had rallied them to the defense of the University, Turlington answered, "Why, our opponents adopted an old political device. They came into the meeting and took it over." When Turlington's comment was reported to young Charles Tillett, he was reported to have laughed and said, "Maybe! And so it goes."

In the ensuing election, Mecklenburg County voters did not return Alexander to the legislature. She and two other anti-evolutionists were defeated by an opposing ticket that included her fellow lawyer, Carrie McLean. At the time of the election, McLean had just completed her term as the first female president of the Mecklenburg Bar Association. Her election as president was a singular triumph for women attorneys, but her colleagues made little of the fact that they had elevated a woman to lead the local bar.

At the Association's annual meeting in late January 1925, at which McLean presided, the evening program, complete with dinner, was held at the sumptuous Southern Manufacturers' Club. Seventy-seven attorneys and their guests enjoyed music and fun, including a series of skits that roasted the local legislative delegation. J. Laurence Jones appeared in "coat suit and wig" as Julia Alexander. One skit singled out little Avery County for special ridicule. Attorney W. M. Smith, impersonating a legislator from that mountain county, said, "All we want is to repeal that obnoxious Eighteenth Amendment to the federal Constitution to permit the legal operation of stills."

Among the matters the new bar officers reviewed each year were the management of the court calendar, now presided over by a committee composed of Plummer Stewart, Carol D. Taliaferro and C. Hundley Gover, and the "rules of the bar," which, loosely interpreted, meant setting minimum fees. The fee schedule adopted in 1921 was to be "accepted as a correct standard of the value of legal services, subject to increases in any particular case by reason of work or skill required or responsibility assumed." The fee for a half-hour consultation was five dollars, with five dollars more for the next half hour and then two dollars and a half for each half hour after that. The rate for an uncontested divorce was $50. The fee increased to $75 in a contested case without alimony. While "charges should never be made on a time basis when it is practicable to charge in some other manner," the per diem rate was $25 to $150, depending on the age, experience and ability of the lawyer, and whether the work was for litigation or office work.

The rate for an uncontested divorce was $50.

These two items, court calendars and fee schedules, were usually the only matters of regular business on the Association's agenda. From time to time, its leaders attempted, always in vain, to have the legislature give Mecklenburg County its own judicial district, one that was separate from Gaston County. During her one term in the House, Carrie McLean advanced another idea that promoted Charlotte's individuality. She proposed the consolidation of city and county government in Mecklenburg County. All public schools would be under one board and some small municipalities would have been eliminated. She said at the time she did not expect the measure to pass, but she wanted to start the discussion about economy and efficiency in government. A similar effort was promoted in the late 1940s. In 1960, all the public schools in the county were consolidated under one governing board, a move that was to have unforeseen consequences in the desegregation of the local public schools a decade later, but further city-county consolidation remained an unresolved issue.

In the 1920s, Charlotte civic boosters enjoyed an exuberant period as they set their sights on building a football stadium in league with the American Legion, on opening a civic center and on an unsuccessful effort to bring the University's medical school to their city. The city's growth seemed to have no limit. Between 1920 and 1930, the population would nearly double to more than 82,000, and the county's population would go from a little more than 80,000 to more than 127,000.

Public facilities, including more paved streets and a replacement for the 1897 courthouse on South Tryon Street, were on the public agenda. Charlotte had become the commercial and retail center of a large part of the Carolinas, and the city attracted lawyers starting a law practice, as well as those who joined the small but established firms. John J. Parker, a native of nearby Monroe, who had practiced first in Greensboro and then in Monroe, came to Charlotte in 1922 to practice law with Plummer Stewart, John A. McRae, and a young lawyer named William H. Bobbitt, a future state Supreme Court Chief Justice. In the years ahead, Parker was to become a national figure.

Bobbitt was just beginning his legal career. He had graduated from the University of North Carolina in 1921, and his undergraduate work had included one year of law classes. He was not old enough to take the bar examination, and so he continued his legal education with Stewart and McRae while he supported himself as a schoolteacher. Bobbitt might have remained a teacher if McRae had not lent him the money to take the refresher courses he needed to prepare himself for the bar examination, which he passed in 1922. In his first year of practice, he took the defense of a client charged with bootlegging to the state Supreme Court.

Fred B. Helms, a Union County native and a World War I veteran, was fresh from the Wake Forest Law School when he applied to A. B. Justice for work as an associate in 1922. In his published biography Helms later recalled, "This was something new in those days. They didn't have associates. You had to start out on your own. As a matter of fact, the few men that were partners wouldn't even take their own sons in. They had to start out and show that they could make good on their own before they would take them in." Justice agreed to Helms's request and offered him a job at $50 for the first month, $75 for the second and, from then on, $100 a month, plus one half the fees from Helms's clients. Helms worked with Justice for a year before opening a solo practice. His income got a boost in 1925 when he was named city solicitor, a part-time job prosecuting minor criminal offenses that paid $175 a month.

Helms was one of many lawyers who haunted the oversized courtrooms in the large domed courthouse on South Tryon Street, where trials remained a form of local entertainment, much as they had been in the middle of the nineteenth century. When word got out that a leading lawyer was arguing a case, "businessmen, bankers, and everybody else would leave their offices and go and sit in the courtroom," Helms recalled. "Unless you went to court and tried cases, you just weren't a lawyer at all."

When it opened in the late 1890s, the South Tryon Street courthouse had been called sufficient "for all time," but with the exploding growth of Charlotte it had become inadequate. In 1922, the county commissioners started planning to replace it, but four years passed before work actually began. They had selected Louis H. Asbury, the first North Carolinian admitted to the American Institute of Architects, to design the new courthouse. Rather than rebuilding on South Tryon Street, the commissioners chose a site on East Trade Street, where it would be a companion building for Charlotte's new 1925 City Hall. Members of the bar were involved in each step, including selling the county the land for the new building. They kept a small strip of the original property for a new Law Building.

The first meeting of the shareholders of the Charlotte Law Building, Inc. was held on January 21, 1926. More than half of the members of the Mecklenburg Bar were on hand to elect the corporation's directors, who included Plummer Stewart, C. Hundley Gover, Carol D. Taliaferro, E. T. Cansler, Jr., J. A. Lockhart, C. A. Cochran, Chase Brenizer, J. L. DeLaney, F. M. Redd, W. C. Davis, Charles Tillett, Jr. and J. A. Bell. The directors approved the purchase of land owned by B. F. Withers, a lawyer, who was to be paid $120,000 and allowed to remain in his house for another eight months. At a meeting three days later, at which Stewart and Gover were elected president and vice president, respectively, the officers approved the sale of the Withers property to the county for $60,000, saving for the corporation a 50-by-145 foot lot for its own at the corner of what was then East Avenue and Myers Street.

Stewart and Gover were the main drivers of the Law Building project, although the Tilletts, father and son, owned about ten percent of the corporation's stock. E. T. Cansler, Sr. and his son were also major shareholders. When stock sales lagged, John McRae suggested that non-lawyers be allowed to invest, but his motion failed. The directors pressed on, feeling ambitious. When they interviewed architects, they talked about a building that would have a foundation suitable for twelve stories. The final building was set at eight stories, with two floors left unfinished and only roughed in.

Years later, two additional floors were added to the original building. After a committee had interviewed seven firms, Asbury, the county's architect, was chosen to produce the plans. He won in a final ballot over C. C. Hook, the designer of the new city hall, fine homes, including James B. Duke's Charlotte mansion, and buildings at Trinity College, now Duke University, in Durham. The law library was to be housed in the new building. The shareholders in the old Law Library Association were given stock in the new corporation equal to the $6,000 value placed on the collection.

The bids for the eight-story building came in higher than anticipated, and shareholders recommended that the size be reduced, but the officers argued that there was sufficient interest from prospective tenants and that the taller building would be necessary to accommodate all those who wanted to rent space. The building committee, Stewart, Gover and the younger Cansler, saved money by buying elevator doors that had been designed for another building. The building was finally erected at a cost of $444,657. In November 1927, three months before the new courthouse was to open,

MAYOR F. MARION REDD AND LAW PARTNER, LEONIDAS L. CAUDLE IN THEIR LAW OFFICE IN THE LAW BUILDING THAT ONCE STOOD ON SOUTH TRYON.

the Mecklenburg Bar Association asked the judges to suspend court for two weeks so that lawyers could move their offices from South Tryon Street to the new Law Building by December 1.

For more than forty years, the East Trade Street Law Building would be the nucleus of the practicing bar. Gover, who as manager of the Law Building became a legend in his own right, managed it under strict rules. The largest shareholders were given first choice of space, with the corner offices available only to those who took at least three rooms – at $30 per month each – and only if the lawyer or firm owned at least $1,500 in stock. All offices were to be painted the same color; any changes to the décor had to be approved by the committee, which frowned on variety. In time, an address in the Law Building was essential to a lawyer's future. Turnover seldom occurred and Gover allocated space as he desired. Some newcomers to the Bar had to wait for the death of a tenant before an office became available.

While law offices and the law library occupied all the upper floors, the ground floor and basement were leased to others. Independent Trust Company opened a branch banking office on the northeast corner, while the Lawyers Title Insurance Company office was adjacent to a smoke shop run by Cliff Stewart. When the building opened, space that had been set aside in the basement for a barbershop was still available. Eventually the space originally occupied by the smoke shop became a coffee shop, a traditional gathering place for the occupants.

The work on the county's new courthouse, its fifth, was not quite complete when the building opened on January 9, 1928. Superior Court Judge William F. Harding convened the first session of court. *The Charlotte Observer* called the building a "million-dollar temple of justice." It actually cost $1.125 million. The four-story building, finished in limestone, was less pretentious than its domed predecessor. The main façade included a Corinthian portico that was

THE "NEW" LAW BUILDING, DESIGNED BY LOUIS ASBURY

flanked by end bays with tall, arched windows on the second floor. Under its roof were the court facilities, offices for the sheriff, clerk of court, register of deeds, extension agents, tax collector, the county commissioners and the county board of education. The top floor housed the county jail. With one round of remodeling of the interior in the 1960s, it was to serve for the next fifty years.

FIFTH COUNTY COURTHOUSE, DESIGNED BY ARCHITECT LOUIS ASBURY, FEATURED AN UNDERGROUND TUNNEL WHICH WAS USED TO TRANSPORT PRISONERS FROM

THE GARAGE TO THE SEVEN COURTROOMS, A ROOFTOP JAIL, A MUSEUM, AND A KITCHEN WHICH FED PRISONERS. JURORS AND OFFICERS OF THE COURT.

Loray Mill Trial

CHAPTER 5

An Historic Trial & Hard Times

A little over a year after the new courthouse opened for business, it became the scene of a drama that was to play out on the national stage. As the textile industry had moved south, the strife between labor and management that played a role in prompting that migration followed it. In nearby Gastonia, the National Textile Workers Union attempted to organize the workers at Loray Mill, the first textile mill in that county owned by outsiders, who worked under conditions that would now be considered inhumane. The mill's owners began to fire those workers who attended union rallies that began on March 30, 1929. Eighteen days later, nearly a hundred masked men destroyed the union's local headquarters, and it had relocated to a tent city, secured by armed guards, on the outskirts of town.

The mill resumed operation with non-striking workers. On the night of June 7, 1929 a group of strikers who approached the mill to call out the night shift were repulsed by sheriff's deputies. Later that night, four local policemen, led by Chief of Police Orville Frank Aderholt, arrived at the tent city, demanding that the guards hand over their weapons. In the ensuing melee, Aderholt was killed and two policemen and several strikers were wounded. Eight of the strikers and eight union organizers were subsequently indicted for murder and conspiracy to commit murder.

The atmosphere throughout Piedmont North Carolina was charged with anger, fear and uncertainty. Recognizing that, the court moved the trial from Gaston County to Mecklenburg County, which, with Gaston, formed the Fourteenth Judicial District. To refute accusations that North Carolina was about to commit a legal lynching, Governor O. Max Gardner sent in Judge Maurice V. Barnhill, who was from Rocky Mount in eastern North Carolina, to sit in for Judge Harding, the local resident Superior Court judge. (Barnhill would later serve on the North Carolina Supreme Court, in his last two years as Chief Justice.)

The state's first attempt to try the defendants ended in a mistrial after a juror was disqualified as insane when three attendants were required to drag him back into the courtroom. The man's collapse followed prosecutor John G. Campbell's display in the courtroom of a life-size, plaster-of-paris effigy of the slain police chief, outfitted in the chief's blood-caked clothing, his signature black hat and neatly tied, scuffed shoes. The presiding judge immediately ordered the prosecutor's creation removed, but not before the jurors got a good look and heard the gasp from the grieving widow at the prosecution table.

Ella May Wiggins

A few days after the first trial ended abruptly, Ella May Wiggins, a mother of five, was shot and killed in Gastonia as a mob chased a truckload of striking workers. A poet and a leader in the strike, her life story was to become the stuff of legends. The second trial resumed just as another strike erupted in Marion, seventy-five miles away in the foothills of the Blue Ridge, where four striking workers were shot and killed by the sheriff and his deputies. Before the Aderholt case went to the jury, the lead prosecutor excused himself from the Charlotte courtroom to go to nearby Concord to participate in a trial arising from the kidnapping and flogging of a British union organizer who had been abducted by the mob that had killed Wiggins.

The Loray Mill case was loaded with ingredients guaranteed to produce sensational headlines: armed conflict, communists, hungry women and children on the picket lines, "hugging and kissing" in the union hall, and "godless Reds," whose testimony was labeled as suspect by the presiding judge. The judge allowed Campbell to challenge the veracity of a defense witness on the ground that he was an atheist. The breathless reporting common to the day included front-page photographs of the jury and the prosecution team, which read like a local political directory.

The first trial had opened in late August before a packed crowd. At Campbell's side was an array of legal talent that included: E. T. Cansler, Sr., who was described as a "most able strategist;" Clyde Hoey of Shelby, a former U. S. attorney and state legislator who was the governor's brother-in-law and who would himself later be elected governor; former congressman A. L. Bulwinkle of Gastonia, who had been hired to look after the interests of Loray Mill and who commanded a troop of special "deputies;" R. Gordon Cherry of Gastonia, whose appearance was delayed so that he could assume command of the state American Legion, and Charlotte lawyer Jake F. Newell, who had been retained by Gaston County, as was Cansler. Also at the table were Gastonia attorneys Edgar Whitaker, A. G. Mangum and A. E. Woltz, the latter two members of the state Senate.

Five Charlotte lawyers and three attorneys from out of state made up the defense team. At the second trial, the chief local counsel was J. Frank Flowers, who was joined by his law partner, W. H. Abernethy. Both were brought into the case by Tom P. Jimison of Charlotte. Jimison was a former minister who had only recently turned to the law after his fondness for drink had disqualified him from his Methodist posting. A zealous supporter of the Gastonia workers, Jimison had been supported since spring with financial aid and advice from the American Civil Liberties Union, which sent its chief counsel, Arthur Garfield Hays of New York, to Charlotte for the first trial. The ACLU also imported Tennessean John Randolph Neal, who had been chief counsel for the defendant schoolteacher in the 1926 Scopes "monkey trial." Another out-of-towner was Leon Josephson, the lawyer for the Communist Party's legal organization, the International Labor Defense, which, along with the ACLU, was paying attorney

NATIONAL GUARDSMEN CAMPED AT THE LORAY MILL

fees and expenses. In the weeks leading up to the trial, Harvard University law professor and future United States Supreme Court Justice Felix Frankfurter solicited support from the local bar, and despite the sentiment against the defendants, two Charlotte lawyers, Johnson D. McCall and Thaddeus A. Adams, joined the defense team. McCall, Flowers, and Adams had served or would later serve as presidents of the Mecklenburg Bar, McCall in 1914, Flowers in 1931 and Adams in 1946.

The second trial, which began in September 1929, did not draw the same crowds, but the sessions produced their own share of headlines and drama, especially after the evidence was in and the attorneys took the floor for their closing arguments. Before the verdict was in, the new courtroom would become the stage for histrionic closing arguments that provoked comment from around the world.

Cansler and Hoey consumed hours as they laid out their versions of the law and the evidence. Jake Newell of the prosecution team brought tears to the eyes of jurors and spectators as he held the blood-stained clothes of the police chief, described the scene and wailed, "O, the criminality of it all. O, the fatal hand and the fatal deed," and then called for the jury to convict the defendants for a crime he said was "black as night, black as hell."

Alternating with the prosecutors were McCall, whom the newspapers called "an entertaining pleader of the homespun school," and Adams, who was described as "a roarer and a cooer, a whisperer and a thunderer." McCall followed Newell to the floor and ridiculed the state's case, saying, "The man that would believe such stuff as this should be tapped at the temples and bled at the frog of the foot." McCall was a former leader in the Anti-Saloon League and a product of the era of New South boosterism that brought textile mills to the region around the turn of the century. Nonetheless, he complained as bitterly as a strike-bound revolutionary about the Gastonia cotton mills "who grind the bones and faces of the working men into shekels to fill their coffers." The gist of the closing arguments was that the defendants were simply hard-working laborers who had fired in self defense.

Adams was as passionate and colorful as McCall. The working man had fought the world's wars, and it was the working man who "plunged into the reddest, hottest battle the world has ever seen, where they rode like centaurs and fought like devils and hurled back the bloody Hun in his march across Europe and made the world safe for democracy. They say these men fought. Well, our forefathers fought. If labor waits till it gets what it wants without a struggle, without opposition, they will forever remain seres [classical Greek for dry vegetation]."

Prosecutor Campbell's theatrics closed the case for the state. The day after his closing performance, a *New York Times* editorial writer wrote, "He wore out two boutonnieres, got dust and grease on his new blue suit, wilted his collar and made a rage of his time. These were merely his physical demonstration. In language, the solicitor soared into the Empyrean and beyond, knocking even at the gates of paradise and called the attention of the Deity and the apostles to what the union agitators had done to Gastonia."

Campbell lay on the floor to illustrate the position of one of the injured officers and then remained there for a full three minutes continuing his argument.

At one point Campbell lay on the floor to illustrate the position of one of the injured officers and then remained there for a full three minutes continuing his argument. Later, he dropped to his knees before the jury to portray the grieving widow at her husband's bedside as he lay dying in the hospital, saying, the chief and his officers were doing their duty to "stop the infernal scenes that came sweeping down from the wild plains of Soviet Russia into the peaceful community of Gastonia, creeping like the serpent crept into the Garden of Eden."

The tumultuous trials that had consumed Charlotte, and Gastonia, for nearly two months ended on October 19, 1929, after the jury spent fifty-seven minutes agreeing on a guilty verdict for all seven of the defendants who had not been dismissed from the case. Judge Barnhill imposed sentences of up to twenty years for the labor organizers from out of state, and lesser penalties for the local workers. All were released on bail, pending appeal. Fred Beal, the leading figure among the accused, fled to the Soviet Union, as did others. He subsequently returned in 1938 and surrendered to Hoey, who by that time had been elected governor. Beal was paroled in 1942 and died in 1954.

The trial had produced more legal theater for the community than it had ever seen. There would be other sensational trials in the county's courtrooms, but none that so closely bound together the passion and emotions of an entire region undergoing a fundamental change. The textile industry, and the workers who filled the more than seven hundred mills that were located within one hundred miles of the Square at Trade and Tryon, were a driving force in the local economy, and mill owners called on the city's bankers and businesses for investment and operating capital. The plants drew their energy from Duke Power Company, which had made Charlotte its headquarters, and the owners depended on cotton brokers and others for both raw materials and the sales of finished goods. The expansion of the industry in North Carolinas had made it possible for merchants like William Henry Belk to grow his network of department stores from his East Trade Street location to communities all across the Carolinas. The Efird chain of stores tracked right along behind, and Ivey's, a store that offered

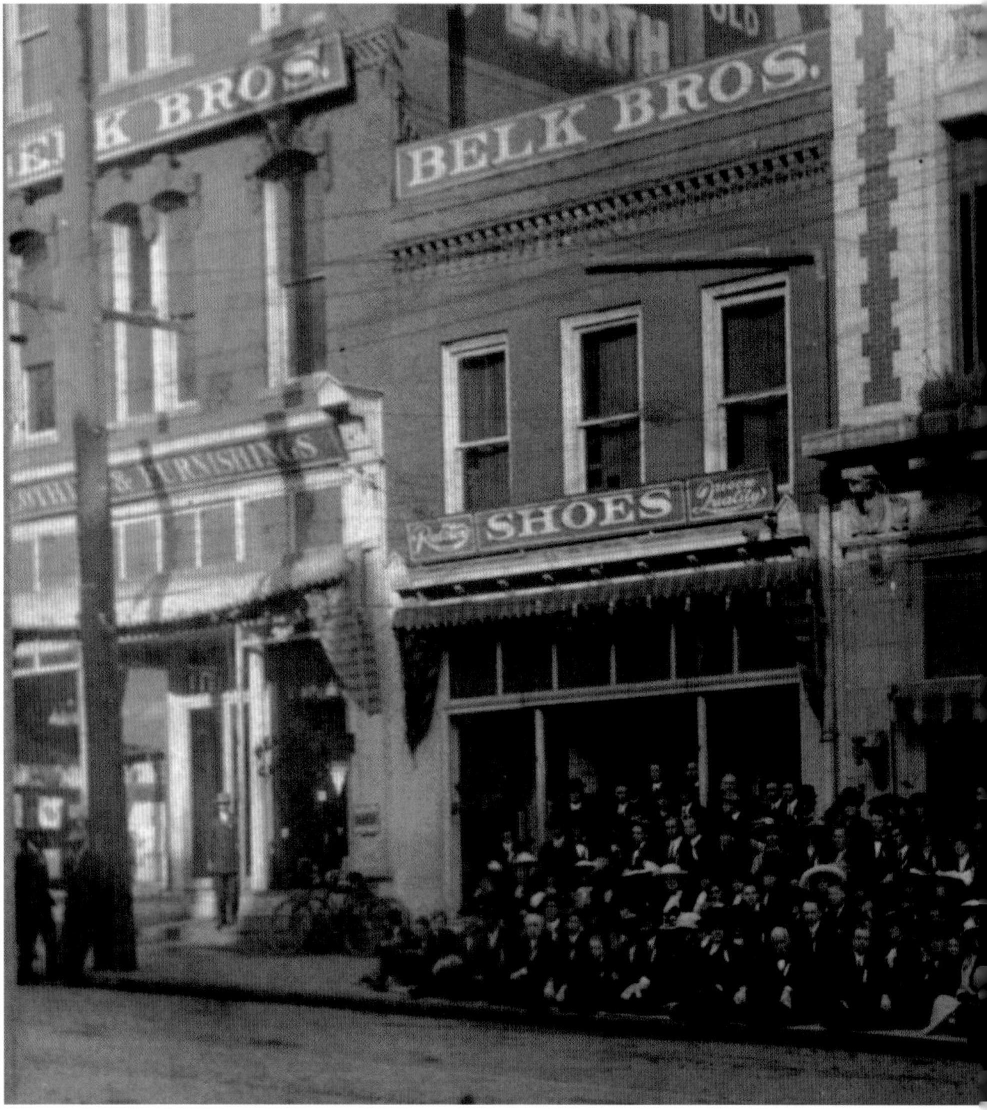

higher-priced merchandise, was soon recognized as a fashion center.

By 1930, the growth of the Charlotte business community had helped to expand the city's population and added to the general prosperity of the county's business and professional citizens. New buildings, some would even call them skyscrapers, were going up on Tryon Street. Many of those who lived in the city's best neighborhoods, notably Myers Park, designed by landscape architect John Nolan, a protégé of Frederick Law Olmsted, lived on fortunes built on the region's expanding business enterprises.

The days of booming business and comfortable bank accounts were, however,

BELK STORES, CIRCA 1910

about to end. Four days after the verdict in the Gastonia case, the Wall Street stock market crashed, and the hard times that had been plaguing the workers in the textile mill villages began to spread across the land. The Great Depression had begun. Reduced wages – or no wages at all – would soon become commonplace throughout the nation. By the end of 1930, the textile mills would slow to part-time operation or cease production altogether. The state's financial institutions would find themselves in deep trouble; within the year, eighty-eight North Carolina banks would fail.

Hard times would bring an end to the prosperity that Mecklenburg County lawyers had enjoyed in the 1920s, when the Law Building had easily filled the available space at its new location on East Trade Street and Charlotte lawyers had enjoyed prominence in state affairs. Governor Morrison had returned to the city in 1925 at the end of his term as governor, along with his new wife, Sarah Watts, the widow of George W. Watts of Durham, one of the wealthiest women in the state. Her resources were such that when Governor O. Max Gardner needed help to save a bank in his hometown of Shelby, he called on Morrison and his wife for the funds to keep it from going under. Upon the death of United States Senator Lee S. Overman of Salisbury in December 1930, Gardner appointed Morrison to serve out the balance of his term. Morrison lost the seat in 1932 after a primary battle with Robert "Our Bob" Reynolds, an Asheville lawyer.

Overman's death came not long after he had urged President Herbert H. Hoover's nomination of Judge John J. Parker to the United States Supreme Court to replace the late Edward Terry Sanford. No member of the North Carolina bar was better known than Parker, who had balanced a legal career with his participation, as a Republican, in state politics. When he began his practice in Greensboro, he had made an effort to become involved in Democratic politics, but being rebuffed, had instead become a perennial Republican candidate. All of his political campaigns had been unsuccessful, but in 1923 his tenacity had been rewarded when he was appointed Special Assistant to the Attorney General of the United States. His 1925 nomination by President Calvin Coolidge to the Fourth Circuit Court of Appeals, the federal appellate court for North Carolina, South Carolina, Virginia, West Virginia and Maryland, had received prompt Senate approval.

Parker's 1930 nomination to the Supreme Court, however, ran into trouble. It was seen by some as an effort by Republicans to reinforce their party's success in the South in the 1928 elections, when Hoover had carried North Carolina and five other southern and border states. The nomination ran into opposition from organized labor and the National Association for the Advancement of Colored People (NAACP), both raising questions about Parker's fitness for the Court. Labor's opposition arose from Parker's decisions backing management in cases involving "yellow-dog" contracts, requiring coal-mine workers to sign an agreement not to join a union in order to obtain a job. The NAACP was outraged at Parker's endorsement of the disenfranchisement of blacks in North Carolina and for campaign statements in 1920 in which he declared that "participation of the Negro in the political life of the South is harmful to him and to the community."

Parker's nomination made it out of the Senate Judiciary Committee, but it failed to win a majority on the floor by the narrowest of margins, forty-one to thirty-nine. He would remain on the appeals court until his death in 1958, at which time he was the senior federal appellate court judge in the United States. He remains the longest-serving chief judge among all the federal circuits. Parker is generally credited with having conceived the idea of holding circuit judicial conferences to provide an opportunity for interaction between bench and bar, a practice later institutionalized nationally by statute. He served as the alternate United States Judge at the post-World War II Nuremberg Trials and was a major figure in urging the international spread of the rule of law in the wake of that experience.

Judge Parker's magnificent portrait looks down from above the bench in the local federal courtroom. He remains the Mecklenburg bar's most famous contribution to the world of law.

JUDGE PARKER

The reversal of economic fortunes took its toll among Charlotte attorneys. Francis Clarkson, Sr., a Marine aviator in World War I, the son of Supreme Court Justice Heriot Clarkson, had joined his father's firm in 1919. He reported that revenues for the work he and his partner, Carol D. Taliaferro, produced had fallen from $33,000 in 1928 to $23,000 in 1930. Three years later, in one of the most desperate years of the Depression, the firm's gross revenues fell to $13,620, leaving a net income for the pair of $4,393. Most of that income resulted from the firm's presence on the list of approved attorneys for the Home Owners Loan Corporation.

Richard C. Thigpen, Sr., who would later serve as president of the North Carolina Bar Association, found himself faced with an even greater challenge. In April 1933, he was trying to launch a new law practice in Charlotte, one that specialized in tax law. Thigpen, a Wilmington native and Trinity College law graduate, chose an office in the downtown business district, on the eleventh floor of the First National Bank Building in the 100 block of South Tryon Street. His practice specialty, a rarity in that day, seldom gave him cause to travel to the courthouse so the South Tryon address suited him, and its affordable $30 dollars a month rent was fortunate because he went many days without collecting a single dollar in fees.

In 1934, when D. B. Smith was elected president, the Mecklenburg Bar Association dropped its dues to $2 a year from $3. That same year, the North Carolina Bar Association's annual dues were reduced from $4 to $2. Their meager bank accounts did not mean that attorneys were not busy. The local Bar Association directed Smith to request additional terms of court to clear a congested docket. At the same time, many lawyers, like others, were having difficulty collecting from their clients. Even the owners of the Law Building were chasing delinquent accounts from its tenants. In 1935, the building's stockholders authorized its management committee, composed of Plummer Stewart, E. T. Cansler, Jr. and Hundley Gover, to employ Carrie McLean to begin collection proceedings against the delinquent tenants.

Meanwhile, despite its economic woes, the growing legal profession was undergoing changes demanded by a new era. Charles Tillett, Jr. was one of the local bar's most active participants in the modernization of the profession. In the 1920s, he had supported University of North Carolina President Harry Chase's efforts to upgrade the university's law school, including the selection of a dean chosen for his academic credentials, rather than his advanced age or his political connections. Tillett had been elected president of the Mecklenburg Bar Association in 1924, and in the late 1920s he had begun working with lawyers from across the state to seek a better system for the licensing of attorneys. The result was a proposal, endorsed at the North Carolina Bar Association's meeting in 1932, to create a statewide regulatory bar that would administer the annual examinations, issue licenses, and discipline attorneys when required.

Since 1915, the North Carolina Bar Association, whose membership was voluntary, had assisted the Chief Justice and two Associate Justices who, as officers of the Court, had traditionally examined and certified applicants seeking law licenses. In response to the Association's proposal, the 1933 General Assembly created a Board of Law Examiners that would operate under a new statutory organization, the North Carolina State Bar. The Chief Justice was named an ex officio member of the examining board. Among the first of the attorneys named to the Board was Tillett, who was elected president of the North Carolina Bar Association in 1934.

THE SMITH BUILDING, FIRST A BALLROOM, NEXT A LIBRARY, THEN HOME TO THE UNC LAW SCHOOL 1905-1925

The creation of the State Bar left North Carolina with both a statutory organization, to which every licensed lawyer in the state was required to belong, and a voluntary statewide organization that was free to take positions on issues of the day, support proposed legislation and create programs to serve both the legal profession and the public, functions that would have been inappropriate for a mandatory organization with compulsory dues. The state has since reaped benefits from this arrangement that its creators could not have envisioned in the 1930s.

This statewide reorganization did not alter the status of the Mecklenburg Bar Association, which continued to be a voluntary organization that focused its attention on local affairs. Its calendar committee remained in the hands of Plummer Stewart, and the periodic calendar calls had become a traditional time for lawyers to gather. Dues-paying members of the Association continued to be guaranteed delivery of a copy of the trial calendars.

In the hot summer months, the courts adjourned from mid-June until Labor Day, with only two weeks of criminal court scheduled to try the cases of those who could not make bail and were confined to the county jail awaiting trial. The Law Building coffee shop had become a gathering place for the local bar, and during the summer, lawyers would pass the time there until the mailman came, returning home if the day's mail brought nothing that called for their attention that day.

Throughout the Great Depression, there was a strong sense of brotherhood in the local bar. From time to time, attorney Elbert E. Foster, a colorful native of Charleston, South Carolina, took up a collection for tenants who were behind on their rent. Before coming to Charlotte, Foster had served as a stenographer in the United States Senate investigation into the Teapot Dome scandal. At the same time, all the lawyers stayed alert to tap potential clients, who knew that the Law Building was the obvious place to seek legal help. Some tenants were reputed to tip the elevator operators to direct potential clients their way. Every piece of business was important. During the depths of the Depression, Mecklenburg County lawyers charged a dollar to draw a deed and $10 to prepare a will.

Even in the depths of the Depression, the reputation of some of the Charlotte lawyers grew beyond the city. In 1937, the year E. T. Cansler, Sr. was president of the Mecklenburg Bar, he and his son, John, represented Anne Cannon Reynolds, the daughter of Z. Smith Reynolds, winning a settlement of $17 million from the Reynolds estate five years after the tobacco heir died under suspicious circumstances at Reynolda, the family mansion in Winston-Salem. Cansler seemed drawn to the unusual case. In 1921, he had successfully defended a will in which two white women in nearby Union County had left their estate to an African American man and his daughter. John J. Parker and Walter M. Clark, who would later become Chief Justice of the state Supreme Court, tried to break the will, arguing that whites would not leave an estate to blacks unless they were mentally incompetent. The case was later highlighted in Gene Stowe's 2006 book, *Inherit the Land: Jim Crow Meets Miss Maggie's Will.*

One of the most exciting days in the Law Building's long history took place in the late 1930s. David H. Henderson, who would later serve as president of the local bar, recounted a day when two attorneys were talking with a client, and a disagreement erupted just as the client was about to enter the elevator. He pulled a gun, shot and killed one of the attorneys and wounded the other. Sarah, the elevator operator, immediately shut the elevator doors and dropped the car to the basement floor. The shooting had occurred just outside the office of attorney Charles W. Bundy, a small, quiet, self-effacing man, who rushed out upon hearing the gunshot, grabbed the assailant's weapon and declared, "Hey, you. You can't go shooting off guns in this building."

In the shadow of Tryon Street commerce, Charlotte had a darker side. At one point in the 1930s, the city's murder rate was the highest in the country. Charlotte

CHARLOTTE POLICE DETECTIVES UPON RECEIVING AWARDS FROM J. EDGAR HOOVER FOR SOLVING A BANK ROBBERY BY THE TOUHY GANG, NOVEMBER 15, 1933. SECOND FROM LEFT IS FRANK N. LITTLEJOHN WHO LATER BECAME CHIEF OF POLICE.

was also notorious for its slot machines and illegal gambling parlors and the ease with which one could obtain bootleg liquor. One of those involved in cleaning up the town was Fred Helms, who earlier had declined to support Heriot Clarkson's crusade for prohibition. Recalling that day some years later, Helms related in his biography that he had told Clarkson, "Judge, with all due respect to you, you don't know what's going on in your home county here. I can pick up the telephone and I can call a certain number and a certain man, and I can have fifty gallons of liquor delivered to any spot in Charlotte in one to two or three hours. That's prohibition for you. It's a farce. It's worse than a farce. It's a criminal operation, and I'm for the liquor stores."

Judge Helms, like others among his contemporaries who had once served as part-time judges, carried that appellation for the rest of his career. He was one of the organizers of the Mecklenburg County Civic League, which successfully cleaned up local elections, abolished the traditional ward system and rid the city of slot machines.

At the end of the 1930s, with the reordering of the way the city was run, the beginning emergence from the Great Depression and the clouds of war gathering in both Europe and the Far East, another era was about to begin.

WASPS at Camp Davis, North Carolina Air Base

CHAPTER 6

World War II & After

Military preparations had begun months before the Japanese navy attacked Pearl Harbor on December 7, 1941. In mid-May 1941, three army officers and thirty-two civilians set up an office for the Charlotte Quartermaster Depot in the former Ford Motor Company assembly plant on Statesville Avenue, just north of downtown. The depot would eventually cover seventy-two acres and employ about 2,500 civilians who received and shipped everything from food and toothpicks to battle uniforms.

A few weeks after the Depot was opened, the army took over the city's airport and turned it into the Charlotte Army Air Base. The principal speaker at the dedication was colorful New York Mayor Fiorello LaGuardia, who warned of the growing challenge of Adolph Hitler. In 1942, the airport was named Morris Field in honor of William Colb Morris, a World War I aviator and a native of Harrisburg, a rural crossroads northeast of Charlotte. At the base, pilots and crewmen were trained, and recovered wounded airmen worked alongside women and civilians there to repair airplanes. Before the War, a group of Charlotte doctors had formed the 38th Evacuation Hospital, and after Pearl Harbor the unit was called to active duty and served in North Africa and Italy.

By 1940, Charlotte was a city of more than 100,000 residents, with another 50,000 living in the county. It was not overwhelmed with service personnel as it had been during World War I, but there was still a decided military presence in the city, and soldiers from nearby Camp Sutton in Monroe and Fort Bragg, outside Fayetteville, regularly came to Charlotte on weekend passes.

In 1941, there were 161 members of the local Bar. Forty-one of these went off to war. Few arrived to replace them; a 1958 directory listed only six local lawyers who had been licensed from 1942 through 1946. The remaining members of the Mecklenburg Bar Association took an active role in providing help for servicemen and their families. Volunteer lawyers worked in a first-floor office of the Law Building, where men facing the draft could receive free advice and help in understanding their obligations.

Attorney Neal Y. Pharr served as chairman of the local draft board and David E. Henderson, president of the Mecklenburg Bar in 1939, who would later serve briefly as a federal district judge, was chair of the regional draft appeal board.

The war effort helped keep the Law Building, still recovering from the Depression, filled. Offices vacated when lawyers left for military service were taken over by government agencies involved in the national emergency. The Office of Price Administration, initially created to control prices and rents during the wartime emergency and later to administer rationing scarce goods, took over a suite of offices.

New laws afforded service members more assistance than they had had in the First World War. The Soldiers and Sailors Civil Relief Act put on hold certain legal proceedings, such as divorce or foreclosure, and servicemen could apply for relief from mortgage and interest payments. In 1944 alone, Mecklenburg County lawyers, in their Bar's first organized public service project, handled at least fifty cases for servicemen. In 1945, Association president Jake Newell noted that this was a decided change. "Our profession," he observed, "has always been inclined to hold back too much and too long against every urge for change, as, to cite one instance, the dominant opposition of so many years to the workman's compensation act, with its consequent elimination of negligence, contributory negligence, negligence of a fellow servant, and assumption of risk in industrial accidents – now generally conceded as a very humane law."

ARMY MESS HALL

In January 1946, at the time of the Association's first meeting after the surrender of Japan in August 1945, the careers of lawyers and lawyers-to-be that had been sidelined by military service were back on track. Eighteen returning members were recognized for their service. Fred Helms had finished presiding over a meeting of the North Carolina State Bar when James B. McMillan, a Harvard Law School graduate, approached him and asked for a job. McMillan, who would serve as president of both the local bar and the North Carolina Bar Association and then become a federal judge, later recalled, "I went to the meeting in the only clothes I had, my Navy uniform."

While McMillan and others whose careers had, like his, been interrupted by the war were looking for jobs, others were finding their way into the nation's law schools. The GI Bill enabled many who would otherwise never have had access to higher education to seek a career in the law. Both returning veterans and the new graduates were a different generation of lawyers. Older, trained to lead, matured by their war experiences, many of them returned to civilian life, as one observer put it, "determined to make theirs a better world." As a new generation emerged from law school and found their place in the profession, no longer would the bar be dominated by those whose professional careers were an inherited legacy and who had in their time seen little change in the law, in the way that law was practiced and indeed in their community.

Charlotte and Mecklenburg County, with a booming post-war economy, would become the destination for many of those who by the end of the 1940s would be looking for a place to practice law. Those who had left their practices two, three, or even four years earlier were seeking new situations, while law schools were turning out men, and incrementally a few women, eager to enter the profession. As a measure of the change this represented, the 1958 Martindale-Hubbell legal directory listed eighty local lawyers who had been licensed to practice law in the seven years after World War II, the years when the GI Bill had its greatest impact. This was nine more than had been licensed in the entire fifteen years from the beginning of the Great Depression through the end of the war. Indeed, by 1958, only seventy-five lawyers licensed before 1930 – before the Great Depression – were still listed in active practice.

Veterans joining the ranks of the bar were sometimes understandably reticent about discussing their war experiences. Few knew that James J. Caldwell was a survivor of the infamous Bataan Death March and had weighed less than ninety pounds when he was liberated from a Japanese prison camp near the end of World War II or that John D. Hicks walked with a cane as the result of a shattered hip he sustained when his jet fighter plane crashed into the ocean. Some knew that as the war in Europe was ending, Army officer Porter B. Byrum had required the inhabitants of a German town to accompany him to view a nearby recently liberated concentration camp. Only a few knew that William H. Scarborough required shoes that were custom made to fit feet badly damaged in the Battle of the Bulge.

Only upon the death of quiet, exceptionally modest Stuart B. Childs did his friends piece together his remarkable history. Volunteering for the Army Air Force at age eighteen, he had piloted a four-engine transport plane in night missions across "The Hump" in the China-Burma-India Theater in World War II. Returning to college on the GI Bill at age twenty-two, he had remained in the Air Force Reserves, learning to fly fighter planes. Again volunteering for active duty in the Korean War, he flew 125 combat missions before being assigned to Edwards Air Force Base. There he was the chief test pilot, testing every one of a succession of supersonic fighter planes up to the first rocket-propelled plane, the Bell X-1. One of the men under his command was the legendary Chuck Yeager, the hero of author Tom Wolfe's, *The Right Stuff*. Other test pilots he had commanded were among our first astronauts. Two years short of retirement, Childs had left the service and entered law school.

The city to which these veterans came was filling out nicely from its center at Trade and Tryon Streets, although Independence Square remained the retail crossroads for many who lived throughout the Piedmont, as stores like Belk's, Efird's and

STUART B. CHILDS AND JET

FEDERAL RESERVE BANK, C. 1945

Ivey's continued to draw shoppers to downtown Charlotte. Indeed, the Belk stores, which were steadily being replicated in other communities, would ultimately become the largest privately-owned mercantile empire in the entire country.

In the years immediately after the war, Charlotte began to establish itself as a commercial and banking center for the Carolinas. The city's economy was founded on three pillars: manufacturing (mostly textiles) wholesaling and banking. By 1951, the city boasted eight commercial banks, two national banks with five branch offices, including one that in 1948 opened the state's first drive-in branch, and five state banks with seven branches among them. The banks' main offices were within a few steps of the Charlotte Branch of the Federal Reserve of Richmond that had opened in 1927 on South Tryon Street. A 1951 profile of the city in *Business Week* approvingly dubbed Charlotte "a paper town" – because most of its business is done on paper.

Tall office buildings lined South Tryon Street and these mid-century "skyscrapers" housed the offices of emerging businesses and a few law firms whose practices focused on commercial transactions generated by the thriving economy. By 1950, Charlotte's population had grown to more than 134,000, an increase of nearly a third in a decade.

The war years had been a time of transition in many ways. Between 1940 and 1945, one generation of attorneys had given way to another. The local bar had lost one of its most highly regarded members in 1943 with the death of E. T. Cansler, Sr., a former president of the Mecklenburg Bar Association. Cansler's legal career had begun in Charlotte in 1887, and for over a half century he worked in small firms that included future Superior Court judges and Supreme Court justices. Herriot Clarkson, another founding member of the local Association, died in January 1942 after nearly twenty years on the North Carolina Supreme Court. The local Association continued a tradition begun in 1936, recording the loss of Cansler and Clarkson with memorial tributes delivered in open court. That tradition survives; over the years, the transcripts of those memorials have been preserved in the office of the clerk of court. The Association also mounted a plaque in the courthouse to recognize those who had served in the armed forces. Judge John J. Parker presided over the dedication ceremony.

Parker remained Charlotte's best-known jurist. In 1945, he held out some hope that a Democratic administration might give him another chance at a seat on the Supreme Court, but that did not happen. President Harry Truman did, however, appoint him Alternate Judge of the International Military Tribunal, created to try Nazi war leaders in Nuremburg, Germany. In 1953, upon the death of Chief Justice Frederick Vinson, the Mecklenburg Bar recommended Parker to President Dwight D. Eisenhower as a suitable replacement. Instead, the President chose former California governor Earl Warren, whose leadership of the Court would be felt for generations.

NUREMBURG TRIALS JUDGES FRANCIS BIDDLE (RIGHT) AND JOHN JOHNSTON PARKER

The veterans reviving their law practices and young lawyers whose careers had been displaced by the war formed a growing block within the Mecklenburg Bar Association. When the time for the election of officers for 1947 approached, the veterans consolidated their support behind William T. Covington, Jr., one of their own, and elected him president. Covington had recently formed a partnership with his law school colleague Hugh L. Lobdell.

J. Spencer Bell, another veteran who would later be president of the North Carolina Bar Association and serve in the North Carolina State Senate and on the Fourth Circuit Court of Appeals, followed Covington as president in 1948. The fee for Bar membership was raised to $10 for those with more than five years of experience and $5 for those with less tenure. Bell also created a committee, led by Joseph W. Grier, Jr, to produce continuing legal education courses for those lawyers who needed to update their skills after their military service.

After Bell's invigorating presidency, the Association then had sixteen committees, ranging from memorials and public information to ones focused on internal matters such as fees, legal ethics and grievances. The most important of these was the Calendar Committee, presided over by Plummer Stewart, a veteran of the courtroom whose dramatic closing arguments often drew crowds of spectators. Stewart paid little attention to his appearance, but even his worn suits and scuffed shoes did not preclude the elegant and precise E. T. Cansler from once asking him for help on a case involving an important New York client. When Cansler introduced Stewart to his client, the New Yorker's decided aversion to his colleague was obvious. But Cansler asked Stewart to tell the story of a girl who had been raised by wolves and by the time Stewart finished the tale, the client and his wife were deeply moved. When Cansler informed his clients that everything Stewart had just told them was a fabrication, they said, "You have the right man."

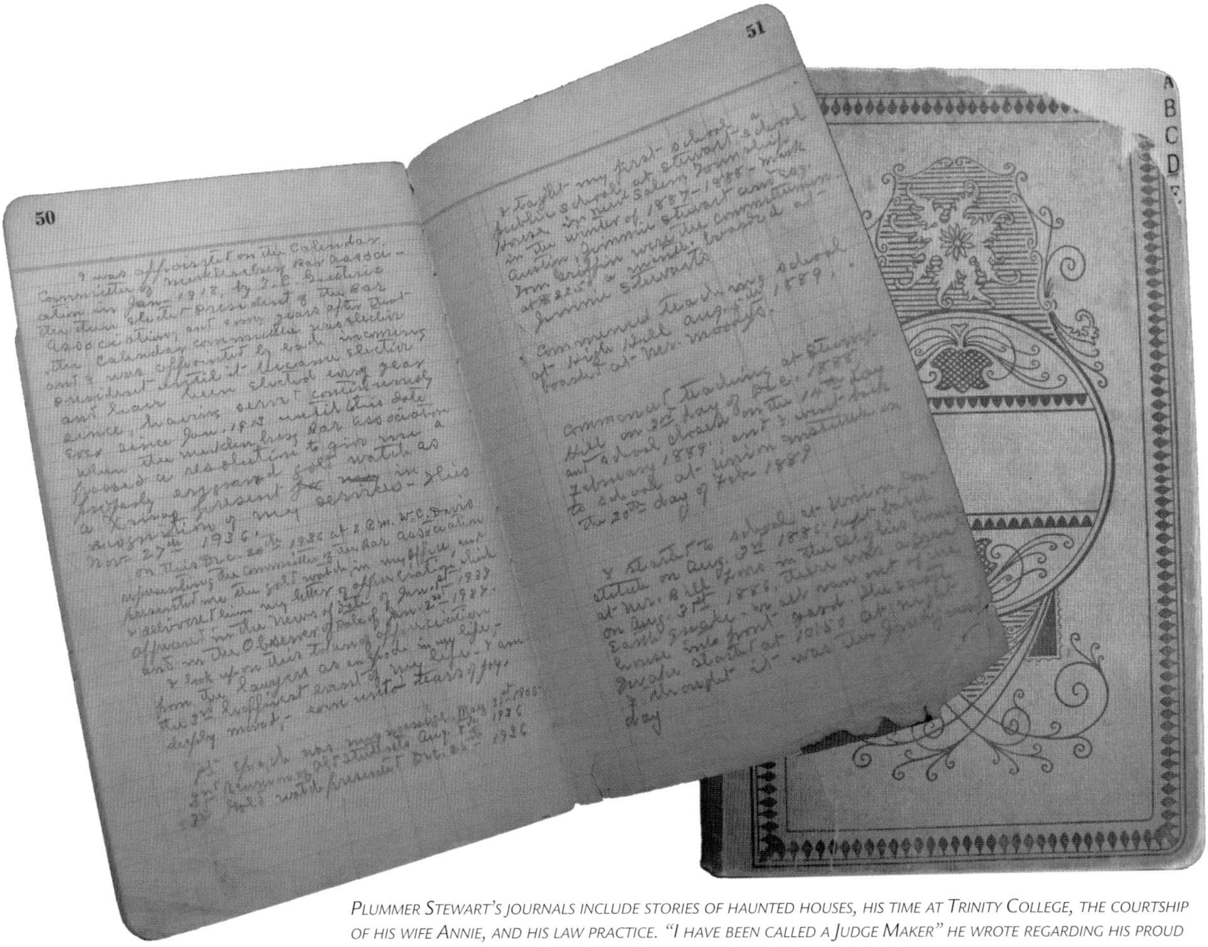

PLUMMER STEWART'S JOURNALS INCLUDE STORIES OF HAUNTED HOUSES, HIS TIME AT TRINITY COLLEGE, THE COURTSHIP OF HIS WIFE ANNIE, AND HIS LAW PRACTICE. "I HAVE BEEN CALLED A JUDGE MAKER" HE WROTE REGARDING HIS PROUD PARTNERSHIPS WITH BOTH JUDGE JOHN PARKER AND JUDGE WILLIAM BOBBITT.

Stewart had been Association president in 1918, had practiced law with Judge Parker and other luminaries of the Mecklenburg bar, and he now kept a firm hand on the scheduling of cases coming before the court. Though his age was showing, he retained the gravitas to move to trial cases that had languished too long on the docket and could withstand the entreaties of lawyers who wanted special favors. He remained chair of the committee until 1950, when the Association recognized his long service to the court. He was succeeded by Hunter M. Jones, who shared the work with committee members Francis Clarkson, Sr. and Hugh B. Campbell, Sr., both of whom would later serve as Superior Court judges and, in Campbell's case, thereafter as one of the first judges on a newly-created North Carolina Court of Appeals.

HUNDLEY GOVER

William B. McGuire, Jr. followed Bell as president in 1949. Later to become president of Duke Power Company, in 2011, he was the oldest living past president of the Bar.

While more law firms were opening offices on Tryon Street, the center of the legal community remained the Law Building, adjacent to the East Trade Street courthouse. During the Depression, the building's owners had worried about rent collections and full occupancy, but those days were over. In the years immediately after the war, the bar grew almost daily. Now, space was at a premium. As he had been from the beginning, the building's manager was Hundley Gover, known by everyone as "Gover" as few called him by his first name. A slim, soft-spoken, pipe-smoker with a shock of white hair, Gover took advantage of the tight rental market and controlled not only the availability of office space, but even the careers of lawyers trying to get a start in the city. Space was so scarce that one new lawyer operated out of the bottom drawer of another lawyer's desk.

"To get an office you had to go see Mr. Gover," Frank W. Snepp, Jr. recalled. Snepp, who would later serve in the state Senate and as a Superior Court judge, was fresh from military service and in need of an office. "He told me I had no chance of getting an office in the Law Building. Then, one day he said, 'You can move in tomorrow.' He gave me an office next to his. He was using me as sort of slave labor." Gover did not ask tenants about their preferences, and they moved as he directed. "One day he came up [to Snepp] and said, 'You are moving to seventh floor tomorrow.'" Interior decorations were forbidden. According to Snepp, "You could not do anything to your office. They were all brown." It was later said that Gover had a soft spot for young lawyers and gave them preference over established firms wanting to expand their offices.

Snepp later joined the firm of Paul R. Ervin and Herbert I. McDougle. Their offices were on the second floor of the Law Building in rooms that overlooked East Trade Street. The building was not air-conditioned, and in the summer the windows were open by necessity. One day, Gover happened by and saw that Ervin was rocked back in his chair with his feet up on the windowsill. Snepp said that Gover reacted immediately to Ervin's relaxed pose, saying, "That is not becoming of a lawyer, and if you ever do that again I will throw you out of the Law Building."

Gover also made a name for himself by aggressively perfecting the process of examining opposing clients and witnesses and evidentiary material long before modern civil rules came to provide more than limited pre-trial discovery. His copy of *Ragland on Discovery*, one of the first textbooks on discovery, was well marked and much-used, so much so that the local bar came to refer to pre-trial discovery as "goverizing." Conducting discovery of one's opponents – goverizing – gradually came to be generally, though often grudgingly, accepted and used by practically all members of the civil trial bar long before the adoption of the modern civil rules that now allow almost unlimited discovery. Gover died at his desk in 1957 while preparing for a pre-trial deposition.

At the courthouse, not yet air-conditioned either, windows were open in hot weather. As a result, the dust and traffic noise from the street drifted into the offices and courtrooms. Lawyers examining witnesses on the stand often had to suspend their questioning until the clatter from outside subsided. Because of the conditions there and in the Law Building, a summer's accumulation of dirt and sweat could ruin a man's clothes. "That was the day of light suits," recalled Marcus T. Hickman, "and they'd last about a season." Hickman, a native of Hudson, North Carolina, had come to Charlotte in 1948 after he finished law studies that had been interrupted by the war. He went to work for Frank H. Kennedy, another of the elders of the bar.

Kennedy was a founding member of a firm with the Charles Tilletts, father and son, that had been organized in 1916. Tillett, Tillett & Kennedy was dissolved in 1936 after the death of the elder Tillett. Kennedy went his own way as did Tillett's son, Charles, Jr., who was as well regarded around the state as his father had been. In addition to his work on behalf of the creation of the State Bar, the regulatory agency, Charles Tillett, Jr. had been elected president of the North Carolina Bar Association in the mid-1930s and was a long-time trustee of the University of North Carolina. He was a staunch supporter of the University's law school, where he lectured often, and he was deeply engaged in the American Bar Association's efforts to establish international tribunals as part of the United Nations after World War II. He was known as a

CAROL D. TALIAFERRO
UNIVERSITY OF VIRGINIA LAW SCHOOL
CLASS OF 1910

serious and intense lawyer with a chilly disposition who kept a set of the *North Carolina Reports* in his home so that he could continue legal research after he had finished his evening meal. A colleague once found himself standing at a street corner with Tillett and asked about a question of law. Tillett's reply was that he had not been paid to find an answer.

The tenants at the Law Building were leaving for lunch two days before Christmas in 1952, and Snepp, Ervin and Ben Horack, who had joined their firm, had just stepped out the door on the Myers Street side of the building when Tillett's body fell onto the sidewalk, landing ten or twelve feet away from where they stood. Tillett had thrown himself out of the window in his sixth-floor office, but he left no note or explanation as to why he took his own life. At the time of his death he was recovering from an illness that had reduced his mental capacities. Those who knew him speculated that his own standards of perfection would not allow him to continue if he could not perform as he had in the past.

One of the most senior members of the Bar of that era, Carol D. Taliaferro, was the sole survivor of one of the city's oldest firms. Clarkson, Duls & Taliaferro had been formed in 1912, the year the Mecklenburg Bar Association had been organized, but its antecedents dated to 1888 when Heriot Clarkson and Charles Duls had become law partners. After Duls went on the Superior Court bench in 1913, and Heriot Clarkson left for the state Supreme Court, Taliaferro remained in partnership with Francis Clarkson, Sr., the justice's son. In 1947, they added Joseph Grier, Jr. to the firm. Two years later, Francis I. Parker, the son of Judge John J. Parker, joined them. The youngest member of the firm, by then known as Taliaferro, Clarkson & Grier, was William E. Poe, who had come to Charlotte after a brief stint as an associate director of the Institute of Government in Chapel Hill. Like Grier, Poe was a Harvard Law graduate.

In the spring of 1952, new Bar under the leadership of its new president, Hugh B. Campbell, Sr., asked members to suspend business on Saturday, June 28, and to use their time to urge their friends and acquaintances to help elect Judge William H. Bobbitt, a Superior Court judge for sixteen years, to a vacancy on the state Supreme Court. Accustomed to having a Charlotte lawyer on the court for the first half of the century, Mecklenburg had not been represented on the court since the Heriot

Clarkson's death in 1942.

Before going on the bench, Bobbitt had worked with the leading members of the Mecklenburg Bar – Plummer Stewart, John J. Parker, and John McRae, the latter a former state legislator who had served as president of both the Mecklenburg and North Carolina Bar Associations. The turnout was strong, but not enough to overcome the support of R. Hunt Parker, an easterner from Enfield, who was elected to the seat. Two years later, Governor William B. Umstead appointed Bobbitt to the Court when Associate Justice Maurice Barnhill, who years earlier had presided over the Loray Mill trial, was promoted to Chief Justice. Fifteen years later, after the death of then Chief Justice Hunt Parker, Governor Bob Scott appointed Bobbitt Chief Justice.

When J. W. Alexander, Jr. was elected president of the Bar in 1955, he was joined by William H. Booe as vice president and John Hicks as secretary-treasurer. Francis H. Fairley was chosen to represent the local Bar on the State Bar Council. Executive committee members were Maurice A. Weinstein, William Covington, Jr., Charles E. Knox, Robert G. Sanders, Frank Snepp, Jr. and Henry L. Strickland. Most of these were veterans of World War II. Alexander, a partner of Whiteford S. Blakeney, one of the region's first labor law specialists, was a physically imposing man who had lost one arm in a farm accident. Booe would later serve on the local school board. Hicks, a naval aviation veteran who had gone to Yale Law School after nearly losing his life when his jet fighter flamed out in a carrier approach, went on to become an officer and director of Duke Power Company. Knox would serve as local Bar president in 1964 and Sanders and Fairley would later serve as presidents of the State Bar and Fairley would sit on the American Bar Association's Board of Governors.

Committee members cross-examined lawyers who sought a continuance and recorded their excuses so that they could not be used again.

The new calendar committee, Knox, long-time City Attorney John D. Shaw and James McMillan, set about revolutionizing the existing civil calendaring procedures by creating a set of rules under which cases automatically progressed toward trial in order of their filing. When a case came up for trial, the committee brooked few excuses for continuances. Committee members cross-examined lawyers who sought a continuance and recorded their excuses so that they could not be used again. Once a case appeared on the tentative calendar, it reappeared every two weeks until it was tried. That lawyers would get together to force their own cases to trial in an orderly fashion was both a remarkable departure from the previous custom and a rare practice among the state's judicial districts.

The weekly calendar call was more than a perfunctory administrative chore. "It was an important event to the lawyers who were anxious to get their case tried or anxious to get their cases put off for whatever reason," recalls Mark R. Bernstein, who began attending for his firm after he came to Charlotte in 1957. "The chair of the calendar committee was a person who made the decision on whether you went to trial or didn't go to trial, so attorneys would appear and argue. Secondly, it was sort of a social occasion, a time to interact with and meet with fellow lawyers. There were moments of high drama, with confrontations and arguments. If you did not get to calendar call, you might end up on the calendar sooner or later than you wanted to. Lawyers had all kinds of ingenuous reasons for not having their cases tried. It was an interesting time."

There were other changes afoot. At an August meeting in 1958, the Association had produced a report critical of the city and county courts that handled routine criminal cases. These Recorder's Courts, as they were called, had been established in cities, towns and counties over the years, and they were usually the average citizen's first contact with the justice system. The Bar officers took particular exception to the use of a city police officer as the clerk in the city courts, saying that this was a dangerous mix of the executive and judicial branches of government. At the time, a state grand jury was investigating irregularities in the operations of the local city Recorder's Court.

The Bar's attention to these lower courts came in the wake of a thorough examination of the state's judicial system by a statewide commission chaired by Charlotte's Spencer Bell. Four years after his term as president of the Mecklenburg Bar Association, Bell was elected president of the North Carolina Bar Association. In his inaugural address, he challenged that organization to be more than a social club that met once a year and to become engaged in real service to the profession and to the judiciary. During his year as president, Bell spoke out in his public appearances throughout the state about the need to update the state's judiciary. In July 1955, Governor Luther H. Hodges endorsed his concern that North Carolina courts "no longer held the high place in the minds of our citizens that they once held." He appointed Bell chair of the Committee on Improving and Expediting the Administration of Justice. It soon became known as the Bell Commission.

SPENCER BELL, 1927 DUKE YEARBOOK PORTRAIT

Bell made his case for improvements so persuasively that three North Carolina foundations agreed to pay for the commission's work, which was coordinated through the North Carolina Bar Association.

The commission's study continued for three years. Out of it came recommendations for a major overhaul of the court system, including elimination of the recorder's courts and justices of the peace, to create a unified statewide court system. It would have upended a judicial system that had been in place for nearly a hundred years. Especially alarming to some were provisions proposing the appointment, rather than the election, of judges. This so offended influential state Treasurer Edwin Gill that he campaigned about the state, warning of the ills of judicial corruption dating to the age of Julius Caesar.

The Commission prepared legislation to effect these changes. Bell himself was a member of the state Senate from 1955 to 1960. These proposals were presented to the 1959 General Assembly, where its proponents failed to get the three-fifths majority necessary to submit approval of constitutional amendments to the electorate. In 1961, with the active participation of the North Carolina Bar Association under the leadership of its then president, James McMillan, the Commission's recommendations finally gained legislative support. The proposed constitutional amendments passed the General Assembly, but only after the provision replacing election of judges with appointment was stripped from the bill. Voters approved the amendments in 1962, setting in motion the creation of the state's first unified and uniform court system, universally regarded as a national model. The continued selection of judges by popular vote has, however, remained a divisive issue.

In recognition of Bell's work, the North Carolina Bar Association presented him with its first John J. Parker Memorial Award. Created to honor Parker, who had died in 1958, the award recognizes "conspicuous service" to the cause of jurisprudence in North Carolina. It is not given every year, but over time, five other Charlotte attorneys would be so honored.

The 1950s were a watershed period in the life of the local bar. The elders who had shaped the county's legal profession in the first half of the century had been replaced by a corps of younger men, many of them World War II veterans, who brought about changes in the way the bar functioned. The practice itself was changing. Charlotte now had lawyers whose work focused on business transactions and who seldom, if ever, saw the inside of a courtroom. Law firms began a modest form of specialization, some handling only transactions, others only civil trial work, while others focused on criminal defense.

Charlotte firms were also growing larger. The largest firm of that era was Lassiter, Moore & Van Allen, a firm that had been formed in 1950 when Robert Lassiter, Jr. and James O. Moore combined their practices. Shortly thereafter, William K. Van Allen joined them. In 1957, the firm had five partners and four associates. By 1960, it would grow to ten attorneys. In 1959, when Clarence W. (Ace) Walker left a New York firm to join Kennedy, Covington, Lobdell & Hickman, he was the seventh lawyer in the group. By 1960, the firm would have four partners and four associates. When Carol Taliaferro retired from Taliaferro, Grier, Parker & Poe in 1958, he was the last direct link to the turn-of-the century firm of Clarkson & Duls. The firm's name was changed to Grier, Parker, Poe & Thompson. The last named partner was Sydnor Thompson, a Harvard Law graduate, who had joined the firm in 1954. By 1960, Helms, Mulliss, McMillan & Johnston had grown to seven lawyers.

The local bar also grew. When McMillan, a Harvard Law School graduate and wartime bomb disposal officer, took over as president in June 1957, succeeding his close friend and fellow Harvard Law classmate Joseph Grier, Jr., the local Bar had 144 members and $4,128.51 in its treasury. In his final report to the Bar in June 1958, McMillan noted that progress had been made on the need for more courtrooms and

SHOPPERS AT THE SQUARE IN UPTOWN CHARLOTTE, CIRCA 1955

more judges. "No calendar system pleases everyone," he wrote, "but I believe it can fairly be said that there has now been developed excellent liaison between the Calendar Committee and the Clerk of Superior Court. . . ."

Indeed, Mecklenburg County had grown so fast that it was handling one out of seven of all civil cases filed in the state, and the Charlotte courts were twelve to fourteen months behind in adjudicating these cases. McMillan had convened a Committee on Courts and Judiciary, appointing William Booe as chairman, and he wrote to Chief Justice J. Wallace Winborne, asking for relief in the form of a third superior court judge. He also noted that committees had been working to stop the unauthorized practice of law by banks in title searches, to provide more continuing legal education and to continue to improve legal aid for the community through volunteers from the Bar.

McMillan was president when the local Bar participated in the first Law Day on May 1, 1958, welcoming as the speaker its originator, American Bar Association president and Charlotte native Charles S. Rhyne of Washington, D.C. In the midst of the Cold War, Rhyne had suggested Law Day as a response to the Soviet Union's celebration of its militaristic May Day. "Charlotte observed the nation's first Law Day with unobtrusive simplicity," *The Charlotte News* said of the occasion. "There was no bombast, no parade, no rally. When you get right down to it, there were just a few words about the dignity of the law. Yet somehow this almost clinically low pressure celebration in Charlotte and other communities throughout the nation emerged as a wholly satisfactory antidote to a different kind of observance today in Soviet Russia and her satellites."

The tradition of the local Bar's Law Day celebration continues to this day. Over the years, most of the speakers on these occasions have been North Carolina justices, judges, law professors, public officeholders and notable citizens of the state. It is also the occasion for the annual awarding of the Bar's Liberty Bell Award, given to a nonlawyer for his or her contribution to freedom under law.

The late 1950s also saw the first glimmer of a new era of banking that later became the driving force behind the community's growth for the next five decades. North Carolina's post-Civil War 1868 Constitution allowed statewide branch banking, though for almost a century that provision had little impact. In the last quarter of the twentieth century and on into the twenty-first, the emergence of Charlotte as a banking center would have a profound effect on the nature and growth of the Mecklenburg Bar.

Class of 1927 at Second Ward High School, the city's first high school for African Americans

CHAPTER 7

RACE IN ITS OWN RANKS

In the midst of the postwar changes that were taking place in Charlotte, and in the law offices on Tryon Street and the Law Building, it was easy to overlook the arrival in 1945 of a young African American attorney named Thomas H. Wyche. He had grown up in Charlotte and graduated from Second Ward High School, the city's first high school for African Americans. Wyche was the son of the Reverend R. P. Wyche, a prominent leader in the Presbyterian Church (USA) and pastor of Seventh Street Presbyterian Church. The Reverend Wyche was a graduate of Biddle University (later Johnson C. Smith University); his wife was principal of Myers Street Elementary School. Like his father, Thomas received his undergraduate degree from Johnson C. Smith and then earned his law degree in 1944 from Howard University in Washington, D. C.

African American lawyers were not unknown in North Carolina, but they were rare. The first African American to practice law in Charlotte had been John Sinclair Leary, Sr., who opened an office on East Trade Street in 1892. Leary, the son of free blacks, was born before the Civil War. He was admitted to the bar in 1873 and began practicing law in Fayetteville, where he was elected an alderman and to a seat in the state House of Representatives. He helped establish the law department at Shaw University and was a leader among black Republicans in the early 1890s. In the 1896 election, he championed a fusion ticket of Populists and Republicans and told a political rally in Charlotte that if Republicans were elected that year, African Americans would be allowed to serve on juries.

Republicans won the 1896 elections, but the white backlash led in 1900 to state constitutional amendments that virtually removed blacks from the electoral process. Leary opposed the amendments in the face of overwhelming white support, much of it fired by young Democrats like Charlotte's Heriot Clarkson, who led a "white supremacy" campaign. Leary encouraged African Americans not to give up hope. In

JOHN SINCLAIR LEARY, SR.

an article in the *Star of Zion*, a newspaper published by the AME Zion Publishing House in Charlotte, he said, "The end is not yet. The Supreme Court of the United States will be the final arbiter in this matter." Leary died in 1904, a half-century before his prediction would become a reality. In 1997, the Charlotte chapter of the North Carolina Association of Black Lawyers renamed its organization in honor of John Sinclair Leary, Sr.

Charlotte's next African American lawyer, John T. Sanders, concentrated his law practice on civil matters and real estate. He passed the bar in 1906 but devoted most of his time to developing a thriving business portfolio that included a drug-store, a barbershop, a boarding house and restaurant and a newspaper called *The Charlotte Advertiser*. In the years just prior to the outbreak of World War I, other African American lawyers were listed in the city directory as having offices at 227 and 229 East Trade Street, the hub of Sanders's business enterprises. Among them were H. H. Cardwell in 1912 and A. Charles Anderson in 1911. Sanders office was in a building that also had offices for the American Life and Benefit Company, a black insurance company. Two African American doctors had offices in an adjacent building. By 1916, Sanders was not listed as an attorney, but he was listed in the city directory as the proprietor of the East Ave. Drug Company, the Queen City Drug Company and the Sanders Hotel.

Because of the racial attitudes that existed at the time, African American lawyers avoided the Superior Court courtroom, where it was generally believed clients stood a better chance with judges and jurors if they were represented by a white lawyer. Sanders followed this convention and engaged white lawyers in his cases that were for trial in the Superior Court. He usually prepared the briefs and drafted other pleadings as a paid service for white lawyers.

By the time Wyche opened his solo practice in 1945, Sanders had died, but there were by then three other black lawyers in the city. A transplant from Oklahoma, Ruffin P. Boulding, had a booming voice and ran a one-man office. He worked without a secretary or assistant and typed his own pleadings. Two other African Americans, Jesse S. Bowser and Leon P. Harris, had opened their offices in the early 1930s and eventually became law partners. They had a more conventional practice, concentrated on civil matters, divorces and real estate. Wyche once talked with Bowser, who was a family friend, about a legal career, and Bowser had urged him to study medicine instead, advice which Wyche ignored.

African American lawyers operated separate and apart from their white counterparts; usually the two races met only at the East Trade Street courthouse. The Mecklenburg Bar Association was restricted to whites only, but cases filed by all lawyers were still scheduled by the Association's calendar committee. Wyche ignored the habits of the past when he started work, and he may have been the first of his race to take a seat in the courtroom in a space set aside for lawyers awaiting the call of their cases. He said in later years he was not trying to make a point, but chose to sit where he did because it was the only chair available.

Wyche was probably more inclined to challenge the local customs than his older colleagues. He finished his legal training at Howard in 1944 with classmates who spent much of their senior year researching legal theories to test *Plessy v. Ferguson,* the 1896 case that upheld separate-but-equal facilities. Leading their discussion was Howard Law professor Leon A. Ranson, a skillful trial attorney who had won the reversal in the United States Supreme Court of the death sentence of one of the Scottsboro, Alabama, defendants known to history as "the Scottsboro boys." William H. Hastie, another faculty member, was Harvard trained and would end his career as Chief Judge for the Third Circuit Court of Appeals. Ranson and Hastie would later play major roles in *Brown v. Board of Education*.

One of Wyche's classmates was Pauli Murray, who had been raised in Durham, North Carolina but lived in New York City. In 1938, she had applied for entrance to the graduate school at the University of North Carolina and had been denied admission because of her race. Five years later, in the spring of 1943, Murray, Wyche, and a dozen other Howard students initiated the first sit-in demonstrations at Washington, D. C. restaurants that served whites only. The first was undertaken in the spring of 1943 at a local eatery in an African American neighborhood near the Howard campus. The following year, the group challenged segregation at a cafeteria at Eleventh Street and Pennsylvania Avenue, a short walk from the White House. Both establishments changed their whites-only policies, although the

THOMAS H. WYCHE

success at the downtown cafeteria was short-lived; it returned to restricted seating and was not permanently desegregated until a few years later.

Just as Wyche was getting his start in Charlotte, the National Association for the Advancement of Colored People (NAACP) was enjoying a surge in membership under the leadership of brothers Kelly and Fred Alexander of Charlotte. The first NAACP chapters had been formed in North Carolina in 1917, and by the 1940s that number had grown to twenty. In 1943, the chapter leaders met in Charlotte to organize a conference of North Carolina branches, and Kelly Alexander was elected president. In 1948, under Alexander's leadership, the NAACP launched a voter registration drive that added 75,000 African American voters to the rolls in North Carolina, nearly doubling the number previously registered.

Charlotte was as rigidly segregated as the rest of the South, both by law and social convention. Wyche's law professors at Howard had despaired at the prospects of a frontal legal assault on *Plessy v. Ferguson*, fearing that any decision might make things worse. Instead, the accepted route to furthering civil rights in the United States was the NAACP's tactic of confronting the inequality of "separate-but-equal" through selected cases around the nation. Wyche's colleague, Jesse Bowser, had confronted this in Charlotte in 1948, when he challenged the city school board to provide black students with the same courses offered to whites in their schools.

In 1951, Wyche carried the challenge of the status quo a step further. After Bowser had died, Wyche formed a partnership with Leon Harris. In December of that year, five days before Christmas, sixteen African Americans petitioned the Charlotte Parks and Recreation Commission to open the city-run Bonnie Brae Golf Course to all players. The Commission asked board member Joseph Grier, Jr. and board chairman J. A. Malcolm to investigate, but largely defended its position with a claim that admitting Negroes was prohibited because a portion of the park land that included the golf course had been donated with a "reverter" clause that limited access to whites only. In April 1952, Wyche filed suit on behalf of black golfers. His co-counsel in the case was the NAACP's regional counsel from Richmond, Virginia, Spottswood Robinson III, who had been on the Howard faculty when Wyche was a student and had participated in the senior seminar debating the future of *Plessy*.

The city subsequently challenged the reverter clause, but the state Supreme Court upheld it. If African Americans were allowed to use the park, it appeared that the city would have to return twenty acres that had been donated by Osmond L. Barringer in 1929. Wyche and Robinson pressed the case, despite the threat that Charlotte would lose the land. In 1956, the case reached Superior Court Judge Susie Sharp, the state's first woman Superior Court judge, herself no stranger to a different form of discrimination, and she ruled in favor of the plaintiffs and ordered the course opened to play without restrictions. It was the first case to break through the segregation of Charlotte public facilities.

PETITIONERS IN THE BONNIE BRAE CASE

FROM LEFT: WALTER BREWER NIVENS, THOMAS HENRY WYCHE, CALVIN BROWN, CHARLES VINCENT BELL, RUFFIN PAIGE BOULDING

While Wyche pressed the *Bonnie Brae* case, the Mecklenburg Bar Association struggled with the exclusionary clause that kept Wyche and other African Americans from membership. At the Association's meeting in June 1954, one month after the United States Supreme Court's decision in *Brown v. Board of Education*, Arthur Goodman proposed that the Association's newly elected president, Warren C. Stack, appoint a committee to study a change in the Association's membership rules to admit all lawyers in the county. Another year passed, however, before the matter was presented to the Association. The study committee was chaired by Hugh Campbell, Sr. and included among its members, Hunter Jones, Carl Horn, Jr., and Henry E. Fisher. The group held only one meeting and recommended that the racial restriction be removed from the bylaws.

The committee forwarded its recommendation in the fall of 1954, but the Association's executive committee failed to act on it. It was not until June 1955 that the recommendation came before the Association's annual meeting. Members seemed in no hurry and voted to receive the committee's report as "information only." *The Charlotte Observer* reported at the time that there appeared to be sufficient sentiment among the members to change the bylaws. In a letter to J. W. Alexander, Jr., the Association's newly elected president, Thomas Lockhart, a young attorney in his fourth year of practice, confirmed the impression. Lockhart wrote. "It was my impression that the members of the Bar Association received the report favorably and would have amended the constitution at that time had it been possible to do so under the terms

of amendment to the constitution."

By the time of a special meeting called by Alexander a month later the issue of changing the bylaws had become moot. On July 25, 1955, statewide legislation replaced the theretofore voluntary Mecklenburg Bar Association with the 26th Judicial District Bar. The new district included only Mecklenburg County. Now made a part of the North Carolina State Bar, the statewide regulatory organization, the District Bar became one of which every licensed attorney, regardless of race, was by definition a member. With this change, the four African American lawyers in the county – Wyche, Harris, Boulding, and Charles V. Bell – became members. Bell, a relative newcomer to the city, had come to Charlotte in 1951 at the urging of the NAACP's Kelly Alexander. He would thereafter establish himself as a leading criminal and civil trial attorney. In 1966, Bell and Walter Nivens, another black attorney who had begun his practice in neighboring Monroe and who would later serve as chair of the county board of elections, took *Davis v. North Carolina*, a criminal appeal, to the United States Supreme Court and won a new trial for Elmer Davis, charged with murder, whose confession was excluded as the product of coercion.

While the 1955 creation of the 26th Judicial District Bar settled the question of membership, it did not resolve a lingering issue over where the organization might hold its social events. Virtually every private club, public restaurant and other venues where the Bar might want to hold a dinner, a cocktail party or celebrate socially refused to serve African Americans. Only on rare occasions, had whites and blacks mixed socially in public, and some resistance among the Bar Association members to including African Americans may have sprung from lingering concerns about the social implications. After the creation of the 26th Judicial District Bar, the Women's Auxiliary, as it was called, eventually took the lead and arranged for a racially integrated social event at a private club at River Hills Plantation, across the state line in South Carolina. "After the entire upheaval," recalled Mark Bernstein, whose wife was involved, "not a black person showed up. They were all very disappointed."

For many years thereafter there were still relatively few African American lawyers in Mecklenburg County. Indeed, in those days, aspiring African Americans found it difficult to gain admission to traditional law schools. In 1964, Julius LeVonne Chambers, a young lawyer who had successfully penetrated that barrier, hung out his shingle to practice law in Charlotte. In the next decade, he and the law firm he set about creating were destined to be instrumental in bringing about a profound change in his adopted city.

Julius Chambers grew up in Mt. Gilead, North Carolina, a small community a hundred miles to the east of Charlotte. He graduated *summa cum laude* from then predominately African American North Carolina Central College (later North Carolina Central University) and afterwards earned a masters degree in history from the University of Michigan. Chambers had decided to become a lawyer after seeing his father, a mechanic, unable to find a white lawyer who would represent him in a breach of contract claim against a white customer. In 1959, Chambers entered the law school at the University of North Carolina, whose undergraduate school had earlier denied him admission, and three years later he finished at the top of his class. He was the first African American to be elected editor-in-chief of the school's law review, the crowning achievement of a law school career. When the press asked law school Dean Henry Brandis to comment on Chambers' election, he responded simply, "He earned it."

Chambers continued his studies at Columbia University, earning an LLM, and working for a time as the first intern at the NAACP Legal Defense Fund. It was here that he came under the tutelage of the lawyer who in the preceding decade had successfully argued *Brown v. Board of Education*, future United States Supreme Court Justice Thurgood Marshall.

In 1964, supported by a small grant from that organization, Chambers opened what would soon become the state's first racially integrated law firm in a cold-water walk-up office on East Trade Street. His first partners were Adam Stein, who was white, and another African American attorney, James E. Ferguson, II, an Asheville native. Over the years, the firm maintained a racial balance in its ranks. Established principally to handle civil rights cases, it soon also found itself meeting a variety of needs for its clients, including handling major criminal cases. In one of his first cases, Ferguson participated in the unsuccessful prosecution of a white man accused of the murder of a black military veteran, a case that was the subject of author Timothy B. Tyson's *Blood Done Sign My Name*.

In 1966, Chambers and Greensboro attorney Henry E. Frye were the first of their race admitted to the North Carolina Bar Association. A voluntary organization, it had been slow to open its doors to African Americans. Its reluctance had come to a head in the fall of 1965, when two law schools, first that of Duke University and then that of the University of North Carolina, withdrew their support of the Association's

Julius Chambers

continuing legal education programs after it had refused the membership applications of two other African Americans, one of them a graduate of Duke Law School. Duke's actions drew support from the dean of the UNC School of Law, J. Dickson Phillips, who declared, "I am confident that the faculty of the law school at Chapel Hill is unanimous in its conviction that Negro lawyers should long since have been admitted to the N. C. Bar Association, in its shame that any may have been denied admission solely because of race, and in its very particular embarrassment that any of its own graduates may have been subjected to this discrimination."

In those days, a membership application to the North Carolina Bar Association required the endorsement of three of its members, a requirement that was itself a barrier to entry. Although it was not widely known at the time, three members of the Mecklenburg Bar played a significant role in Chambers' successful application. It was endorsed by two of its past presidents, Joseph Grier, Jr. and James McMillan, the latter also a past president of the North Carolina Bar Association itself, and by Senior Resident Superior Court Judge Francis Clarkson, Sr. Frye, who was also admitted, had been a member of the law review at UNC and would one day become the first African American Chief Justice of North Carolina,

Duke and Chapel Hill law schools withdrew support from the NC Bar Association after it refused membership to African Americans.

Chambers' firm, originally Chambers, Stein and Ferguson, was to prosecute hundreds of cases brought to implement *Brown v. Board* and the various civil rights acts of the 1960s. Four members at this firm argued and won cases before the United States Supreme Court. Chambers alone argued and won eight cases in that Court.

A firm that never numbered more than a dozen lawyers at any one time produced the state's first appellate public defender, a chair of the National Institute of Trial Advocacy (NITA), a long-time general counsel of the ACLU, two judges of the North Carolina Court of Appeals, seven state court trial judges, the second African American president of the North Carolina Bar Association, one of the state's first two African American members of the United States House of Representatives since the nineteenth century, two members of the North Carolina General Assembly, a general counsel of both the Charlotte-Mecklenburg Board of Education and the University of North Carolina, the current Executive Director of the Z. Smith Reynolds Foundation, five Fellows of the American College of Trial Lawyers and one of the one hundred members of the Inner Circle of Advocates. Ten past or present members of the firm have been adjunct professors or instructors at law schools that include Harvard, Columbia, Penn, the University of Virginia, the University of North Carolina and

Duke. The government of South Africa decorated two of its members for their years of teaching trial advocacy to its young African lawyers.

Chambers became the third Director Counsel of the NAACP Legal Defense Fund, after Thurgood Marshall and Jack Greenberg, then became the Chancellor of North Carolina Central University and finally the director of the Civil Rights Center at the University in Chapel Hill. In 2005, he delivered the graduation address and was awarded an honorary Doctorate of Laws by the University of North Carolina at Chapel Hill.

Over time, the local bar has been led by four African American lawyers and the local bench has become more representative of the ethnic mix of the county's population. While the Mecklenburg Bar thus confronted the issue of race within its own ranks in the 1950s and 1960s, the daunting task of dealing with that issue in the community at large was yet to be addressed. Indeed, that task was to occupy much of the next decade.

Attorney David Simpson with Legal Aid client John Wilson

CHAPTER 8

Responding to Growing Needs

Well before 1963, when the U.S. Supreme Court decided *Gideon v. Wainwright*, requiring legal representation for criminal defendants who could not afford counsel, Charlotte lawyers Thomas Lockhart and Ernest S. Delaney, Jr. knew that securing legal services for all citizens in civil and criminal matters was not something that many of their peers wished to discuss. Lockhart had already upset some of his elders by vocally urging admission to the local Bar of the handful of African American attorneys then practicing in Charlotte. Proposing that the Bar support an organized program to provide free legal services was something else again.

When Lockhart received his law license in 1951 at the age of twenty-two, Hundley Gover refused to give him an office in the Law Building. A call from Lockhart's uncle, Judge John J. Parker, seemed to change Gover's mind. To pay the $50 a month rent – and he was sure Gover would put him out if he missed a payment – Lockhart, by his own account, became a proficient two-finger typist to produce without the aid of a secretary the lengthy wills he turned out for his clients. In 1956, he and Delaney began an uphill battle to establish a system in which indigent defendants would have representation.

Members of the Mecklenburg Bar had long provided some free legal services, usually in special cases that came to an individual lawyer's attention. "I remember there was a fairly strong, unorganized ethic for the obligation of lawyers to represent people who could not afford them," recalled Russell M. Robinson, II, who began practice in 1956 and became president of the Mecklenburg Bar in 1970. Robinson had learned this from his father, John M. Robinson, who had been president of the local Bar in 1919. "When I got here," Russell Robinson continued, "lawyers were expected to take on representation, not just in those appointed by the court, but in non-litigation matters, to see that justice was served by representation of people who couldn't afford it."

THOMAS LOCKHART

That practice had gained some formal structure during World War II, when the Bar provided counsel at no charge to servicemen and their families. In 1949, the Association's legal aid committee had recommended the creation of a Legal Aid Society for Charlotte, but nothing came of the proposal. The committee did continue to consider finding assistance in hardship cases brought to its attention. William F. Mulliss, the chair of the Legal Aid Committee at the time, reported in the mid-1950s that the committee was hearing from about a dozen or so clients in need each year. What Lockhart had in mind was something more far-reaching. In 1956, he and Delaney proposed that the clerk of court be authorized to call on lawyers who volunteered to provide services to clients in criminal cases.

Services for the poor or persons of modest means had been on the legal profession's agenda since before the Great Depression, when the American Bar Association had proposed a limited referral system that put the cost of legal services within reach of those with little or no ability to pay. Privately funded legal aid societies were already operating in more than a dozen cities around the country. In 1921, the ABA formed a standing committee on legal aid, an effort that Boston lawyer and legal aid pioneer Reginald Heber Smith of Boston led for the next fifteen years.

After some discussion, in the mid-1950s, the Mecklenburg Bar opted to follow the ABA's model, but only for civil matters. On March 1, 1957, the local bar's Lawyer Reference Service (later to be renamed the Lawyer Referral Service), the first in the state, opened for business. Attorney Lelia M. Alexander staffed the new service's office in the courthouse on weekdays from 9 A.M. to 10 A.M. She collected a $1 fee for an initial interview to review the client's problem before assigning the case to one of the seventy-seven lawyers who had signed on as volunteers. If a follow-up session was desired, a client was charged $5 for the first half-hour of consultation with the lawyer assigned to assist the client. The client could then decide whether to engage the lawyer to handle the matter. A Charlotte native in her forties, Alexander was one of the more well-educated lawyers in the bar. A graduate of Columbia Law School, where she had enrolled with the encouragement of a local lawyer for whom she had been a legal secretary, she had received the law school's highest academic recognition, a Harlan Fiske Stone Award.

The referral service proved popular, and it won support from the community.

Charlotte banks inserted notices of the service in monthly bank statements and the Charlotte media spread the news. *The Charlotte News* said, "The Bar's new service is worth commendation and worth patronizing." For many years thereafter, until the North Carolina Bar Association created a statewide referral program, this was the only such service offered to local citizens.

This modest local referral program came at the beginning of a period of dramatic change in the delivery of legal services that would shake the legal profession and challenge some of its most sacred traditions. The delay in creating legal services programs for the poor was caused in part by the reluctance of lawyers to be seen as violating Canon 27 of the Code of Professional Ethics, which prohibited "the solicitation of professional employment." The North Carolina State Bar was quick to pounce on any form of solicitation of business. It once disciplined a lawyer who left his business cards on the counter at a towing company. Not long after the referral service was organized, it drew the attention of the State Bar and its ethics committee, which reported that it had received an anonymous complaint. The inquiry was answered by the chair of the Lawyer Reference Service Committee, Fred H. Hasty, who along with John O. West, Jr. and Francis Fairley traveled to Raleigh in December 1957 to meet with the State Bar committee, which subsequently tabled the matter.

In his report to Bar president James McMillan, Hasty, who would later become the local Senior Resident Superior Court Judge, pointed out that Canon 27 "does not prohibit the employment of advertising facilities by an organized Bar to acquaint the lay public with the desirability of securing legal services . . . ." Hasty's report contin-

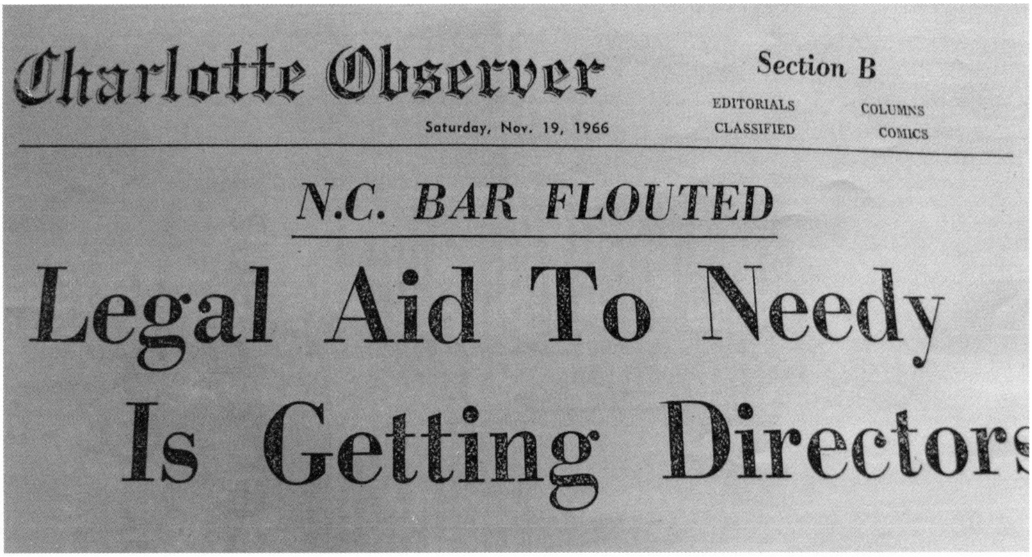

HEADLINE, NOVEMBER 19, 1966

ued: "We must never forget that the primary objective of the Lawyers Reference Service is to benefit the public and not the members of the legal profession . . . . The service is designed chiefly to aid those of moderate means who have or think they have a legal problem and desire to consult a lawyer but are not acquainted with a lawyer and do not understand how to engage one."

He emphasized that, "It has been discovered that people of moderate means are not seeking charity of the legal profession. They are willing and able to pay a moderate fee for legal assistance," he wrote, but "perhaps they do not clearly understand how to engage the services of a lawyer, . . . are fearful and ignorant of the ways and charges of lawyers."

The experiment proved its worth. In the first fourteen months of operation, Alexander handled 123 referrals. Hasty optimistically reported, "Experience indicates that the activities of the service increase as time goes on." That prediction proved altogether too modest. Twenty-five years later, the Service's report for 1984-85 was to show that 1,286 persons had applied for help that year.

Lockhart and his committee continued to press for something more. In 1959, he told *The Charlotte Observer* that Charlotte was one of five cities of its size without a public defender program for criminal defendants who could not afford a lawyer. "We believe," he said, "that legal aid is a community responsibility just as are Family and Children's Service, Red Cross, mental health and the other agencies sponsored by United Community Services."

In October 1961, the Mecklenburg Bar established a legal aid office that would provide free legal services for poor and indigent clients in civil matters. This free legal service was available to single persons making no more than $20 a week or married persons making no more than $40 a week. Domestic and criminal cases involving court appearances would not be eligible "as a general rule," *The Charlotte Observer* reported. A non-lawyer, Nadine Keating, was hired to staff the office in the courthouse for two hours daily. Keating also took over the administration of the Lawyer Referral Service.

Keating helped legal aid applicants complete paperwork, and their cases were then assigned to one of the seventeen lawyers who donated their time. Among the first attorneys who volunteered were both senior attorneys and relative newcomers. The original list included Thomas C. Creasy, Jr., James B. Craighill, James O. Cobb, Francis Parker, Larry J. Dagenhart, James Moore, Richard E. Wardlow, William J. Waggoner, Benjamin Horack, Henry C. Lomax, John G. Golding, Ernest Delaney, Jr., Ernest W. Machen, Jr., Mark Bernstein, Hugh G. Casey, Jr., William A. Shuford and Sydnor Thompson. In its first year, the office handled seventy-nine cases. Twenty cases were refused because clients were found to be able to pay.

A year later, in September 1962, then president John S. Cansler appointed a committee to investigate extending services to indigents charged in criminal cases. Nine months later, the committee proposed a public defender system that would assist those charged with both felonies and serious misdemeanors. The program was to be organized as a non-profit corporation and be supported by public and private funds. The committee recommended that defense attorneys handle cases without compensation, except in those felony cases in which the state was required to provide attorney fees. The committee proposed that the local Bar recommend legislation to permit a public defender system to be operated by municipalities.

The committee's report was released just as the United States Supreme Court decided *Gideon. V. Wainright*, holding that indigent defendants were entitled to legal representation in non-capital criminal cases, representation theretofore required only in capital cases. In June 1963, the North Carolina General Assembly authorized the appointment by the courts of lawyers to represent indigent defendants in criminal cases. About sixty members of the local Bar volunteered to accept such appointments. This arrangement remained in place for more than a decade, even after state-funded public defender offices were established in other counties. The local program was discontinued in 1975 when the legislature finally created a public defender office for the 26th Judicial District. Governor James Holshouser appointed Michael S. Scofield, then an Assistant United States Attorney, as the district's first state court public defender.

The local federal court had long exercised its authority to appoint members of its bar to represent indigent criminal defendants. Over the years, as federal criminal law and procedure became more complicated, it came to rely on panels of volunteers. Finally in 2004, the first federal public defender office was created. Its first director was Claire J. Rauscher.

Over the 1960s and 1970s, money from government programs, decisions from the United States Supreme Court and agitation from within the profession itself would create publicly funded legal services offices, preclude sanctions on attorneys who advertised their services and see an array of cases that challenged governmental authority as never before. In particular, the 1960s would prove as disruptive to the way that lawyers had traditionally operated as the decade would be to the rest of society.

The early debate within the bar over legal aid for the poor was but a prelude to a more expansive effort that grew out of the nation's anti-poverty programs of the mid 1960s. The creation of what later became known as Legal Services of Southern

Piedmont (LSSP) began with open conflict between organizers of the Charlotte Area Fund, a government-funded anti-poverty program, and the local Bar.

On May 11, 1966, Mecklenburg County lawyers were stunned to read in *The Charlotte Observer* that the Area Fund had prepared an application for $200,000 in federal funds to hire a director and six full-time staff lawyers to handle a variety of civil cases. The program proposed to serve 13,000 low-income families that lived in the area. "We hope the Bar association will come along on this thing," the newspaper account quoted a Fund spokesman. This extraordinary gaffe on the part of the Area Fund, announced with no prior communication with the local Bar by a spokesperson who was a stranger to the community, produced a furor. At a called meeting of the local Bar, the Fund spokesman, who was not a lawyer licensed in North Carolina, was called on to describe the proposed program, and the Fund's plan was then challenged from beginning to end.

This extraordinary gaffe on the part of the Area Fund produced a furor.

The money was to come from the federal government's Office of Economic Opportunity, created two years earlier by the Economic Opportunity Act. At the time, U. S. Attorney General Nicholas Katzenbach had spoken of a "new breed of lawyers . . . dedicated to using the law as an instrument of orderly and constructive social change." Such pronouncements were not especially welcome in parts of the South, where groups like the NAACP had used the law to effect social change through desegregation of public schools, hospitals and public accommodations. Some of that sort of sentiment was heard at the bar's called meeting. Attorney Basil M. Boyd, Sr. was quoted in a newspaper account as asking who the "clients" of the Charlotte legal services office would be: "Who are these people? Where are they? I want someone to name me one destitute person the Area Fund has helped. They won't work."

Other long-time members rose at the meeting to point out that the Bar already had a tradition of furnishing legal services to those who needed but could not afford them and indeed had in place its own voluntary legal aid program. Even the most level-headed members present made no attempt to hide their displeasure at what appeared to them to be a potentially constructive proposal brought forth in a confrontational manner by an outsider who was a stranger to them.

Bar President Richard M. Welling navigated through the emotionally charged meeting, allowing everyone who wished to speak to do so, then announced that he would appoint a committee to study the Area Fund proposal. Named to the committee were legal aid committee chair Nick J. Miller, the son of a Greek immigrant, Julius

Chambers, Alvin A. London, Sydnor Thompson and the Association's incoming president, James E. (Bill) Walker. All of the members except Chambers had been active in the local Bar for many years.

In a series of meetings, the Charlotte lawyers ultimately resolved their differences with the Area Fund proposal. An agreement emerged to create the proposed federally funded legal services office in partnership with the local Bar, to be managed by a board representative of the potential client community and the Bar. Wisely, since the organization was to provide legal services, the Bar would have a one-vote majority on the board. In substance, the Bar helped to create a law office to serve the indigent with far more resources than it could have mustered alone, but one that appropriately remained in the control of lawyers. Originally called the Legal Aid Society of Mecklenburg County, the organization was expanded in 1979 to include Cabarrus and Gaston Counties and was renamed Legal Services of Southern Piedmont (LSSP).

The new plan drew opposition from the State Bar, which called the proposed office "illegal and unethical" and called on the state's congressional delegation to prohibit such use of federal funds. The State Bar argued that the program's lawyers would be in-house lawyers practicing law for a corporation, which was illegal, and threatened action through the office of the Secretary of State to withdraw the charter of the non-profit corporation.

LEGAL SERVICE OFFICES ON ELIZABETH STREET IN CHARLOTTE

BILL WALKER

At a special meeting on October 7, 1966, the State Bar condemned the idea, saying that it would render a lawyer answerable to a government agency rather than to the individual client and that such representation would constitute unauthorized practice of law. The State Bar's resolution asserted, "The independence of the legal profession will be seriously imperiled and the independent representation of the individual before the Courts and before administrative and executive bodies will be jeopardized and the freedom of the individual will be endangered. Lawyers should not stand idly by and see this happen without at least trying by all means to prevent it."

The resolution concluded, "The concern of the lawyers is not just for lawyers, but for the citizens of this state and nation of all races and creeds and all walks of life. It is their freedom which is at stake, whether they realize it or not; and it is vitally important to them that a free and independent legal profession is not killed or seriously crippled."

Local Bar president Bill Walker, who had followed Welling in office, and his law partner, Robert G. Sanders, then the Bar's representative on the State Bar Council, took the matter to the General Assembly and successfully lobbied for a change in state law that removed the legal obstructions and allowed lawyers employed by a legal services agency to represent individual clients. Clearly, a key to their success was the local Bar's foresight in having a majority of the board that controlled the agency composed of lawyers. Years later, in a more enlightened era, the preamble to the State Bar's Rules of Professional Conduct was amended to assert that lawyers have a responsibility to provide legal services to those unable to pay for them, both by providing such services themselves and through financial support for organizations providing those services.

An editorial in *The Charlotte Observer* noted that "the State Bar, almost from the outset, has taken the view that the legal profession somehow had to be protected first and the poor people had to be served second, if, indeed, they could or should be served at all. President Walker and others of the Mecklenburg Bar have taken a different and proper attitude. They know and understand the need for and value of a community-wide legal aid program which will give poor people the benefit of good legal counsel."

With this foundation, the local legal services office quickly became an accepted part of the legal community, another local law firm, albeit one with a special mission, and the "us" versus "them" mindset disappeared. At first led by a succession of three local lawyers, Marvin K. Gray, who was later to be a Superior Court judge, William J. Eaker and Thomas Wyche, LSSP's stature grew to the point that it was able to attract in succession two leaders, Terrence S. Roche and Kenneth L. Schorr, both of whom had established national profiles in the legal services movement and whose leadership brought to Legal Services of Southern Piedmont both statewide and national recognition.

Walker considered the new program to be the highlight of his year as president. He later recalled, "The idea of the federal government sending money down here to take care of poor people was unsettling as hell for a lot of people. My message was, 'Let's be the lawyers that are going to do it.'" Among the first members of the agency's board were attorneys Paul Ervin, Hugh Lobdell, James McMillan and Julius Chambers.

Over the ensuing years, as available federal funds were reduced, members of the local bar stepped forward with generous financial support, as well as active participation in LSSP's mission. In the face of declining federal financial support, the need of legal services offices throughout the state for additional funds prompted the creation of an annual Access to Justice fund drive. At first a statewide effort, in subsequent years it was transformed into local campaigns. In 1991, the first local campaign was led by the Bar's immediate past president, Sydnor Thompson. His successor turned that role into a tradition, and with one exception, in the fall of every one of the nineteen years since, the immediate past president of the Bar has led the campaign. In the one year when the immediate past president had become a judge and was precluded by the Code of Judicial Conduct from soliciting funds, Robert W. King, Jr., a past president from twenty-one years earlier, stepped forward to lead the effort. When in the late 1990s, the Bar Foundation began its own annual solicitation of contributions, its campaigns were timed so as not to conflict with the Access to Justice campaign. Over the years from 1991 through the 2010-2011 campaign, local lawyers have contributed over $2,870,000 to the Access to Justice Campaign, over two million of that in the last six years.

Walker's successor as president was Benjamin Horack. The law firm he joined shortly after World War II later became McDougle, Ervin, Horack & Snepp and, in its present-day iteration, Horack Talley, PA. Horack was a gregarious sort with a keen

BENJAMIN HORACK

sense of humor. One of his hobbies was collecting arcane metes and bounds references he had discovered in his years of poring over real estate records in the office of the Register of Deeds. One that stuck with him called for a corner at "a nail in the center of a bridge, since washed away." When Horack assumed the office, he was concerned that Charlotte lawyers did not enjoy the camaraderie within the profession that he had known in the late 1940s and 1950s when he was starting out because the Association had grown to include more than 400 members. He instituted a monthly brown-bag lunch that included the judges. "It worked pretty good for a few months, before it petered out," he later wrote. "I was sorely disappointed."

Horack was still in office when the announced retirement of United States District Judge Wilson Warlick of Newton, a Truman appointee, provided the opportunity for the local bar to have one of its own replace him. Charlotte, with by far the busiest federal caseload in the district, had not had a member of the local bar on that bench since the recess appointment of Judge David Henderson that expired in 1949. The county had lost an earlier chance to have a Mecklenburg lawyer nominated to the district court bench when local lawyers could not agree on a candidate to fill a vacancy created by the elevation of Judge J. Braxton Craven, Jr. to the Fourth Circuit Court of Appeals. Exasperated by the lobbying for more than one candidate from Mecklenburg, Senator Sam J. Ervin, Jr. had recommended a former congressman, Woodrow Wilson Jones of Rutherfordton, to replace Craven.

Senator Ervin had let it be known that the next nominee should come from Mecklenburg, but that the local bar needed to get behind one candidate. Horack and his executive committee decided to solicit an expression of interest from those who wished to be considered and to submit their names to a confidential bar referendum. Two candidates came forth: James McMillan and Joseph Grier, Jr. The two were about the same age. They had been classmates as undergraduates at the University of North Carolina and at Harvard Law School. They had succeeded one another as president of the Mecklenburg Bar in the mid-1950s. Grier was a partner in Grier, Parker, Poe & Thompson. McMillan, a partner in Helms, Mulliss, McMillan & Johnston, had also been president of the North Carolina Bar Association and had remained involved in the implementation of the statewide court reform movement of the early 1960s.

Two members of the Bar's executive committee, one from Grier's law firm, one from McMillan's, counted the ballots. When they reported the result of the count to the two candidates, Grier withdrew and gave his support to McMillan, asking the Bar's choice be made unanimous. Then on November 8 the 425-member Bar voted unanimously to forward McMillan's name as its choice for the judgeship.

McMillan worried privately that his old friend Joe Grier's candidacy might have been disadvantaged by Grier's earlier principled stand in favor of desegregating the local parks. Little did McMillan know that he would soon be called on to decide a case that would put Charlotte-Mecklenburg in the national headlines as it wrestled with the desegregation of its public schools.

McMillan, then 51, told *The Charlotte Observer*, "I'm real happy that it is apparently possible for lawyers in this county to unite behind somebody who they think will do a good job. I'm grateful to the lawyers who have thus expressed this amount of confidence in a man who had been fighting with and against them in court for a fifth of a century." McMillan appeared on May 8 before the Senate Judiciary Committee and was readily approved and his nomination was then confirmed by the Senate.

McMillan was sworn in on June 24, 1968, in Charlotte with his friend, Judge Craven, presiding. Fred Helms presented his former law partner. McMillan's pastor, Dr. Lee Stoffel of Charlotte's First Presbyterian Church, delivered the invocation. Remarks followed by local Bar president Ben Horack, James M. Poyner, Jr., of Raleigh, president of the North Carolina Bar Association, Robert Sanders, by this time president of the State Bar, and Beverly C. Moore, Jr. of Greensboro, who represented the American Bar Association. Judges Warlick and Jones, his new colleagues in the Western District, also made remarks.

The new judge had an impressive resume and a reputation as a successful trial lawyer. E. Osborne (Ozzie) Ayscue, Jr., a young lawyer who had practiced with McMillan, later wrote that his mentor believed "there were no complicated lawsuits, only lawsuits that lawyers made complicated." He always limited his files to essentials. "He would strip his file down to nothing more than the materials he needed to try the case, walk in when the case was called for trial, placing a file that was at most a quarter of an inch thick on the table in front of him. The implicit message as a defense lawyer was that 'there's really not all that much to this case.' He was a masterful teacher. . . . He was low key, quiet, almost shy. . . . The late Judge Spencer Bell once commented that trying a case against Jim McMillan was like going up against a blue-eyed Boy Scout."

JAMES MCMILLAN

McMillan had been elected president of the North Carolina Bar Association in 1960. In his outgoing speech to 800 lawyers and guests at Asheville on June 29, 1961, seven years earlier, McMillan urged the members to take the leadership in race relations. He said that most lawyers "have thus far failed to speak with clarity in the area of race relations." He expressed concern that North Carolina had not moved further along in desegregating its schools in the wake of *Brown v. Board of Education*. "After many years, these requirements remain more honored in the breach than in the observance," McMillan said. "Our local school boards often shrink from serious effort to recognize valid requests for assignment to unsegregated schools. The pressures for recognition grow higher and the constitutional validity of the system grows weaker with each passing school assignment season." He told the assembled group that a fair question would be, "Have we done all we should to help create a climate of encouragement of school authorities?"

"Trying a case against Jim McMillan was like going up against a blue-eyed Boy Scout."

It was a strong speech that covered much ground, and he also listed three ongoing goals for the Association – court reform, law reform and lawyer reform. "We need to keep a close eye on new practices and trends in the law," he said. "We deserve our monopoly only if we earn it."

Until 1917, the local federal court was located in a post office building erected in 1891 at the corner of West Trade and Mint Streets, next door to the 1835 United States Mint building. That 1891 Victorian style building was replaced in 1917 with a modern structure shared by the post office and the court. By 1934, that building had become inadequate. The old Mint building next door was torn down and its parts carefully labeled and stored, later to be reassembled as the original Mint Museum of Art on Randolph Road. The 1917 building was then more than doubled in size to create the existing building at 401 West Trade Street. Ultimately, the post office moved out, leaving the entire building to the federal courts.

For years that courthouse had been a virtual graveyard for civil cases, and the court's criminal caseload consisted principally of low-level crimes such as tax evasion and the unlawful production of corn whiskey. With the arrival of Judge McMillan, that picture changed. On the bench, Judge McMillan's experience as a trial lawyer quickly shaped his judicial persona. He became known as a judge who tried cases rather than "managing dockets," and the federal courthouse quickly became a sought-after venue for litigants who wanted to get their cases tried and could find a basis for bringing them in that court

For many years, McMillan and Judge Woodrow Jones, who held court principally in the divisions west of Charlotte, later joined by Judge Robert D. Potter, who took over the Charlotte criminal docket, consistently ranked annually in the top three or four courts among the ninety-odd federal districts in both cases tried and cases disposed of per judge.

McMillan came to the bench at the beginning of an era when the federal courts all over the country were forced to reexamine fundamental principles that had long been taken for granted. He was called on to handle many high-profile cases arising during the civil rights era. Although he may be principally remembered for his role in some of those cases, over his career, the bulk of the trials over which he presided were the major civil actions that are the grist of federal courts – antitrust, patent validity and infringement, securities fraud, breach of contract, indeed every kind of litigation that came with a growing local economy. At the end of a multi-week trial in late 1978, a multimillion dollar case involving an array of national corporations, lawyers from distant places, reams of documents and over sixty depositions, a *Wall Street Journal* editor found it so incredible that the case was only eighteen months old that he had his reporter call to verify his facts. Indeed, the reporter learned that it was the second oldest pending case in the Western District of North Carolina, the oldest being a patent case remanded for trial by the appellate court.

Over the years, this revitalization of the local federal court, first in the civil arena and later in the criminal, was to be a major factor in the development of the community's remarkably strong trial bar.

CMS PARENTS PROTESTING BUSING STUDENTS

CHAPTER 9

A Defining Moment

McMillan had been on the bench less than a year when a dormant case that challenged the racially segregated local public school system came back to life. The case was to thrust the community – and the new judge – into the national spotlight and to test the community's adherence to the rule of law.

Julius Chambers had originally filed *Swann v. Charlotte-Mecklenburg Board of Education* on January 19, 1965, two months after he had opened his office. Darius Swann, a missionary, had returned to his alma mater, historically all-black Johnson C. Smith University, for a two-year sabbatical. His son, who had never known racial discrimination, had been assigned to an all-black elementary school. The class action that Chambers filed on behalf of the Swanns and nine other families prompted the local school board to adopt a "freedom of choice" pupil assignment plan. In July 1965, Judge Braxton Craven had ordered the immediate desegregation of school faculties and staff and had approved the assignment plan as adequate progress. The Fourth Circuit Court of Appeals had affirmed.

In May 1968, the game changed with the United States Supreme Court's ruling in the *Green v. New Kent County*. Expressing impatience with the slow implementation of *Brown v. Board*, the Court held that local school authorities had an affirmative duty to proceed to dismantle racially segregated school systems and that freedom of choice was an insufficient remedy. When Chambers then moved to reopen the *Swann* case, the local school system had 83,000 students in more than a hundred schools, but only 822 of the more than 20,000 black students in the system went to school with white students.

After days of hearings, on April 23, 1969, McMillan issued his first order, finding a generalized pattern of discrimination in public policy – housing, zoning, location of schools – that had created a segregated society onto which had been superimposed a pupil assignment plan that perpetuated racial discrimination. This finding of fact was never seriously challenged. The community wrestled for years to find an appropriate remedy to address the problem. Relying on the *New Kent County* decision, McMillan asserted that the school board had an affirmative duty to eliminate all-white and all-black schools. He gave the board three weeks to submit a plan for complete desegregation of facilities by the beginning of the next school year and partial desegregation of the student bodies at the same time, with full compliance to follow the next year.

North Carolina law had long required that students living a certain distance from their assigned school be furnished transportation. Charlotte and Mecklenburg had merged their school systems in 1960, so that there was no city-county issue. McMillan had grown up in Robeson County, perhaps the most racially segregated county in the state, one with separate schools for whites, African Americans and Lumbee Indians. In his order he observed, "Buses for many years were used to operate segregated schools. There is no reason except emotion (and I confess to having felt my own share of emotion on this subject in all the years before I studied the facts) why school buses cannot be used by the Board to provide the flexibility and economy necessary to desegregate the schools. Buses are cheaper than new buildings; using them might even keep property taxes down."

Joseph Grier

McMillan's order created an uproar in the community. He was hanged in effigy, received death threats at his office and on his home telephone and for a time he and his wife were forced to take refuge in the home of his minister. He and his law clerk, Fred A. Hicks, went to a firing range, where McMillan practiced firing his old .45-caliber handgun. A few calls of support and letters of encouragement arrived, including ones from Charlotte author Harry Golden and former United States Senator Frank Porter Graham.

"Immediately after Judge McMillan decided the case, an angry crowd picketed his home on Mecklenburg Avenue," Mark Bernstein recalled. "I went to the office on a Saturday morning and found Joe Grier [his law partner] . . . in our firm's library, researching *pro bono* whether the First Amendment would permit him to enjoin the crowd from picketing the McMillan residence."

In response to McMillan's initial order, the school board submitted a plan that involved few changes, and the judge rejected it. Its next plan proposed closing seven predominantly black inner city schools, reassigning their students. Reluctantly accepting the plan for the 1969 school year, McMillan ordered the submission of a new plan for 1970. Then in December, seeing no progress from the school board, he appointed the plaintiffs' expert witness as a consultant. The plan the consultant submitted involved large-scale cross-town busing to achieve some semblance of racial balance. On February 10, 1970, the court issued an order implementing that plan.

McMillan outlined recent federal court decisions, pointing out that these decisions were binding on his court. "Unless that were true, the Constitution would mean whatever might be the temporary notion of whichever one of 340-odd federal judges happened to hear the case. This is a matter of law, not anarchy; of constitutional right, not popular sentiment." He asserted that the decision was not based on "racial balance." "The School Board, after four opportunities and nearly ten months of time, has failed to submit a lawful plan, one which desegregates all the schools. This default on their part leaves the court in the position of being forced to prepare or choose a lawful plan."

McMillan continued, "The court claims no infallibility and does not seek to prevent appeal from all or any part of this order and will allow the making of any record needed to present on appeal any contention the parties desire to make, and will do what this court can to expedite such appeal. However, . . . this order will not be stayed pending appeal, and immediate steps to begin compliance are directed."

Public reaction was quick to follow. On Sunday, February 8, more than 1,700 persons demonstrated in front of the federal building on West Trade Street and others showed up in front of McMillan's house carrying signs of protest. "Charlotte's known as a Hornet's Nest," one demonstrator told *The Charlotte Observer*. "We showed one king, now we're going to show King James." After the photographs of picketers at his home appeared in the newspaper, the local Bar's executive committee passed a resolution condemning such action and called for restraint, recalled Russell Robinson, who was the president of the local Bar at the time. "He is a federal judge, this is his decision, it needs to be obeyed," Robinson later remarked. "Any attack on this decision by encouraging disobedience of it, or any attack on the judge for entering it, is unacceptable." Robinson, a graduate of Princeton and of the Duke Law School, the son of a lawyer, the grandson of a Supreme Court justice and the author of the definitive treatise on North Carolina corporations, was well prepared to lead the Bar in this trying time.

One of the organizers at the courthouse rally read a telegram from Senator Ervin, who wrote, "Once again we are confronted in America with the old issue of governmental tyranny versus liberty. I am glad that the Concerned Parents of Mecklenburg [the anti-busing group] stand on the side of liberty. Let us all remember that God gives liberty only to those who love it and are always ready to defend it." Ervin, who had from the beginning been outspoken in his criticism of the Supreme Court's decision in *Brown v. Board of Education*, apologized for having recommended McMillan to the bench. The irony of McMillan's having been selected on the Senator's request that the local Bar choose the nominee seemed to have gone unrecognized.

As the case continued to wend its way through the courts, McMillan found himself shunned by former friends, ostracized at his church and avoided at his country club, where former golfing buddies suddenly became unavailable. Julius Chambers was to pay an even higher price. His automobile had been blown up in an eastern North Carolina town. On November 22, 1965, shortly after the *Swann* case was filed, his home and those of two other civil rights activists in Charlotte were firebombed. Chambers nailed a sheet of plywood over his front door, and he and his family spent the rest of the night there. In August 1970, Chambers' mechanic father's garage in Mt. Gilead had been set afire. It was again torched on New Year's Day of 1971. Then on

JULIUS CHAMBERS' LAW OFFICES AFTER BOMBING

Julius Chambers inspects the damage

February 4, 1971, an arsonist set fire to the Charlotte office of his law firm. In his characteristically understated, unemotional way, Chambers later referred to these incidents as "things that made life interesting." He later told another lawyer that after his car was bombed, he began to leave his car door open and to keep one foot on the pavement while he turned on the ignition to increase the chance that he might be blown out, instead of blown up. Chambers' partner James Ferguson put it this way: "You can't do this work and be scared."

The torching of Chambers' office brought immediate response. Opposing counsel in the firm's pending cases offered to help rebuild Chambers' firm's files. The firm set up temporary quarters in an aging hotel in downtown Charlotte. The local bar had no mechanism to provide direct assistance – it still had no office of its own – but in a February 11, 1971 letter the Bar's executive committee expressed regrets and offered: "Realizing that the disruption caused by this occurrence may require the continuance of some of your cases and the reconstruction of files, we wish to advise you that we shall be happy to assist you in procuring the cooperation of the Bar to the end that you will not be put at a disadvantage in the resumption of your practice. Please feel free to call upon us regarding any matter in which you feel that we can be of assistance."

Individual members of the bar also pitched in. Queens College professor Norris Preyer, whose brother was a federal district judge in Greensboro, and attorneys Hugh B. Campbell, Jr., who, like his father, would later serve on the bench, and W. Thomas Ray, who would later become the chair of the Mecklenburg County Commission and whose wife was to play a seminal role in resolving the local school crisis, held a fund-raising event. Twenty-two of the thirty members of the faculty at the UNC School of Law took up a collection. "You, as a student, ranked No. 1 in your class," read an accompanying letter from the group in Chapel Hill. "You as a lawyer have been No. 1 in representing the minority and disadvantaged citizens of North Carolina. Your arguments in all levels of all tribunals on behalf of all kinds of clients and causes give hope and example that change can be made peacefully, and under the law."

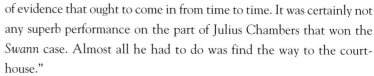

"Almost all he had to do was find his way to the courthouse."

Ironically, one leading figure in the opposition to the busing order was Joe Grier's law partner, William Poe, the chairman of the school board. Poe was a staunch defender of the board's opposition to the busing plan ordered by McMillan, which he thought went beyond the law. The tension between what many in the community, like Poe, believed was settled law and what others saw as a moral imperative requiring the judiciary to act to right a wrong that the executive and legislative branches of government had too long allowed to fester divided the community and friends, families and law firms.

"Judge McMillan took that one over from almost the word go," Poe later said. "And McMillan, I think, dictated the course of the trial and even suggested the kind of evidence that ought to come in from time to time. It was certainly not any superb performance on the part of Julius Chambers that won the *Swann* case. Almost all he had to do was find the way to the courthouse."

The school board's lawyer was William J. Waggoner, and the board recruited Benjamin Horack to assist in the case. The two literally worked day and night in preparation of the appeal to the Fourth Circuit. At one point, Horack was hospitalized for exhaustion. From there, the two carried on to the United States Supreme Court, where Horack had to be sworn in as a member of its bar in order to appear. *Swann* was argued before that court on October 12, 1970. The two had apportioned their time, but Horack found that their plans were for naught. "I had hardly opened my mouth with the customary, 'If the Court please,' when

WILLIAM POE

I was bombarded with questions from one end of the bench to the other." Before he could finish his summary, he heard Chief Justice Warren Burger say, "Thank you Mr. Horack. Your time has expired."

Some years later, Horack recounted the experience in a short memoir. He was opposed to segregation as both "morally wrong and unconstitutional." He, like Poe, believed that the court's order was not based on sound law. "Like any experienced lawyer, I know you can't win 'em all," he wrote. "I don't mean to beat a dead horse, but I'm still convinced that the *Swann* decision was prompted by social engineering, i.e., subjective notions of social justice and equity, rather than Constitutional imperatives."

William Booe, who had gained a reputation as a bulldog chair on the Bar's calendar committee, carried his outspoken opposition to *Swann* to the political arena. One of a majority of new school board members elected by parents angry with McMillan's decision, he later carried his new-found fame as a conservative into an unsuccessful race in 1974 for the Republican Party's nomination for the United States Senate.

The greater significance of *Swann* had not been lost on anyone. If the Supreme Court accepted segregated housing patterns and school locations that were in part the result of public policy as a ground for altering geography-based school assignments, if racial balance was affirmed as a legitimate goal, if busing was approved as an appropriate remedy, then school desegregation would no longer be just a Southern issue. The urban ghettos of large cities would become targets as well.

Chambers was only thirty-four years old when he argued *Swann* in the United

U.S. Supreme Court whose bench upheld McMillan's rulings

States Supreme Court. It was his first appearance before the Court. Arrayed against him were the school board's attorneys, older and more experienced than he, and the Solicitor General of the United States.

Then, on April 20, 1971, the Court unanimously affirmed McMillan's order in an opinion issued over the signature of perhaps its most conservative member, Chief Justice Warren Burger. Most notably, it found the remedies that had been employed in Charlotte-Mecklenburg to be within the court's discretion. This decision was to have a profound effect on accelerating the progress of public school desegregation throughout the United States.

The Court's deliberations in *Swann* are the subject of extensive portions of Woodward and Armstrong's 1979 inside look at the Supreme Court, *The Brethren*.

The Court's decision did not end the story. The court-appointed expert's pupil assignment plan proved temporal and unstable. The board's own suggested plans transparently favored affluent areas of the district and exempted the vast majority of white students from busing. But the tide of public opinion was changing. The 1972 elections produced a new set of more moderate school board members. In the meantime, a group of citizens drawn from all over the community, all devoted to preserving public education, calling themselves the Citizens' Advisory Group, emerged under the leadership of Tom Ray's wife, Maggie Ray. In the end, that group crafted and submitted an assignment plan that the school board accepted and the court ordered implemented. It was to serve the community well for many years.

Poe accepted the authority of the Supreme Court's decision in *Swann* and for the remainder of his tenure on the school board worked to accomplish the desegregation of the local schools. On July 11, 1975, ten years and six months after the case was originally filed, McMillan entered a final order. With his characteristic humor, he entitled it "Swann Song."

Poe and McMillan, who had faced one another as trial lawyers many times in the past, knew one another well. Few, however, knew until many years afterwards that in January 1975, after *Swann* had essentially been laid to rest, McMillan sent a handwritten letter to Poe on his personal stationery that read in part as follows:

"For people who both think deeply and feel strongly, any form of contest is a trial, and I have been aware of the pressures and problems you have faced, even while trying to cope with those I have seen and felt from my own point of view. . . . I know you can and will always know that your part has been carried out with strength and integrity. As a poet once said,

> 'Honor and shame from no condition rise;
> Act well your part; there all the honor lies.'"

A few years later, in 1981, a different school board cancelled its regular meeting so that is members could attend a banquet at which the Charlotte Chapter of the National Conference of Christians and Jews presented its Brotherhood Award to both Judge McMillan and Julius Chambers.

Chambers' role in *Swann* won him national recognition and led to a remarkable career as an advocate, a leader and an educator. McMillan continued on the bench for almost two more decades. One of his law clerks from a later era recalled, "Some of my most vivid memories are of jurors who approached Judge McMillan after a trial to state that his unshakeable fairness on the bench had dissolved all of their worst prejudgments about the man who had ordered busing in their community."

In a 2003 paper delivered to the local bar, Osborne Ayscue observed, "[F]rom the vantage point of over thirty years, it [*Swann*] takes on many of the characteristics of a Greek play. However much heat it may have generated at the time, it is difficult . . . to label the conduct of any of the players in the drama as 'right' or 'wrong.' Each player was destined by who he was and where he came from to do exactly as he did, to take the positions that he took. It is also apparent that the one person who clearly understood all that at the time was Jim McMillan."

"*Swann* accomplished more for Charlotte-Mecklenburg than the desegregation of its schools," Ayscue continued. "It pricked the conscience of this community and the community ultimately responded with a spirit and a quality of leadership that have set it apart ever since. Much of that leadership came from lawyers who were not involved in the lawsuit, who were just citizens doing that they felt was right and persuading others to do the same."

The story of the Swann case is superbly told in author Frye Gaillard's *The Dream Long Deferred.*

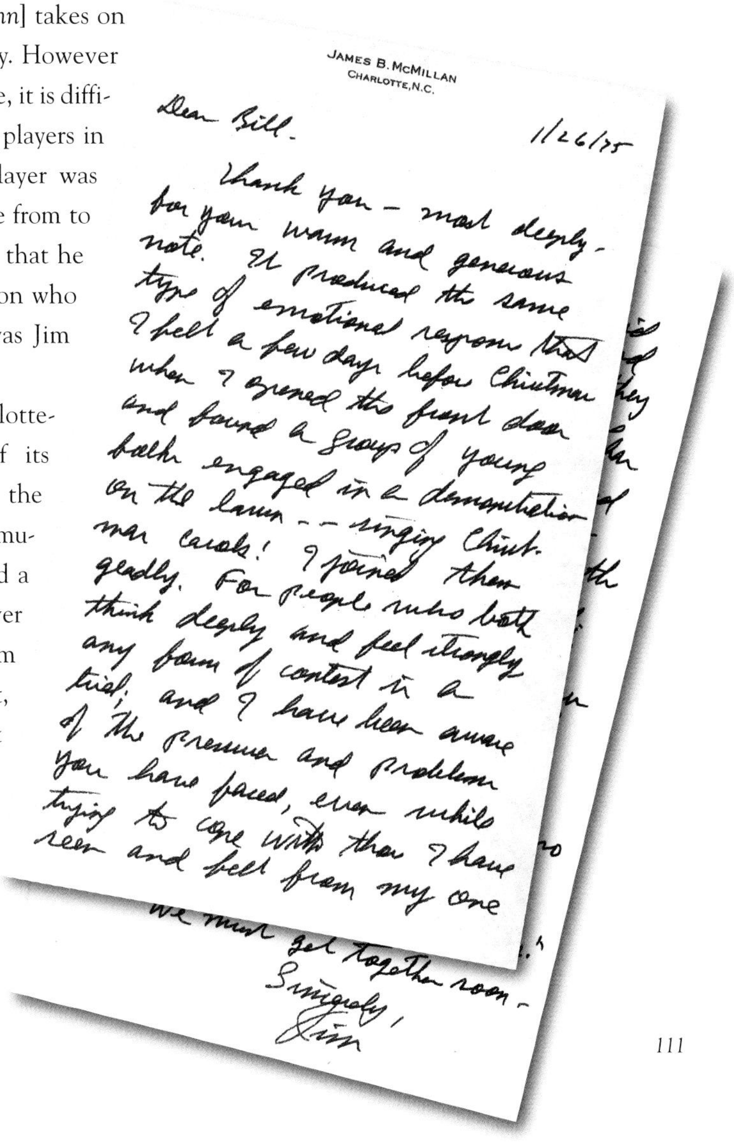
JAMES B. McMILLAN
CHARLOTTE, N.C.

Dear Bill - 11/26/75

Thank you - most deeply - for your warm and generous note. It produced the same type of emotional response that I felt a few days before Christmas when I opened the front door and found a group of young blacks engaged in a demonstration on the lawn -- singing Christmas carols! I joined them gladly. For people who both think deeply and feel strongly any form of contest in a trial, and I have been aware of the pressures and problems you have faced, even while trying to cope with those I have seen and felt from my own

We must get together soon -

Sincerely,
Jim

The 1954 Brown v. Board of Education decision, civil rights, and desegregation became some of the defining political issues of the 1960s.

CHAPTER 10

The Shift to a Regulated Society

Beginning with *Brown v. Board of Education* in 1954 and civil rights and voting rights legislation in the 1960s, the entire country was undergoing a significant shift. A society in which the law was the last arbiter in the lives of most people – and indeed of most businesses – was fast becoming a regulated society in which law would be the first arbiter of all their lives. Some observers have characterized this as a response to a declining moral consensus in post-World War II society; others have attributed it to a renewed utilization of the law to right long-standing societal wrongs. Whatever the cause, the result was a wide variety of federal, and some state, legislation imposing new regulations – Truth in Lending, stricter regulation of publicly held companies – and creating government agencies to enforce them – the Environmental Protection Agency, the Equal Employment Opportunities Commission and a host of other such new entities. Further, the law governing such subjects as health care, disability and taxation were becoming more and more complicated. Increasing regulation brought with it a growing body of administrative law. In a regulated society, clients were beginning to need more and more lawyers, whose practices would, over time, become more and more specialized. These changes were to have a profound effect on the practice of law in the rest of the twentieth century.

On top of this, the 1960s and 1970s were a time of social upheaval, as a new generation began to question the authority of its elders and controversy over the United States' involvement in Vietnam became a focal point of widespread protests. As never before, the law was being used to bring local governments to account, as the predictions of U. S. Attorney General Katzenbach from a decade earlier were being played out in the federal courts. More and more the federal courts, called on to enforce new national legislation, were becoming the principal legal battlegrounds.

A federal court in Charlotte that had already begun to attract a flow of conventional business-related litigation began also to see more than its share of civil rights oriented cases, particularly in the wake of Judge McMillan's handling of *Swann*. Over the next few years, McMillan was to preside over class actions that dismantled the discriminatory employment and promotion policies of many local industries, including notably the long-haul trucking firms that called Charlotte home. More than a few of these rights-oriented cases found their way to the United States Supreme Court.

Not everyone was pleased with this role of the court. Some of Judge McMillan's critics, conservatives like William Poe, who in a lawyer-like way had accepted the Supreme Court's opinion in *Swann*, nevertheless believed that McMillan invited legal challenges to proper government authority and allowed cases to be heard that would have been dismissed by other jurists. "I thought that anybody who was a member of the ACLU was a little bit kinky," Poe later said. "McMillan showed his colors pretty quick when he got on the bench. There was something almost every day; and several lawyers in town made their living just bringing these way-out claims that McMillan would entertain."

George Daly, 1972

One of those whose cases often drew considerable public attention was George S. Daly, Jr., a, Oxford, Mississippi native who had gone to law school thinking he would become a business lawyer. Instead, he became perhaps the most visible plaintiff-oriented civil rights lawyer in the local bar outside the Chambers firm. Daly subsequently developed a clientele that ranged from the countercultural local haven for "dropouts" of the hippie generation who had labeled themselves the Red Hornet Mayday Gang to the Ku Klux Klan and the Black Panthers when their First Amendment rights were threatened. "I liked doing them," he said many years later. "I enjoyed being a lawyer within a system that allowed you to do things like that." A graduate of Princeton and of the Harvard Law School, Daly often added something to his briefs to make them good reading. In a complaint against the Charlotte police, who had raided a "hippie house" and charged its occupants with vagrancy, he wrote a section entitled, "Literary and Historical Vagrants" and included a quote from actor Errol Flynn: "Anybody who dies with $10,000 left is crazy."

BILLY GRAHAM AND PRESIDENT RICHARD NIXON WAVE TO A CROWD OF 12,500 IN CHARLOTTE ON OCT. 16. 1971

Perhaps Daly's most celebrated case arose in 1971, when Charlotte's elite dressed up the city to honor its native son, Billy Graham, an event that brought President Richard M. Nixon to town to honor his friend. The original Charlotte Coliseum was rented for the occasion. Free tickets for the occasion were widely distributed. Public schools were recessed for the day. An advance guard had visited the local VFW post and enlisted an ad hoc group to help police the event. That group, led by one Ernie Helms, equipped with armbands, essentially took charge of deciding who would be admitted and who excluded. Young people with long hair, tie-dyed clothes and other indicia of nonconformity had their admission tickets, indistinguishable from those of others, invalidated on the spot and were thus systematically excluded from the public event. Daly brought a class action on their behalf against an array of defendants, including the Secret Service and members of the White House staff. White House Chief of Staff Bob Haldeman, who was later shown to have approved in advance the exclusion of those who appeared to be dissidents, was ultimately compelled to come to Charlotte to testify. The trial court's initial findings of fact, expressed in Judge McMillan's low-key humor, set out the events of the day from the point of view of each of the participants except for Ernie Helms, who had chosen to invoke his Fifth Amendment rights in a civil case. On First Amendment grounds, McMillan enjoined the defendants from further conduct of this sort. The court's findings and order, *Sparrow v. Goodman*, 361 F.Supp. 566 (1973), are a revealing window into the temper of the times.

The community clearly was not of one mind. In 1968, the 26th Judicial District Bar had honored Charles Crutchfield, the president of Jefferson Standard Broadcasting, whose television station, WBTV, had produced the documentary, "Weep for the Innocent." That program criticized the United States Supreme Court's 1966 decision requiring police to inform people they arrested of their constitutional rights. Ironically, it was the Charlotte Chamber of Commerce, of which Crutchfield was then president, that three years later conceived the idea of Billy Graham Day. The principal speaker at the 1968 event honoring Crutchfield with the Bar's Liberty Bell Award was the Chief Justice of the Supreme Court of Maine, at the time Chair of the National Conference of Chief Justices, who spoke against Senator Sam Ervin, Jr.'s proposed amendments to limit the powers of the Supreme Court.

> "The worst of our youngsters are growing up to become booted, sideburned, unwashed, leather-jacketed beatniks and hippies."

On the other side of the coin, many lawyers, particularly those of his generation, agreed with Chief Justice R. Hunt Parker of the North Carolina Supreme Court. Speaking in 1968 to the 35th annual meeting of the North Carolina Bar Association, Parker, said, "The worst of our youngsters are growing up to become booted, sideburned, ducktailed, unwashed, leather-jacketed beatniks and hippies . . . ." He also castigated the United States Supreme Court for opinions "which have thrown God out of our public schools." Going further, Parker said, "I wonder how the gentlemen of the Supreme Court will feel about what they have done regarding prayer in the public schools when they lie on their deathbeds."

The conflict between governmental power and individual freedom would play out over time as the rulings of federal courts, some of them coming from McMillan's court, and the line they drew between these conflicting imperatives gradually came to be accepted by a new generation of citizens and lawyers as the law of the land.

Daly was just one of the members of the local bar who were often good for a lively or provocative quote. When local attorney Allen Bailey had taken up the defense of a police officer charged in a suit filed by Daly with assault on his client, a May 1971 article in *The Charlotte Observer* compared and contrasted the styles of the two. Bailey had long been allied with conservative causes. He had chaired the unsuccessful 1964 gubernatorial campaign of segregationist candidate I. Beverly Lake and was a devoted opponent of extending the sale of alcoholic beverages. He had recently been in the forefront of the opposition to consolidation of government functions of Charlotte and Mecklenburg County. Bailey had a flamboyant style of his own. He favored well-tailored suits and good cigars and was not above crowing about his success in the courtroom.

Some of his peers took exception to what they considered Bailey's self-aggrandizing comments in the front-page news article, which included four photographs of him. They took their complaints to Mecklenburg Bar. At the direction of the Bar's ethics committee, president Russell Robinson responded with a letter to the more than 500 members of the Bar that criticized "certain lawyers" for using the media to improve their business. "It is our opinion that such articles indeed lower the tone of our profession and seriously impair the reputation and respect of our bar," Robinson wrote. The bar's executive committee published a resolution reminding members that Canon 20 prohibited attorneys from making comments to the media about pending cases and that Canon 27 prohibited such comments as being indirect advertisements.

Bailey fired back. He told a reporter, who asked about the letter, "Unfortunate but true is the fact that jealousy of the success of others fills the hearts of too many members of the local Bar. They prefer to sit in their chairs and criticize others rather than put out the effort to make a success of themselves. I learned a long time ago that if you had an opinion of your own, and sought to get things done according to your own convictions, you were going to be criticized. I have chosen to have an opinion and to do that which pleased me and help my fellow man. Those that would deny me that right can make a flying trip to the moon."

He told the complainers to "get off your seat, go to work and stay there from 12 to 18 hours a day as I have done for the last 21 years, deal honestly and fairly with the people of this community, and you too might get asked a question by a reporter some day and even get your photograph in the paper."

The canons of ethics of the profession prohibited self-promotion, and a lawyer risked sanctions from state licensing boards if he did not adhere to this principle. Another tradition, reflected in local minimum fee schedules, curbed what had been regarded as unseemly economic competition. Lawyers in Mecklenburg were therefore as disturbed as were their peers elsewhere when in the 1970s the United States Supreme Court's rulings in two cases changed these traditional precepts.

First, in 1975, *Goldfarb v. Virginia State Bar* held that minimum fee schedules were price-fixing and therefore illegal. The decision had little practical impact on most segments of the local bar. The fee schedules indeed suggested only a minimum charge.

Beginning in the late 1960s, liability insurance companies, who were involved in a large portion of the civil litigation of that era, had begun to insist that the lawyers defending tort cases against their insureds charge for their services on an hourly basis. Although some lawyers saw in this practice a conflict between the lawyer, who had a major hand in deciding how much needed to be done to defend a case properly and how long it took to do that, and the client, this method of billing for lawyers' services had fast become the norm in many areas of practice. Aside from those lawyers who represented claimants on a contingent fee basis, criminal defense lawyers who traditionally charged a set fee to be paid in advance, lawyers handling real estate transactions for buyers and those who handled the estates of decedents, most lawyers had begin to charge, and their clients had begun to accept, charges computed on an hourly basis. The admonition of the local Bar's 1921 minimum fee schedule that, with certain exceptions, "charges should never be made on a time basis when it is practicable to charge in some other manner" had long since become an anachronism.

Larry Dagenhart, who was president of the Bar at the time, recalls, "It was pretty much a non-event except for the real estate title lawyers and the trust and estate lawyers. Indeed, the fee schedule was only a suggested minimum, and most of the litigators and corporate lawyers were charging on a time basis or value basis. But the title lawyers went by the schedule, and they fought the change. Also, some of the trust and estate lawyers charged according to the size of the estate, not by the amount of work. I think the intent of the discretionary language in the fee schedule was to enable the lawyer to charge a higher fee, though there was some thought to the contrary. Otherwise, I think the fee schedule went quietly."

In the second case, *Bates v. State Bar of Arizona*, decided in 1978, the prohibition against lawyers' advertising their services was held to violate the First Amendment to the United States Constitution. Thus, the flap over the Daly and Bailey news articles now appears a quaint reflection of an earlier time. S. Dean Hamrick, the Bar's president at the time of the *Bates* decision, said that the Bar's executive committee left all comment on the Supreme Court's holding to state and national legal organizations. The ruling had no immediate effect among Charlotte-Mecklenburg lawyers, he said. "I don't remember anyone openly advertising. Only low-class people would have done that. It was just a matter of honor." The decision did bring to an end, albeit indirectly, to an old practice that skirted the earlier prohibition on advertising: Hamrick noted that a few lawyers were reputed to have engaged in what some considered a form of advertising by paying "runners," who would receive a portion of the fees collected for steering clients to them.

Hugh Campbell, Jr. was a member of the State Bar's ethics committee at the time of *Bates*. "The traditional bar hated that," he said some years later. "They struggled with how not to allow it. The first people who did it [advertised] were anathema." In time, however, lawyers would be using every conceivable form of advertising, from direct solicitation of those charged with traffic offenses to billboards and television ads.

Over time, the workload of the local federal court increased exponentially due to civil rights-oriented cases, major litigation resulting from Charlotte-Mecklenburg's growth as a business, commercial and banking center, and criminal prosecutions arising from drug wars and the federalization of conduct once considered the domain of the state courts. The United States Courthouse on West Trade Street, built on the site of the nineteenth century United States Mint, became as familiar to the county's trial lawyers as had been the succession of state courthouses in the past.

That growth, however, did little to relieve the pressure on the local state courts. The court reforms of the 1960s had added a second layer of courts in Mecklenburg County. The Superior Court remained the court of general jurisdiction. Its judges were elected in statewide elections, and they rotated among the counties in the one of the three geographical divisions in which their county was located. The newly created District Courts were assigned many of the functions that the Superior Courts had theretofore handled alone, as well as replacing the traditional Recorder's Courts and Justices of the Peace. Their judges were selected locally and they normally held court only in their own county. The number of district judges in a county varied with the local caseload. Mecklenburg, with the largest caseload and the largest number of judges, had outgrown its 1928 courthouse. A county office building had already been built across Fourth Street to house some offices previously located in the 1928 courthouse, including the register of deeds, but the need for courtroom space and offices for the judges had become critical.

On May 19, 1978, members of the Bar turned out for the dedication of the county's sixth courthouse, located at 800 East Fourth Street, across from the 1928 courthouse and adjacent to the new county office building. Retired Chief Justice William H. Bobbitt delivered the dedicatory address. The new courthouse was the first to be built to house only courtrooms and judicial offices. The $5.3 million building, designed by Harry Wolf, III, won an excellence in design award from the American Institute of Architects.

The new courthouse may have won awards, but because of the defeat of a local $13 million bond referendum, it was built with the limited funds available from general tax revenues. As a result, there were significant access problems: judges found themselves riding elevators with people they had just sentenced to jail. "They say this isn't big enough, but it's better than what we had," former Mecklenburg County commissioner W. T. Harris told *The Charlotte Observer*. Eventually, the sleek, modern Wolf-designed building was connected by an overhead bridge to a seventh courthouse, one constructed solely for criminal courts, built in 1989 at 700 East Fourth Street.

Among those holding court in the new 1978 building was Clifton E. Johnson. A graduate of North Carolina Central University and of its law school, in 1969 he became the first African American in the state to serve as a District Court judge. In 1974, he became the Chief Judge of the local District Court, also a first. In 1978, he became the first African American elected a Superior Court judge in North Carolina since the nineteenth century. In 1982 Governor James Hunt appointed him to the North Carolina Court of Appeals, also a first. Twice reelected, at the time of his 1996 retirement, he was the Senior Associate Judge on that court. While on the appeals court, he had chaired the state's Judicial Standards Commission, which handles disciplinary cases against sitting judges. He died in 2009 at age sixty-seven.

CHARLOTTE'S SIXTH COURTHOUSE

Judge Clifton Johnson

One of the more colorful District Court judges was World War II veteran William Scarborough. Each year in the days when public drunkenness was still regarded as a crime, in early December he would call into court from the county jail all those serving sentences for that offense, interrogating each to find out which ones would have a place off the streets – home or family – to spend the holidays if they were released. He would then commute the sentences of those who had such a place, knowing that they would be back in his court – and back in jail – shortly after the holidays.

The local Superior Court's docket had grown exponentially over the years, but as the 1978 courthouse was under construction the scheduling of civil cases remained under the control of the bar's elected calendar committee, as it had been since 1912. Then, one day in the 1970s, Hugh Campbell, Jr. was chairing a meeting of calendar committee when Senior Resident Superior Court Judge Frank Snepp, Jr. arrived and announced that the court, and not the bar, would thereafter set civil cases for trial. For more than sixty years, the Bar had essentially run the civil calendar under strict mandatory calendaring rules that pushed cases to trial. Over those years, Superior Court judges, who rotated from county to county in six-month cycles, had accepted the practice. Having a set calendar to work with expedited their sessions. Indeed, once the county had been given additional judges, under the watchful eye of the calendar committee, Mecklenburg's civil docket had become perhaps the most current in the entire state. It was not a county where the judge was likely to run out of cases to try and motions to hear before the end of the week. With the increasing caseload in the county, Campbell conceded that the three-member committee's job had become quite time-consuming. A short time after Snepp's unannounced visit to the calendar committee, the scheduling of cases became the responsibility of a newly appointed full-time trial court administrator.

The need for the 1978 courthouse reflected the dramatic growth of the city since mid-century. Charlotte had outgrown its dependence on the textile business and had become a major commercial, retail and financial center. The county's population was about to reach 400,000. The city was on the verge of breaking ground on a $55.6 million airport terminal. When it was completed in 1982, Douglas Municipal Airport became the Charlotte/Douglas International Airport, with overseas flights offered by US Airways. The first plane to take off on a new 1979 runway was a cargo carrier bound for Saudi Arabia with a load of North Carolina tobacco. Business leaders were

TERMINAL AT CHARLOTTE DOUGLAS MUNICIPAL AIRPORT, MARCH 1975; LATER THAT YEAR, AIRPORT RENAMED CHARLOTTE DOUGLAS INTERNATIONAL

still hopeful that a large tract of land purchased near the campus of the University of North Carolina at Charlotte would become the home for research facilities for international corporations, duplicating the success of the Research Triangle Park that lay between Raleigh, Durham and Chapel Hill. Although that ambition did not materialize, University Research Park did acquire offices of several national and international firms, including IBM, one of its first tenants.

As early as 1958, some of Charlotte's leading law firms had begun to leave the relatively cramped quarters of the Law Building to move "uptown," a historic local reference to the fact that Tryon Street ran along a ridge that had been the highest point in the community. Offices built to serve one, two or three lawyers working together were no longer adequate for firms with growing numbers of partners and associates. The county courthouse was becoming less and less the center of gravity of the bar. With the growth in the local business community, many firms' clients were located in the center city. A senior partner of one firm, heavily involved in a growing client's mergers, had a desk in the client's offices while his firm searched for downtown office space.

The Law Building progressively came to be occupied by single practitioners and small firms. In 1958, there had been only twelve firms with four or more lawyers and eleven of the community's seventeen largest firms still called the Law Building home.

By 1968, there were twenty-six firms with four or more lawyers, the largest still numbering only twelve lawyers, and only eight of those remained in the Law Building. In 1978, though there were still only twenty-nine firms with four or more lawyers, the largest with twenty-seven, only four of those firms remained among the Law Building tenants. By 1988, when there were forty firms with five or more lawyers, the largest firm still had only sixty-two lawyers – the law explosion was yet to come – but only two of the largest forty remained in the Law Building. Then in 1993, the building that had for sixty-five years been the heart of the local bar was razed to make way for a new county jail. Before it was demolished, the law library that had been created more than century earlier was given to the Public Library of Charlotte Mecklenburg County. That law library was later closed, a victim of the new age of technology. The library collection was eventually to be housed in the community's first law school, the Charlotte School of Law, which enrolled its first class in 2008.

Meanwhile, the 26th Judicial District Bar was struggling to keep up with its growth. With a membership approaching 900 in 1979, it still depended on the support of part-time help. Its office consisted of two hundred square feet on the eighth floor of the Law Building. In recognition of the growing number of new attorneys in the city, the Bar had created a Young Lawyers Division. In a nod to better communication among its members, a newsletter – one page mimeographed – came into being.

View of Charlotte skyline with North Carolina National Bank, now the Bank of America and Wachovia Bank in the foreground, 1961.

From the post-war years on into the 1970s, the accepted method of picking Bar officers was for a group of those most involved in the Bar's work to gather annually in the Law Building office of Frank A. McCleneghan, a gregarious cigar-smoking senior partner in another of the older local firms, originally Cochran, McCleneghan, & Miller. McCleneghan, who had been president of the local Bar in 1940 and who represented many of the construction companies that were building a new Charlotte, had once, with tongue in cheek, told a younger lawyer that he had chosen law school because there were no labs. "We would get together in his conference room, filled with smoke, and we would select who was going to be president of the Bar," recalled Mark Bernstein. "It was done informally. It was not a very organized kind of thing. There were fewer lawyers and most of them were together. It was easier to reach consensus."

Before long, however, the local bar was looking outward. In April 1980, president-elect Ayscue was preparing for a planned meeting in Charlotte of the ABA Board of Governors. ABA President Leonard S. Janofsky of Los Angeles explained in a letter to Ayscue that the visit was part of the ABA's decision to meet in different locations to confer with local and state bar leaders. The Charlotte visit would include invitations to the North Carolina State Bar, North Carolina Bar Association, South Carolina Bar Association, Atlanta Bar Association and State Bar of Georgia, each of which had representatives in the ABA House of Delegates. "We are delighted that you are meeting here," Ayscue wrote to Janofsky. "We welcome the opportunity to participate . . . ." Ayscue explained in his letter that the local bar embraced the Twenty-Sixth Judicial District of North Carolina, which was composed of only one county, Mecklenburg. "At our last annual meeting in 1979 we exercised an option available to one-county judicial districts and changed the name of our organization to The Mecklenburg County Bar."

In an age of change, the old historic name had been resurrected.

Mel Watt, Mary Howerton and Lloyd Baucom at the East Boulevard Bar Center—the state's first local bar center.

CHAPTER 11
GEARING UP

Mary Howerton knew more about doctors than she did lawyers in the summer of 1984 when another parent at her son's soccer match, Dr. Andrew W. Walker, president of the Mecklenburg County Medical Society, passed along word that the Mecklenburg County Bar was looking for an executive director. "He thought I might be interested," she said.

At thirty-four years old, Howerton had learned something about how professional organizations worked. She had been executive director of the local chapter of the American Cancer Society and most recently had been the first chief executive officer of a new palliative care program in Charlotte, called Hospice. Managing the affairs of medical professionals and health-care volunteers could not be that much different from lawyers, she thought. Besides, when she learned that what Bar President Ray S. Farris was looking for was someone to help bring a seventy-two-year-old organization into the modern world, it was clear that her experience might be just what the lawyers needed.

At the time, the Bar was a hip-pocket organization whose affairs were only as detailed and orderly as the person who was elected president each year chose. There was some continuity from one administration to the next, but little more than annual meeting minutes and notes from committee meetings. In fact, the organization performed only a few useful chores for its membership or for the community. The annual dues of $30 raised enough money to cover the expenses of periodic mailings, the cost of secretarial services and the rent on a small office in the Law Building on East Trade Street, where Nadine Keating kept the files.

Farris, and others, wanted to change that. The idea for creating a fully functional organization to better serve the profession and the public had begun to take shape five years earlier, in 1979, after President Robert King, a Navy veteran of the Korean War era, traveled to Chicago in the dead of winter in response to an invitation from the ABA. King had been invited to the ABA's Chicago headquarters to attend a pilot leadership institute for local bar leaders. Sixty-seven years after its formation in 1912, the Mecklenburg County Bar had grown large enough – 862 members – to attract the ABA's attention. It was the largest local Bar in North Carolina and it had a membership larger than the bars of some states. The ABA, in turn, had begun to give more attention to local bar organizations that were a growing component of the profession, and the local Bar was an early beneficiary of that development.

There were now as many lawyers in Mecklenburg County as there were residents in some North Carolina towns. Charlotte's population had grown from 133,129 in 1950 to 315,473 in 1980, and 970,000 people lived in the three-county area, a 16 percent increase since 1970. During the 1970s, the city had attracted nearly three thousand new businesses with a net worth of $3 billion. The city's workforce now included more than 37,000 new employees. It was the home of two large and growing banks, NCNB and First Union. Tryon Street was beginning to look like a genuine center of regional commerce. The population growth also had spawned a major expansion of new subdivisions and retail centers, including SouthPark, a huge, upscale shopping center on the city's south side, destined to become the center of North Carolina's second largest business district.

There were now as many lawyers in Mecklenburg County as there were residents in some North Carolina towns.

Along with this growth had come a corresponding growth in the number of local lawyers. Each year, the Bar traditionally held a joint swearing-in ceremony for those who had just passed the bar examination. Each new lawyer was introduced by a member of the Bar. By the turn of the century this ceremony and a similar one held after the mid-year bar examination would be introducing upwards of two hundred new lawyers each year. It was becoming increasingly difficult for established practitioners to get to know all the new members of the Bar.

RAY FARRIS, BAR PRESIDENT, 1984

Although King returned from his Chicago trip infused with new ideas, it would be more than four years before the Bar would be ready for organizational change. At King's suggestion, the Bar asked for consultation from an ABA representative. "Bob King was the invitee to the first ABA Bar Leadership Institute in 1979," King's successor, Osborne Ayscue recalled. "I was going to ABA conventions anyway – I started going in 1969 and realized that once you are president of the local Bar you become a member of the National Conference of Bar Presidents, and so I kept on going. I found out that was a way of keeping up with what was going on in other local Bars."

Conversations about the Bar's future role took place among the leadership during the next two presidencies, those of Francis O. Clarkson, Jr. and Hamlin L. Wade, but it took several years for the Bar to digest the need and the opportunity for change. In 1983, President Francis M. Pinckney, Jr. and the executive committee once again retained an ABA consultant to survey the local Bar's resources and programs and to "offer recommendations as to how the Bar might serve the profession more responsibly." Out of that came an impetus for change just as Farris, a lawyer's son, was about to assume the presidency in June 1984. Years earlier, Farris had proved his tenacity. As the sophomore quarterback of the UNC Tar Heels, he had thrown back the kicking tee after a touchdown, called an option play, kept the ball and carried it across the goal line for a two-point conversion, making the final score of the annual season finale against the Duke Blue Devils 50-0.

Among the recommendations the latest consultant made was the need for a full-time director. After four months of study, Farris called a special meeting of the members for August 23 to accept or reject major changes, including a dues increase from $30 to $60 per year. By 1984, the Bar had reached a membership of 1,265 – up from just over 700 in 1977 – and the previous year had an annual budget of $41,500. The proposal would increase revenue for the coming year to $97,000. In his report to the members, Farris said that despite "commendable volunteer efforts, it is impossible to provide continuity of programs, consistency of performance, and adequate planning with present staff and other resources." Further, he said, "The work of the Bar has simply outgrown the capacity of volunteer lawyers without greatly increased administrative support and improved facilities. The Bar requires a full-time Executive Director and at least a part-time secretary . . . ."

At Farris' request, Ayscue, who had just assumed the presidency of the North Carolina Bar Association, had written in support of the proposal, saying, "Our local Bar is larger than the Bars of one or two of the smaller states in the United States. There are many things we should be doing that we are not doing. We owe both the profession and the community a much higher level of activity and service than we can possibly generate without an

MARY HOWERTON
FIRST MCB EXECUTIVE DIRECTOR

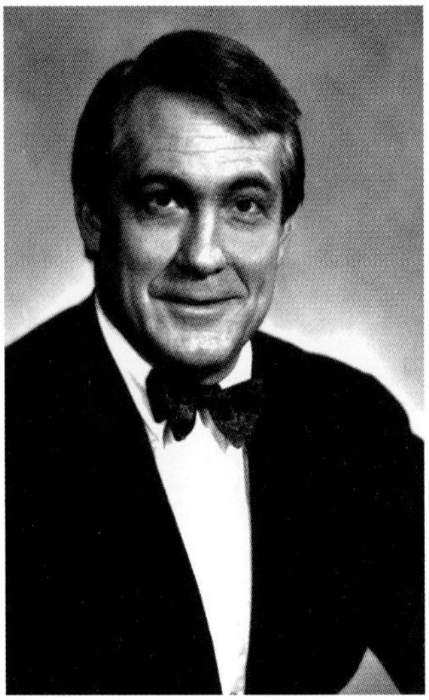

E. OSBORNE AYSCUE, JR.
PRESIDENT, NC BAR ASSOCIATION
AND FORMER MCB PRESIDENT

Executive Director and an expanded budget." His letter, which Farris forwarded to all Bar members, explained, "We toyed with the idea of suggesting what you are suggesting now several years ago, but we concluded that the pressure for a higher level of activity on the part of the local Bar needed to build up a little bit more before we undertook to ask the membership for a substantial dues increase."

The members approved the dues increase and the search for an executive director began. A committee of nine was appointed, headed by Farris, and an outstanding list of candidates emerged. Howerton's organizational experience and her enthusiasm for the job made her the leading candidate.

The bright-eyed brunette knew her way around Charlotte, the city where she had been raised before heading off to attend Marymount and Sacred Heart Colleges. She subsequently earned an English degree from Charlotte's Queens College (now Queens University of Charlotte). Her family name was one of the best known among musically inclined school children. Her father owned and operated Charlotte's Howren Music Company, where for years local children got their first clarinet, drumsticks or trumpet, as they joined their school band or orchestra.

Howerton (married to lawyer and District Court Judge Phillip F. Howerton, Jr.) began work on October 1, 1984 at a salary of $25,000 per year. "One of the board members gave me the Bar's checkbook balance as the financial statement," Howerton recalls. "It was written on the back of a napkin. I thought, 'Oh dear, we've got a long way to go.'" Years later, she said, "I remember thinking this would be an exciting and challenging position. I also had the idea it might be fun." She got on well with Farris, who paced back and forth in his office as if he were still on the gridiron, while talking about what needed to be done in the Bar. She said, "A pat on the shoulder and the softly spoken words of encouragement, 'Go get 'em, kid' were his parting acts of support."

"My learning curve was addressed initially through interviews with about twenty lawyers, asking each the same questions so that I could arrive at themes," she said. "These included their thoughts on vision, strategic initiatives and specific ideas for quality programming. From there, and under the guidance of the executive committee and other committees which were being established, we initiated new programming."

She explained that her experience with the American Cancer Society and later as CEO of Hospice made her familiar with organizational development. "Frankly there were many things to be attended to in those early years and it took some time to get organized," she said. "One such structural issue dealt with financial matters. These involved making certain we ended in the black for events such as Law Day and the annual meeting, dues collection from all members and producing financial statements that were both accurate and informative."

In her first month, she hired a part-time secretary and moved the Bar's office from the spare 200 square feet on the eighth floor of the Law Building to quarters over five times larger on the first floor. While the building was showing its age, it remained a vital center of activity for the legal profession. More firms were moving their offices to other locations, however, and finding more room at the Law Building was not the problem it might once have been.

Farris recalled the early months. "With Mary came organization: agendas at every committee meeting; assigned specific responsibilities; follow-up with chairs; cross-section participation by all members of the Bar; timetables for results; other accountability of volunteer lawyers as well as staff, encouragement and cheerful prodding. And new ideas abounded."

During her second year on the job, Howerton hired LueAnn Whitten, a graduate of a job training program instituted by then City Council member and later Mayor Harvey Gantt for low-income residents. A resident of a low-rent subsidized housing project, at first she literally walked over a mile to work each day. First hired as an administrative assistant and Lawyer Referral coordinator, Whitten brought computer skills that no one else on the staff had. She later became coordinator of events and of the Bar's growing number of sections and over her career touched every aspect of the staff's growth and its operations. Whitten would ultimately become what Howerton described as "the face of the Bar."

As the staff grew, Lisa Armanini was hired to coordinate the Bar's Legal Services for the Elderly program, and she later transitioned to coordinator of its growing Continuing Legal Education (CLE) programs. When, under the leadership of past president Hamlin Wade, the Bar received a grant from the State Bar's Interest on Lawyers' Trust Accounts program to support a coordinator of a Bar-sponsored program to match volunteer lawyers with *pro bono* clients, Sara Pressly was hired to fill the position.

Some of the ideas for new programs dated back to King's 1979 trip to Chicago and what Ayscue had learned during his year as president in

LUEANN WHITTEN, "THE FACE OF THE BAR"

1980-81 and through his earlier long-range planning experience with the North Carolina Bar Association. Howerton herself began to attend annual meetings of the ABA, where she would learn of bar activities around the country, but she said that the ideas for the Mecklenburg programs came largely from local attorneys whom she consulted to gather suggestions after she took the job. "As we evolved from those early interviews, the Mecklenburg Bar became a model of programming for other bars throughout the country," Howerton said. "For example, in 1987, we established the first Lawyer Assistance Program in the country offered by a metropolitan bar. During that same time we began our sports programs—softball, basketball and re-instated an annual golf tournament. These were initiated so that our members could meet one another in venues other than the courtroom."

There were other innovations. "We began a fee arbitration program," Howerton said, "to assist clients who disputed their legal fees and continued to take a very serious approach to the local grievance process." The fee arbitration system used panels of experienced lawyers and a non-lawyer member to resolve such disputes. As for grievances, other local bars in the state routinely forwarded all complaints about lawyers' conduct to the State Bar for handling. Howerton recognized that many of these complaints involved the failure of a lawyer to return a client's calls or disputes over the lawyer's fee. She and the local grievance committee undertook to resolve these kinds of problems, problems that did not appear to involve ethical violations, through communication with both lawyer and client. Those complaints that did appear to involve genuine issues of lawyer misconduct that violated the State Bar's ethical rules were investigated locally, so that a complete file could be forwarded to the State Bar, instead of leaving it to start from scratch in investigating the complaint. "Those early years," Howerton recalled, "were full of creative ideas that resulted in new programming and an overall extension to the community of lawyers and the community at large."

One project that Howerton inherited and helped to bring to fruition was the publication of a Bar Handbook. Ten years in the making, the first edition, a compilation of local court rules, was completed in December 1984 through the dedicated work of District Court Judge Robert P. Johnston. "Bob and I worked together," Howerton recalls, "from September to December to get the first edition printed by *The Mecklenburg Times*. The first copy of the Handbook was presented to Al London, who, as president of the bar, conceived the idea years before." Her work on that project provided Howerton with a quick education about the Bar of whose organization she had assumed responsibility. For years thereafter, a copy of the Handbook and annual revisions were given to all the members of the Bar. An ongoing encyclopedic reference for the entire Mecklenburg Bar organization, the local courts and law-related offices, including their fundamental documents, policies and operating rules, it was eventually made available online on the Bar's website.

Howerton also found that the Bar's only communication with all its members, save for an occasional letter, was a newsletter, produced sporadically, sometimes once a year, sometimes twice. Beginning in 1984, the Bar produced a monthly newsletter, the last issue each year being an annual report of the Bar's activity. Judge Johnston, a graduate of Stanford Law School, who served on the District Court for eight years before going on the Superior Court bench in 1991, was instrumental in producing the newsletter and served on the committee that produced it for over twenty years.

One of the early programs in Howerton's tenure replicated a "buddy system" for young lawyers that other local bars had found successful. At the time, the legal profession remained largely one of small firms and sole practitioners. In 1984 fully forty-nine percent of the nation's 441,000 lawyers were sole practitioners. Of the more than 40,000 law firms, ninety-three percent consisted of ten or fewer lawyers. Many young lawyers simply lacked the kind of mentors that had been a mainstay of the profession in earlier days. Silent Partners was designed to help newly licensed lawyers adjust to life in the profession. Young lawyers, those just beginning their careers, needed some guidance to help them transition from what they had learned in law school to the law practice they would encounter in the courtroom, across the desk from a client or across a negotiating table. The Silent Partners Program was designed to make the transition go more smoothly.

"Years ago, when there were comparatively few lawyers in Charlotte and only a handful of new lawyers each year, it was not difficult for a new lawyer to find an older lawyer to whom he could turn for general advice," President Farris wrote to the membership. "Now that we have nearly 1,200 lawyers and 70 or more new lawyers each year, a haphazard approach to provide help for inexperienced lawyers is no longer feasible." He encouraged members to volunteer both as young and old Silent Partners. Seventy-seven bar members signed on to mentor new members. According to James B. Craighill, the first chairman of the new program, of the fifty-five new lawyers in 1984, seven signed on to be mentored.

Pender R. McElroy, who next chaired the committee and became Bar president in 1994, said, "The Silent Partners Committee was started because the Mecklenburg Bar was experiencing significant growth in numbers, and there was concern that young lawyers just out of law school could easily get lost in the rush and the crowd and should have a mentor or a silent partner outside of his or her firm whom he or she could consult on issues and questions facing new lawyers."

McElroy said that the new program did not include technical aspects of the law and procedure, but included just about everything else, such as how to generate clients and communicate with them, how to use the continuing education programs, a survey of areas of practice, how to avoid burnout and how to interact with staff. "We were able to recruit veteran lawyers to serve as mentors to new lawyers for one year," he said. "The mentors were expected to communicate with their young lawyer at least once a month. Lunch was suggested, and I think that is how most mentors connected with their mentees."

Erik Rosenwood was one of the first to take advantage of the program. Years later, when he was a partner in Hamilton, Moon, Stephens, Steele & Martin, he recalled, "I was encouraged to participate in, and told about, the Silent Partners program by now federal magistrate David Keesler, who was my mentor at Moore & Van Allen. I'm not from Charlotte and didn't know anyone other than law school classmates and the folks at MVA."

His mentor was Sydnor Thompson, who became something of a gregarious uncle for Rosenwood. "We were both pleased to learn we had each studied at St. Andrews in Scotland. Sydnor definitely filled the stated role of the Silent Partners program, as I understand it – to allow a new attorney to have an experienced resource not within his or her own firm. But more than that, he invited me to breakfast with his wife, Harriett, at Charlotte Country Club, took me to political events and introduced me to dozens of Charlotte leaders, such as Parks Helms [long-time legislator and county commission chair], and invited me to his annual Christmas party which is a veritable *Who's Who* of Charlotte."

Rosenwood said he especially appreciated the invitation as a way to start his necessary networking. "Sydnor has become not just a mentor but a friend," he said. "I fully plan to participate in the Silent Partners Program as a mentor in the future, and if I can give young lawyers half of the experience I had, I'll consider it a resounding success."

The new energy and programs coming from the Bar prompted President R. Cartwright (Cart) Carmichael to convene a three-hour meeting of the executive committee in December 1985 to consider the Bar's mission in the face of changes taking place in the profession and within the community. The Bar's dual role – as a membership organization and as a regulatory body – often left its "public service obligation dangling in between," Carmichael said in the January 1986 Bar newsletter. Out of the meeting came a new mission statement: "The purpose of the Mecklenburg

County Bar is to render appropriate service to the public and the District Bar membership in improving and preserving the administration of justice, and to assist the North Carolina State Bar as prescribed by statutory requirements."

The mission of the Bar had never before been so clearly defined. It had simply evolved over time, from the days when lawyers got together for a meal and fellowship and left the work of the Bar to a few earnest members who set the calendar. Seventy years after it was first organized, however, the Bar and the members were part of a more complex and structured legal system. A *pro bono* case was no longer something a lawyer was moved to accept when he had some free time; it was now understood that this kind of service was part of being an attorney.

The mission statement focused attention first on the support that the organization would provide to its members, especially in continuing education. It also emphasized the Bar's commitment to ethical standards and to providing legal services to all who were in need. The role of attorneys in the judicial system, as a liaison between the courts and judges and the public, was a part of the statement of purpose.

A *pro bono* case was no longer something a lawyer did when he had some free time; it was now part of being an attorney.

In 1987, the Bar found another, and different, way to reach out to the community, through its annual Law and Society programs. Conceived as a way of presenting speakers of interest to both the Bar and the public, thereby educating the entire community on the role of law in a democratic society and, through that, creating a better sense of community, the first speaker was legendary Harvard Law School professor Arthur Miller, who spoke on "The Media and the Right to Privacy." These programs, to which lawyers and law firms traditionally invite friends and clients, have since brought to Charlotte twenty more speakers, including former United States Attorneys General Griffin B. Bell and Janet Reno, FBI Director William Sessions, consumer activist Ralph Nader, Whitewater Independent Counsel Kenneth Starr, Associate Supreme Court Justice Anthony Scalia, Homeland Security Secretary Michael Chertoff, 9/11 and BP oil spill victim fund administrator Kenneth Feinberg, UNC-CH Chancellor Holden Thorp, legal reporter Nina Totenberg and the local Bar's own Julius Chambers.

As the Bar continued to grow in the early 1980s, outgoing president King told his successor that the organization needed to find a way to create its own permanent headquarters building. "Whatever other conclusions a long range study committee might reach, I feel that they are certain to identify a foundation as the most practicable way for us to ever have a Bar Center," King wrote.

The expansion of the Bar's program portfolio and the idea of a free-standing building to use as its headquarters presented Howerton and the Bar leadership with a challenge. All lawyers in the 26th Judicial District were required to be members of the Mecklenburg County Bar, but programs that went beyond the traditional bar services to lawyers would need financial support, and that money could not come from mandatory membership dues. Howerton found an answer in the Bar archives. While preparing for the move to new offices in the Law Building in the fall of 1986, she opened one of the ancient army-green file cabinets and found a stack of file folders. One was entitled: "Lawyers' Educational Foundation." "I thought here was something we might possibly use," she recalled. "I called Bob Sink, who was president then, and told him that it looked like we had some kind of fund that had been started in 1962."

Indeed, the Bar had established a Foundation on June 18, 1962, funded by stock in the Wachovia Corporation valued at $3,000 that had been donated by Bar member Guy Carswell. Carswell, a Wake Forest Law graduate, and his wife, Clara, who had no children, were later to leave the bulk of their estate to his alma mater, Wake Forest, to establish the Carswell Scholarships. He had hoped the local Bar would use his $3,000 gift as incentive to raise more money for law school scholarships, but that hope had never materialized. With the exception of a fund drive in 1970 to raise funds to buy books on law enforcement to be donated to the growing University of North Carolina at Charlotte, the Foundation had been dormant. Most Bar members were not even aware of its existence. In April 1980, President Bob King had even asked tax attorney Mark B. Edwards to explore the possibility of creating such a foundation.

After Howerton's discovery, the Foundation was revived and renamed the Mecklenburg Bar Foundation. A committee composed of Judge Robert Johnston, Henry W. Flint, and Howerton decided it should be used to establish programs that would "enhance public awareness and knowledge" of the law and the role of lawyers in the community. In his newsletter message to the Bar in December 1986, President Sink wrote, "There exists, at some level, a latent 'community of spirit' among our members. There exists a desire to continue traditions represented in the lives of the best of our present and former members. There exists a need for a vehicle to support and enhance that continuity and those traditions. Why not a foundation centered in that community, in those traditions and in the continuity of purpose?"

The Bar's executive committee agreed, and the Foundation was registered as an organization totally separate from the Mecklenburg County Bar. The revitalized Foundation soon became the focus of the long-time desire of Bar leaders to have a permanent headquarters. In the mid-80s under the leadership of Leslie J. Winner, the Bar had created a thoughtful set of continuing legal education programs, created to supplement those offered by the North Carolina Bar Association and other statewide providers. Winner, a former law clerk to Judge McMillan and a partner in the firm founded by Julius Chambers, would go on to serve three terms in the state Senate, would become the general counsel of the local Board of Education and then of the University of North Carolina System before assuming her role as Executive Director of the Z. Smith Reynolds Foundation.

The new center would be seated in the Foundation, which in turn would lease it to the Bar. The center could thus support any number of activities that could not otherwise be paid for out of mandatory dues. It could also host the Bar's growing continuing legal education programs. Sessions could be held there rather than at hotels or other venues that charged for use of the space. The Foundation's board of directors launched a $600,000 fund drive to buy or build a new bar center, establish a first-class law library, offer scholarships, create new awards and sponsor programs like the Law and Society Lectures.

The first Mecklenburg Bar Center, created during the presidency of Lloyd F. Baucom, was located in a house on East Boulevard in what had been Charlotte's first modern residential development, Dilworth. In 1987, the Mecklenburg County Bar became the first local bar in the state with its own headquarters building. Over time, the level of the bar's activities outgrew that rented facility. The search for permanent headquarters bore fruit in 1993, when Howerton discovered that a 1912 Georgian style house at 438 Queens Road, located in Charlotte's second early twentieth century residential development, Myers Park, was for sale. The owner, George Pittman, who operated his decorating business out of the location, was willing to sell, but there was a major problem. The $435,000 property would have to be rezoned before the Bar could use it. James Y. Preston, who had earlier served as president of the State Bar, took the lead in the negotiations.

When the Myers Park Homeowners Association retained counsel to oppose the Bar's rezoning request, *The Business Journal of Charlotte* noted the irony of lawyers versus lawyers. The Bar ultimately secured the zoning change by agreeing to lease offsite parking at nearby Theatre Charlotte and by buying a nearby nineteen-car parking lot for $105,000. These concessions appeased the Homeowners Association and the center's neighbors on Queens Road.

"One of the first things we did," Howerton recalled, "was to set up a capital campaign through the Foundation to buy the property." The campaign was led by William M. Claytor, who in 1996 would

LESLIE WINNER

serve as president of the local Bar. Prospective donors were asked to contribute $450 each, payable over three years through the Foundation. Since the Foundation was a non-profit organization, the contributions were tax deductible. The Foundation became the owner, with the Bar itself paying rent to the Foundation. The Bar's headquarters were finally moved to that location in 1995 during the presidency of Pender McElroy.

With space available at no cost, hosting the CLE sessions quickly became a major source of income. In 1984, the Foundation's income from CLE was zero. That changed after January 1988, when annual CLE courses became mandatory for all the state's licensed lawyers. In 2004, income from CLE brought in $184,557. By comparison, in that same year the Bar's income from membership dues was $490,135.

The revived Foundation would receive an unexpected and significant infusion of funds as a result of a *pro bono* effort led by Mecklenburg lawyers that had a national impact and provided relief to a large class of citizens. In 1983, members of the Bar had gathered over lunch to hear United States Court of Appeals Judge Sam J. Ervin, III talk about the history and importance of *pro bono* representation. The occasion was the

MCB OFFICES ON QUEENS ROAD

inauguration of the Bar's Lawyers Volunteer Program, a new effort designed to encourage more members to participate in *pro bono* work in conjunction with Legal Services of Southern Piedmont. Soon after Ervin's talk, Robert C. Sink, who would serve as president of the local Bar in 1996 and of the State Bar in 1998, told his Robinson, Bradshaw & Hinson colleague, John R. (Buddy) Wester, a future president of the North Carolina Bar Association, what he had learned about a new internal ruling by the Social Security Administration (SSA).

This ruling, issued without prior notice, denied disability payments to thousands of claimants, including a man named Patrick Henry Hyatt, who subsequently lost his home and his car because he could no longer support his family. The SSA had simply declared that Hyatt and, as was later discovered, an estimated 500,000 other recipients across the nation, were suddenly ineligible. Without his SSA payments, it was not long before Hyatt could not pay his bills. Creditors even repossessed his recliner chair, the only thing that gave him relief from searing back pain.

Hyatt had sought help at LSSP, whose executive director, Terence Roche, and the agency's litigation director, Theodore O. (Ted) Fillette, had heard complaints similar to Hyatt's from others in the Charlotte area. Complaints were also being registered at legal aid offices in other parts of the country. With LSSP lawyer Jane Vandiver Porter, who would later become a District Court judge, taking the lead, the Legal Services team began to pursue Hyatt's case through the administrative appeals process, and when these appeals failed, it filed suit on his behalf in the federal court in Charlotte. LSSP needed the help of a major law firm to prosecute a class action of this magnitude, and Wester and his firm stepped up to take on the assignment.

As the case began to move through the judicial process, the lawyers discovered that the SSA had secretly changed eligibility standards. Three decisions by the Fourth Circuit Court of Appeals supported the claims of people like Hyatt, and the class action asserted that SSA had not complied with these rulings. According to an internal memorandum unearthed in the discovery process, SSA said that it did not have to "acquiesce" in the Fourth Circuit's rulings because those rulings did not conform to what SSA was doing in other jurisdictions. The agency had issued orders to its administrative law judges not to follow the Fourth Circuit rulings – even in the states in the Fourth Circuit – pending a final decision by the United States Supreme Court. The SSA's strategy was simple: the Supreme Court reviews so few cases – then less than 2 per cent– that SSA apparently thought the odds were that it would not suffer an adverse ruling from the Court. Its "non-acquiescence" policy thus appeared safe.

District Judge James McMillan was assigned the *Hyatt* class action. After a January

1984 trial, he issued an injunction against the Secretary of the United States Department of Health and Human Services, the parent agency for SSA, and had it typed, for emphasis, in all capital letters as an expression of his outrage over the agency's actions.

The government appealed. In the first of what would be five arguments to Fourth Circuit Court of Appeals, the government's counsel, by now an appellate specialist from the Department of Justice, relied on a recent Supreme Court decision indicating that disability claimants must comply with administrative rules to be eligible for relief. Wester argued that these rules were unfair, because many of the probable recipients could have had no idea that the rules had changed. More emphatically, he said the crux of the case was not in administrative rules, but in the fact that the SSA was defying the orders of the court to which it was appealing.

"I said I had an older case in mind, a much older case than the ruling the government was relying on," Wester recalled. As a former *Duke Law Journal* editor, he had helped edit articles on the subject, never imagining he would have an opportunity to base an appeal on *Marbury v. Madison*, the landmark 1803 United States Supreme

TED FILLETTE, LSSP LITIGATION DIRECTOR

LSSP EXECUTIVE DIRECTOR, TERENCE ROCHE

Court decision that had established the principle of judicial review of executive actions.

The Fourth Circuit upheld the basic merits of McMillan's order, but applied the administrative rules to reduce dramatically the number of claimants who would secure new hearings. Now, there was only one court left to provide relief. When Wester, with his partner Dan T. Coenen who had clerked for Supreme Court Justice Harry Blackmun a few years earlier and who later became a professor at the University of Georgia Law School, pursued the case to that Court, McMillan's order was reinstated in full. Over the next fifteen years, Wester would argue *Hyatt* on four separate occasions in the Fourth Circuit, and at numerous other times before McMillan. He was joined by new teammates from LSSP, Charles M. (Mac) Sasser and Douglas S. Sea, whom he credits, along with Coenen, as outstanding advocates in the battle, "critical to the team's success." Ultimately, more than 50,000 disabled citizens of North Carolina received benefits pursuant to the lawful disability standards McMillan enforced. McMillan made a "conservative estimate" that the potential benefits totaled $470 million for one year.

JOHN (BUDDY) WESTER

Although *pro bono* cases proceed without expectation of compensation, a federal statute allowed recovery of fees from the federal government upon a showing of "no substantial justification" for the government's position. McMillan ordered the government to pay the plaintiff's attorneys' fees. "The United States has acted in bad faith, voraciously and wantonly in this action," McMillan wrote, "and those actions justify an award of fees . . . . The government's position in this case is neither 'substantially justified' nor 'reasonable.' To the contrary, the Secretary's position is not even marginally justifiable, and it may be fairly characterized as outrageous at best, both before this case was filed and during the course of this suit . . . ."

His ruling continued, "Plaintiffs have succeeded in forcing the Social Security Administration to halt application of a secret, unlawful policy to its determination of hundreds of thousands of disability claims in North Carolina and, perhaps, to many hundreds of thousands more outside North Carolina. [As a result of this case, plaintiffs have effected] fundamental change to a recalcitrant agency which brought all of the power of the federal government to bear on Plaintiffs and their counsel while it resisted Plaintiffs' efforts to enforce the orders of this court . . . each step of the way."

In August 1984, the ABA gave the first national *pro bono* award in its 106-year history to Robinson, Bradshaw & Hinson, which had ultimately contributed more than 4,500 hours of its lawyers' time to the case.

LSSP's Roche thanked the Mecklenburg Bar for its support. "What we have accomplished together is, of course, a credit to us corporately as the Mecklenburg Bar. But, even more importantly, it has made a critical difference to a huge number of low income North Carolinians and, thanks to the Mecklenburg County Bar and the

Foundation, will continue to do so through the efforts of future volunteers and our staff." The plaintiffs' legal bill in the first round was $242,086.43 in fees and interest. A subsequent order increased that by $1,172,825.40. Wester's firm donated its $450,000 share of the award to the Bar Foundation. It would support both the training of lawyers to represent individual *Hyatt* claimants in pursuing their disability claims and new programs that Howerton and the Bar's leadership hoped to create as the Bar moved beyond its traditional role.

The *Hyatt* case would prove to be one of the milestones in the life of the Mecklenburg County Bar. It demonstrated a new working relationship between the private bar and the public legal services agency that served the poor – two groups that had initially been at odds with one another. Indeed, it occurred to some of the older members of the Bar that its foresight in bucking tradition to help create LSSP twenty years earlier had borne fruit. *Hyatt* also raised the stature of the Bar in the public's eye by demonstrating that *pro bono* work was something that lawyers, even those in the large, prestigious firms, took seriously and valued as part of the tradition of the profession.

PAST PRESIDENTS OF THE MECKLENBURG BAR ASSOCIATION AND THE FOUNDATION
FRONT ROW: BEN HORACK, JOE GRIER, SHIRLEY FULTON
SECOND ROW: PENDER MCELROY, ROBERT STEPHENS, MARK MERRITT, RAY FARRIS, CATHERINE THOMPSON, JON BUCHAN, NANCY BLACK NORELLI
THIRD ROW: DAVID H. HENDERSON, BOB HENDERSON, WILLIAM M. CLAYTOR, JOHN GRESHAM, MARION COWELL.

CHAPTER 12

A Diverse Group Emerges

When Nancy Black Norelli returned to her native Charlotte in 1977 to practice law, the first woman associate at Helms, Mulliss & Johnston, she knew that women were a decided minority in the Mecklenburg Bar, but she did not know how many women lawyers were in the county. The State Bar was no help; it did not record the gender of the lawyers it licensed, and so Norelli and two other women lawyers, Jean Cary and Leslie Winner, went name-by-name through the roster of the local Bar and mailed about forty invitations to an after-work party for women lawyers. Although Bernice (Bernie) Farmer turned out to be a man and asked to be excused, Norelli later wrote, "Our invitation struck a chord and twenty women attended our party."

One of those who came to the 1977 event was Lelia Alexander. In the early 1950s, she was the first woman to open an ongoing law practice in Charlotte that did more than handle research and write briefs for male lawyers, as the few local women lawyers had done since the 1920s. In subsequent years, she was followed by a few other women, including Lila G. Bellar, who was educated at New York University and received her North Carolina license in 1962. After working as a law clerk for the firm of Goodman & Levine, Bellar began her own general practice. Unlike most women in the profession, her work carried her into the courtroom, where she developed a reputation as a tough and aggressive advocate in criminal cases. It was the kind of legal work that most women had avoided in the past.

In 1968, Claudia E. Watkins, caught the attention of her peers when she was elected one of the state's new District Court judges, becoming the first female judicial officer in the county. After finishing at the UNC School of Law, Watkins had worked as a hearing officer for the Clerk of Court, handling juvenile and domestic relations cases, and was in general practice before becoming a candidate for judge. Later, after her marriage to Charlotte Mayor John Belk, she left the bench, citing potential conflicts of interest.

NANCY BLACK NORELLI

The first African American woman lawyer to open an office in Charlotte, Patricia King, arrived in 1971.

By the time of that 1977 meeting, women in court, especially criminal court, remained rare and noteworthy. The first woman lawyer in the Mecklenburg District Attorney's office was Barbara Dean, who was hired in 1973 and stayed for two years. Assistant District Attorney Catherine Cooper made her first court appearance in 1976 in a case where the defendant was represented by Ann Villar, a University of Kentucky law graduate who worked in the public defender's office. A *Charlotte News* account of the trial carried the headline, "Two Women Have Trying Day."

Norelli did not neglect the effort she had begun in 1977. Two years later, when her law partner Osborne Ayscue, as president-elect of the local Bar, was considering committee appointments, she gave him an annotated list of all the women lawyers in town and persuaded him to have lunch with as many of them as she could muster at the Ivey's department store's Tulip Terrace restaurant. Years later, in 1999, Norelli herself would assume the Bar presidency.

In the 1970s, women had begun to make up a larger proportion of the student population of the nation's law schools. Yet, despite the success that women seemed to have practicing alone or finding jobs in the judicial system, women had difficulty finding work as associates in law firms. One of the early pioneers in this new era was Sarah E. Parker, who was hired in 1969 by Thomas Lockhart to work in his firm, the Cansler firm, whose roots went back into the 1800s. In the year Norelli came to Helms, Mulliss, Heloise Merrill became the first woman lawyer at Grier, Parker, Poe, Thompson, Bernstein, Preston & Gage. By that time, Moore & Van Allen had two female associates among its eighteen attorneys. In 1977, however, only two women had become partners in their firms.

Even with the changes taking place in society, with women occupying jobs traditionally held by men, many private law firms avoided hiring women at all or hired only a token woman lawyer. According to Norelli, "Sorry, we've already hired a woman," was a common refrain. Even when women did secure positions, they were not universally well received. Some senior male members of firms worried that clients would not take a female colleague seriously. They feared this lack of confidence would adversely affect their law practices.

Throughout the 1960s and the 1970s, North Carolina had repeatedly elected and reelected Susie Marshall Sharp to the state Supreme Court, but Katherine S. (Katie) Holliday, a 1980 Duke University Law School graduate and a former McMillan law clerk, remembers that her first day at work with a Charlotte firm was nevertheless difficult. "One of the senior partners, the day I started, took me into his office and said, 'I just want you to know that I basically didn't want them to hire them [women]. I don't approve of women practicing law. And my wife doesn't want there to be a female attorney in this office.' I'm giving you bottom line. He was much smoother about it than this, but that was bottom line," she recalled. She also was told that if she attended firm meetings, this lawyer would not be there, and he vowed never to work on a case with her. "And then the kicker was, he said, 'If I should, for instance, ever run into you at the opera or the symphony, don't even attempt to speak because we're not going to do this introduction thing.' I have very vivid memories of being at home that night in the bathtub crying and saying, 'Do I go back tomorrow?'"

By 1984, when Mary Howerton came on board as the Bar's executive director, women lawyers were becoming more organized. "There was a strong, growing movement to place women lawyers in high offices," Howerton recalled. One result was the 1985 election of Julia V. Jones to become the first woman State Bar Councilor. The local Bar also united behind Governor Jim Hunt's 1984 appointment of Sarah Parker to the state Court of Appeals. Parker had been one of the twenty who had met in 1977 to talk about women in the Bar. She would ultimately become the Chief Justice of the North Carolina Supreme Court. In 1988, Shirley L. Fulton, an African American, became Mecklenburg's first woman elected to the Superior Court bench. She would later become its Senior Resident Judge. Two years later, Julia Jones was elected to the same court, and over the ensuing years an increasing number of local women lawyers, including Chambers, Stein alumna and Wellesley and Duke Law School graduate Yvonne Mims Evans, joined the Superior and District Court bench. The last all-male enclave would disappear only in late 2011, when Laura Turner Beyer became a Federal Bankruptcy Judge, the first full-time female federal judge in the Western District of North Carolina.

The number of women in the profession was on the rise in the early 1980s when a young Catherine E. Thompson, joined Helms, Mulliss & Johnston. A *summa cum laude* graduate of Duke (though ironically a direct lineal descendant of UNC founder William Richardson Davie) and a Yale Law graduate, she been a law clerk for Fourth Circuit Court of Appeals Judge Sam J. Ervin, III in his first full year on that bench. A decade later, in 1991, when Thompson became president of the local Bar at age thirty-six, about half of those attending law schools across the nation were women.

Thompson talked with *The Charlotte Observer* about the challenges female lawyers faced. "There are special challenges, I think, for women lawyers," she said. "One of the important parts of the quality of life issue is the challenge for women lawyers who want a family and want to be a lawyer. By talking to lots of women lawyers in this community, I know they find it very difficult to do all that. The firms need to figure out how to keep women lawyers over the long haul. It's going to require an accommodation of scheduling [and] alternative compensation."

Speaking some years later, Thompson said, "There was a sorority of women lawyers ahead of me always looking after the new women lawyers that came, so I benefited greatly from that. I'd like to think that the year went well. I was treated fine. Maybe having a woman president was no longer a big deal; we had one and it wasn't a threat. That was past. The pressure was off. I was not conscious that this was going to be singular. I thought this was going to happen again and again, and it did." Six years later, Judy D. Thompson, no relation to Catherine Thompson, followed her as president and in 1999, the Bar elected Norelli to the presidency. After her retirement from the bench, Shirley Fulton was elected president in 2005, the Bar's first African American woman president.

"Thinking of mentors, there were several men in the Bar who were key for me," Catherine Thompson reflected. "They just let me become part of the structure of the executive committee, Bob Sink, Ray Farris, Sydnor Thompson, and Jim Preston. They were always so good to me, and so kind. I loved to spend time with them. And they were not in my firm and that was something I liked also."

Although the Mecklenburg Bar never had a separate section for women, the Charlotte Women's Bar, formed in 2003, would provide a unique and personally supportive professional network. "Women attorneys have come a long way," Chief Justice Sarah Parker observed. A Charlotte native, she received her law degree in 1969 from UNC, where she had earned her bachelor's degree in 1964. She served two years in Turkey with the Peace Corps between undergraduate and law school. "And we have far fewer miles to go than we did forty years ago; but we cannot forget the struggle, and, like our male counterparts, we cannot rest if we wish to continue succeeding in the profession. I, of course, from time to time in the earlier days encountered lawyers and judges who were not comfortable with or accustomed to the idea of a female lawyer. One time after I had been practicing law for three or four years, one judge told me that if I wanted to sit at the counsel table, I should get admitted to the bar."

JUDGE SHIRLEY FULTON
FIRST AFRICAN AMERICAN WOMAN JUDGE

HARVEY GANTT, ELECTED MAYOR OF CHARLOTTE 1983

Parker recalled a District Court hearing in 1971 in Forsyth County that may have been the first time in the state that all three courtroom positions were filled by women. "Rhoda Billings [herself later to serve as Chief Justice] was the judge; Barbara Westmoreland, an African American lawyer in Winston-Salem, was representing the plaintiff, and I was representing the defendant."

Parker joined the Court of Appeals after the retirement of Chief Judge E. Naomi Morris, its first woman member and its first female chief judge, and except for a brief period in 1990 was the only woman on the court. While Parker herself was the only woman on the Supreme Court for more than a dozen years, by 2011 a majority of that court was female.

One of Charlotte's most dramatic breaks with old traditions and habits came in 1983 when Harvey Gantt, an African American, was elected Mayor. An architect who had broken the color barrier at Clemson University when he was admitted as an undergraduate in the early 1960s, Gantt first served on the City Council before becoming Mayor. He was re-elected in 1987. One of those who helped attract Gantt to Charlotte was Julius Chambers, who was constantly on the alert for promising young African American professionals he thought could add to the quality of life in his home town.

"Harvey Gantt was working on Soul City," recalled Melvin L. (Mel) Watt, who at the time had himself recently been recruited to the Chambers firm and who was to go on to be the local bar's first African American president. "We were out in the middle of nowhere one night and I happened to be with Julius. Harvey had clerked with Odell [Charlotte architect A.G. Odell] one summer, and Julius made that same pitch [to come to Charlotte]. So Julius was responsible for me and for Harvey coming to Charlotte. Julius was basically the Charlotte black chamber of commerce at that time. At that time, not a single black professional was coming to Charlotte that was not being recruited by Chambers."

The changes taking place in society were not lost on members of the Bar. "The leaders of the Mecklenburg Bar were becoming very concerned about the lack of diversity in top jobs," Howerton said. "There was a real emphasis on our Bar leading the way." In 1985, the Bar elected Karl Adkins and Ronald L. Gibson, both African Americans, to serve along with Julia Jones on the fifty-member State Bar Council, the governing body for all the state's lawyers. The Mecklenburg Bar had grown so large that it could name three councilors instead of the usual one. At one time, Adkins and Gibson had both practiced in the Chambers law firm. Gibson had earlier clerked for Judge McMillan, and he was later Associate General Counsel of Duke Power Company. Adkins was later to serve on the Superior Court bench.

"It was a very interesting time," recalled Geraldine Sumter, an African American woman who had joined the Chambers firm in 1984. "There were lots of changes. Of course it was a very interesting time to have Terry Sherrill and Shirley Fulton go to the District Court bench. Before that, Cliff Johnson had been the only African American who had been on the District Court and Superior Court here. He was then on the state Court of Appeals. It was an incredible thing because we were also trying to make sure that there were African Americans and women in the District Attorney's office and the Public Defender's and over at the U.S. Attorney's office and the EEOC and all of the federal sectors. It was such a time that if there was an appointment of an African American or a female, everybody knew about it. It was noteworthy. It was sometimes historical."

> If there was an appointment of an African American or a female, everybody knew about it. It was noteworthy. It was historical.

In the years to come, Sumter and her partner James E. Ferguson, II were to be honored by the government of South Africa for their years of mentoring young black lawyers in that country, a program they undertook under the auspices of the National Institute of Trial Advocacy, of which Ferguson later served as chair. Some of the people they mentored are now, in post-apartheid South Africa, helping to run its government.

Mel Watt was forty-three in 1988 when he became the first African American elected president of the Mecklenburg Bar. In his first letter to the members, he suggested that he was like the first black quarterback to lead a team in the Super Bowl; neither could avoid being under scrutiny. "How I perform may well bear on your perception and the public's perception of how well I as a black lawyer and, indeed, how black lawyers in general, can lead. That is wrong but it's a fact. . . . But," he continued, "I accept the position of President of the Bar in that same spirit – the spirit that I'm a lawyer who happens to be black; your president and leader for this year who happens to be black."

MEL WATT, 1988
FIRST AFRICAN AMERICAN
MCB PRESIDENT

Watt grew up in Charlotte, raised by a single parent, and as a high school student in the early 1960s had joined other student leaders from the county's all-white high schools under the auspices of the National Conference of Christians and Jews to talk about race relations. A Phi Beta Kappa graduate of UNC-Chapel Hill in 1967, where he had the highest academic average in the business school, he earned a law degree in 1970 from Yale, where he was a member of the Yale Law Journal. Chambers hired him to expand the firm's business beyond its base in civil rights litigation. Watt organized the firm's corporate division, which played a major role in removing barriers to economic development for African Americans. He managed Harvey Gantt's 1983 mayoral campaign and a year later launched his own successful campaign for the state Senate, where he became widely known as "the conscience of the Senate." Remembering his own upbringing by a single parent, after one term he declined to run for reelection, withdrawing from public service until his children finished high school.

"Obviously an African American was going to be president at some point," Watt said some years later. "African Americans had been an important part of the Bar for a number of years. Some had suffered substantial indignities in the courtrooms and before judges, but that was passing on into the night except for a couple of die-hard judges. We were moving in a transition period to a more modern Bar that was inclusive, and I think symbolically it was important for somebody to make that first step, and it was important for somebody who had been active in the Bar. You knew the process we were going through that someone had to be that first person, and I happened to be in the right position at the right time."

Watt appointed African Americans and women to vital Bar roles. Leslie Winner became chair of the CLE committee, Catherine Thompson headed the communications committee and Sherri L. McGirt was named co-chair of the Lawyers Volunteer

Program. He summed up his service a year later in another letter to the members, saying that he had undertaken the position with humility and hoped that he had preserved the great tradition of past presidencies. And, he added with humor, "Perhaps I shouldn't admit it to my law partners, but my time records tell me that I have spent 289.5 hours of time on Bar business." He reported that he had attended thirty-seven early morning meetings, twenty-two luncheon meetings and forty-three late afternoon or dinner meetings.

"My most amazing morning accomplishment was getting in my car at 7:25 one morning for a 7:45 meeting at the Bar office, realizing that my car wouldn't start, running next door to borrow a car and jumper cables, getting my car started, returning my neighbor's car and making it to the Bar office for the meeting still with one minute to spare."

In 1992, Watt was elected one of the first two African American members of the United States House of Representatives from North Carolina since the nineteenth century. In his ninth term in 2011, he has served on a number of House committees, including the Judiciary Committee, and served a term as chair of the Congressional Black Caucus.

According to Sumter, who later would become the Chambers firm's managing partner, she was at the center of change for both blacks and women in the 1980s. "So the Bar grew as Charlotte grew and the diversity grew. It was probably ahead of other bars in the state. In terms of gender and racial equality, all of North Carolina probably lagged behind the nation. It is remarkable that I can remember when there was only one person of color as a partner in one of these big law firms in the state of North Carolina. His name is Tony Brett. He was in Winston-Salem's Womble, Carlyle & Rice office. The next person to become a partner in one of these big firms was when Frank Emory left Ferguson, Stein [and] went to Robinson, Bradshaw laterally as a partner in the early nineties."

One of the fastest growing segments of the Bar during the 1980s was young lawyers. During that decade, on average fifty-five new lawyers were sworn in each year. By the end of the period, almost as many young lawyers had taken their oaths as there were total members of the Bar in the early 1970s. Those numbers would double in the next decade, with more than a hundred new lawyers taking their oaths in a single year. A Young Lawyers Division had been created years before for members no older than thirty-six. It was organized to supplement the ongoing mentorship programs and to promote the interest of young people in the law. The Division created a speakers bureau that made Bar members available to civic clubs and it started a Law and the Arts

Committee to assist artists with legal problems. It sponsored a high school moot court competition and a Boy Scouts of America Law Explorers Post, and it helped create a high school orientation program to acquaint students with the legal profession. The Young Lawyers also worked with a pre-law counseling committee and sponsored an appellate advocacy CLE program and a Bridge-the-Gap program to acquaint new lawyers with the various courts and personnel. They also sponsored a tennis tournament and various social events.

Later, the Bar was to create a Bar Leadership Institute, in which promising young lawyers first went through a weekend together, then met in regular evening sessions in which the subjects ranged from the history of the local community and its current problems to developing leadership skills. Over time, its graduates have had a growing impact on the Bar and the community.

The Bar's Legal Services for the Elderly, which had been established as a committee in 1981, had attracted 100 volunteer members who devoted up 337 hours of service to 155 persons in 1984-85 alone. In October 1985, the Bar took the unprecedented step of reaching out to work with the local medical community. A joint committee of lawyers and doctors from the Mecklenburg County Medical Society negotiated a six-page agreement that outlined suggested witness fees for a doctor's testimony and rules for subpoenaing physicians that accommodated both the needs of the court and the physicians' own professional practices.

The Bar also began to focus on members' personal problems that appeared to be linked to the demands of increasing complexities in the law and competition within the profession. By 1987, Howerton and others had begun to see an alarming increase in suicides among lawyers. In a later study, Howerton quoted from a note left by a young lawyer who took his own life in 1987. "I am so sorry for all the pain I have caused you in our marriage," the lawyer wrote to his wife. "I don't know that I can explain what I have done: the simple explanation (and there is no simple explanation, really) is that I am so tired and I don't see any way out of the box I am in. Please understand that you are not to blame. I am, and I know that what I am doing is selfish. But it is a reasoned decision and one I must carry out." He left the note and called the police before going into his backyard to shoot himself.

In the year this young man died, the Bar established the Lawyer Support Committee, one of the first such local initiatives in the nation. Its purpose was to provide a confidential resource to members who needed support because of personal, job or health-related problems. If the issue was related to chemical dependency, lawyers were encouraged to seek assistance from the statewide Positive Actions for Lawyers

(PALS) program. The State Bar had established that program in 1979 to assist lawyers dealing with depression, addiction and other debilitating problems. W. Donald Carroll, Jr., a member of the Mecklenburg Bar, a former McMillan law clerk and Helms, Mulliss partner, would become the first permanent PALS executive director in 1993. Other matters, such as depression, were referred to committee members who serve as trained peer support volunteers.

In a statewide quality-of-life survey conducted by the North Carolina Bar Association in 1991, fifty-four percent of the lawyer respondents agreed that Bar-related organizations should sponsor programs to help lawyers balance their personal and professional lives.

The Mecklenburg Bar's pioneer 1987 Lawyer Support program, similar to a corporate employee assistance program, offered immediate help to the individual seeking assistance. The contacts were confidential, with no records or notes of engagements. This program was not a faceless voice over the telephone. The lawyer-to-lawyer contact communicated a sense of caring and promoted an element of trust, which organizers considered critical to the success of the program. Trained volunteers provided resource information and, if necessary, appropriate referrals.

The Lawyer Support Committee was assisted by two psychologists and one psychiatrist who acted as volunteer therapists. They attended monthly meetings and provided support, information and training to committee members. The Mecklenburg Bar Foundation provided funding to assist members who needed professional services but could not afford to pay for a clinical assessment.

The committee struggled to keep up. In Howerton's first nine years on the job, the Bar lost eight members to suicide. They included solo practitioners and lawyers from small and large firms. At the average age of forty-two, five took their lives at home, two in motel rooms and one in the conference room adjacent to his office. At least half of the deaths resulted from alcohol and drug abuse. Depression and various mood disorders were, Howerton found, underlying causes in the rest.

"These are disturbing statistics," she later wrote. "They have created a stir among Bar associations and Lawyer Assistance Programs (LAP) throughout the United States. We believe they may be among the highest incidents of suicide within such a time frame of any bar association in the country. Suicide is a subject that most of us would rather not address. But for those who worked with and were close to the Bar members who took their lives, it became a poignant reality. We address the issue of suicide because of that reality. In discussing it, learning more about it and becoming more aware of the warning signs, we hope we may be able to provide support to our members and prevent future deaths."

Howerton wrote in an article for the ABA, "While chemical dependency underlies a number of problems afflicting lawyers, we felt we needed to focus on a growing subset of problems arising from depression. For the busy lawyer, it may mean that the very ordinary conditions of living, raising children, marital relations, family illness and death, long hours of continuous work, can lead to a state of chronic depression. And untreated depression may cause a lawyer to neglect personal needs and client affairs. It was under these conditions that the program was launched as a safety net for our members."

Later, in 2004, Howerton presented to the LAP Board the results of her doctoral research. Her thesis, entitled "The Relationship of Attribution Style, Work Addiction, Perceived Stress and Alcohol Abuse in Lawyers in North Carolina," showed that, in comparison with earlier studies, the rate of depression among lawyers had increased significantly. Howerton noted that the data showed an increase in the level of dissatisfaction with the practice of law among younger lawyers, particularly those in practice less than five years.

Responding to these developments, the local Bar's effort ultimately evolved into the Lawyer Life Resource Committee, which sponsored CLE programs, special educational events, support groups and stress management courses in cooperation with a local hospital. Its members, including the clinical advisors, routinely contributed articles to the Bar's newsletter and provided speakers for section, legal auxiliary, and other Bar meetings.

Habitat for Humanity volunteers, Judge James McMillan, lawyer Jackie Shannon and Kathy Jones working on a Habitat for Humanity house in 1991.

CHAPTER 13

Reaching Outward

Friends told Sydnor Thompson that he had seen enough in his years of law practice that he ought to write a book, and so in 2006 he did, calling it *Sydnor Knows the Answer*. Included among his recollections were his days as a young associate working with legendary trial lawyer John W. Davis in preparation of a defense for a South Carolina school district that was a part of the appeal in *Brown v. Board of Education* and his abbreviated stint as a judge on the state Court of Appeals. There also is a paragraph or two on his 1990-91 year as president of the Mecklenburg Bar when it built its first Habitat for Humanity house.

It is a long way from the company of a nationally known lawyer like Davis and the polished wood of the Court of Appeals, to smoothing the concrete driveway of a modest house in north Charlotte. Yet, along with other members of the Mecklenburg Bar, Thompson helped bring the driveway to a level finish, and the home to completion, in the early 1990s, as the organization began efforts to establish itself as a civic-minded group that was involved with the community. The Mecklenburg Bar was not only a professional organization that served the legal profession; it was also involved in many dimensions of Charlotte and Mecklenburg County.

"The great thing about watching lawyers build a house is that there are no whereases, no continuances and no appeals," *The Charlotte Observer's* Allen Norwood wrote. "A mashed finger is a mashed finger, and all the precedents in all the law books on all those walnut-paneled offices won't take the sting out."

The Bar's executive director, Mary Howerton, reflected, "The leaders of the Bar were determined that the time had come for more community involvement." In addition to Law and Society luncheons and Liberty Bell Awards to outstanding non-lawyer citizens, the Bar, through its Foundation, began to sponsor summer internships among local high school students to give them exposure to what lawyers and law firms do, and the Bar collaborated with the Center for Mind-Body Health at Presbyterian

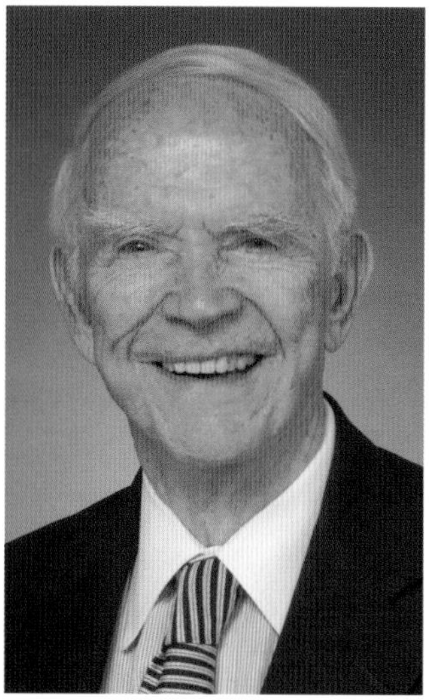

SYDNOR THOMPSON

Hospital to offer stress-relief courses for lawyers.

The work expanded under Catherine Thompson, Sydnor Thompson's successor as president and the first woman elected to lead the Mecklenburg Bar since Carrie McLean's term in the mid-1920s. She and Sydnor were not related, but they shared a common interest in developing the Mecklenburg Bar's service in Mecklenburg County. The new president was a partner in Smith Helms Mulliss & Moore, a firm of about 65 lawyers, the product of a merger of legacy Helms, Mulliss with a Greensboro firm, and one of only a few women who had achieved partnership status in the city's large firms.

Since its founding in 1912, the Mecklenburg Bar had focused its attention on the needs and interests of its own members. Those functions were largely procedural at first, but in the years after World War II, it began to work to improve the professional competence of its members through post-graduate training. These activities were member-focused, dealing directly with the administration of the courts and the support and management of the profession. In the 1950s, the Bar introduced programs like the Lawyer Referral Service that reached out to the community, but even those efforts were tied closely to the legal system. Broader based non-legal community service was left to individual members who had long assumed important roles in community service. By the 1970s and 1980s, increasing demands of clients and the need to stay abreast of fast-paced changes in the law made it difficult for many lawyers to find time for community involvement. Many who earlier had time for community work no longer volunteered.

CATHERINE E. THOMPSON

Catherine Thompson took office deciding that she wanted to move the Bar into a more active role in the community. "I thought the timing was good," she recalled. "Having an African American Bar president and then having a woman president a couple of years later made for more diverse leadership."

In her first letter to the members, Thompson said, "The Bar has exceptional people, and I believe that if we work together on these two particular challenges – first, strengthening our professional commitment to public service and community involvement, particularly focusing on the criminal justice system, and, second, starting to address the quality of life issues that a number of our Bar is facing, we will see good results."

She later recalled, "I can actually remember sitting in my den at home wondering what it was I was supposed to do my bar year. Was it supposed to be a maintenance year? Sometimes that's what you need to do. Was it supposed to be sort of a refreshing or refurbishing of existing programs? Then it struck me that a way for the Bar to make a contribution was through a partnership with a school."

She explained her interest to *The Charlotte Observer* in an August 19, 1991, interview: "There is an interesting tie between the education system and the criminal justice system; it's reaching children and youths who are at risk of becoming drug dealers or getting caught up in crime and getting swept into the criminal justice system. Trying to intervene and making a difference in those children's lives – that push is going on around the community."

Thompson appointed a committee of Charles F. Bowman, Frank Emory, Jr. and Ellen T. Ruff to interview school principals and other educators. (Bowman would later head a major department at Bank of America, Ruff would become President of Duke Energy's Nuclear Power division and Emory would become the first African American partner in a large local firm.) "They all felt Devonshire Elementary was the best school for us," she recalled. Eulada Watt, the wife of former Bar president Mel Watt, was its principal at the time. More than 70 Mecklenburg Bar members signed up as tutors, lunch buddies or in other volunteer roles. They started a mediation training program and speaking contests.

EULADA WATT

It was not just about improving the public image of lawyers, Thompson insisted. "Image follows action," she said. "It is part of the whole package of being a lawyer, which is being part of the community. In the early 1990s the pressure on lawyers to be involved in the community was getting harder and harder. People were getting more insulated in their firms and corporations. I think it's something they can carve out because they are doing something that actually can make a difference."

During Thompson's administration, the Bar addressed another change in the practice of law. "The law in 1957 [when he began practice] was relatively simple," Mark Bernstein reminisced. "You could be a general practitioner and feel pretty comfortable that you could render professional service to your client in most areas. Those of us who came along in my generation were general practitioners. One day you would be in courtroom and the next day you would be drawing a will and the next day you would be down doing some other kind of work." The transition to a regulated society triggered tremendous changes in the profession. "The lawyer as a public figure, as someone who could help a client with all sorts of things, and could commit to the community and provide leadership and all that began to evolve," Bernstein observed, "into a specialist who made a great deal more money than an old general practitioner. You had all that taking place."

Thus, during Catherine Thompson's presidency, for the first time in its 79-year history the Bar re-organized into sections for lawyers practicing in a specialized area. The first were criminal law, family law and real property law sections. There were already twenty-five committees working within the Mecklenburg Bar, and some members complained that creating sections divided the membership. The sections, however, helped to bring segments of the large and diverse membership of the Mecklenburg Bar with a common professional interest closer together.

> The transition to a regulated society triggered tremendous changes in the profession.

"The membership had become so large that it was becoming difficult for lawyers to relate to each other, so the sections were a way to break into more intimate relationships," Thompson said. "It was a chance to let people share expertise or information as they wanted and maybe to have meetings that were more relevant to what they were doing just as the Bar got bigger."

Edward T. Hinson, Jr. took on the leadership of the new Criminal Law Section, Fred Hicks led the Family Law group and Claude Q. Freeman chaired the Real Property Section. The Criminal Law Section was particularly important, Thompson said, as a way to help deal with the under-funding of courts and various programs. "Funding for prosecution is a critical need," she told *The Charlotte Observer* in the August 1991 interview. "Funding for indigent defense is a critical need. But we have a terrible shortfall of funds in doing that. There's a tension between safety and freedom. Those can be at odds with each other. All those things I think lawyers are uniquely position to help sort."

By 2011, as specialization continued, there were to be eleven sections, the three created in 1991 and ones dealing with business law, civil litigation, immigration and nationality, juvenile law, estate planning and probate, sole practitioner/small firm issues and taxation, as well as a section for corporate counsel.

Certainly, the community service work of the Mecklenburg Bar helped to repair some of the damage that the legal profession had inflicted on itself over the years. Thompson had just taken office when a tragic fire at a chicken-processing plant in Hamlet, a town about fifty miles east of Charlotte, left 25 workers dead. Another 56 were injured. The incident drew national attention, both from the media and from attorneys in out-of-state firms eager to sign on clients. "These lawyers are known as 'parachute lawyers'," former State Bar president Emil F. (Jim) Kratt of Charlotte said. "They appear any time there is a major disaster."

A Washington, D. C., lawyer, John Coale, who had represented clients after the Bhopal, India, disaster, was subsequently charged in a criminal action with unlawful solicitation of the victims of the Hamlet fire. Coale defended his actions in a comment to the media dismissing the State Bar officials as "sanctimonious yahoos." Thompson responded on behalf of the Mecklenburg Bar. "After the fire," she wrote

A PADLOCKED FIRE DOOR AT IMPERIAL FOOD PRODUCTS PLANT IN HAMLET, NC LED TO WHAT BECAME THE STATE'S WORST INDUSTRIAL DISASTER.

in a letter to *The Charlotte Observer*, "the State Bar and the [North Carolina Bar Association's] Young Lawyers Division sent volunteer lawyers from across the state to Hamlet to staff an information center. The volunteers provided, at no charge, information about unemployment benefits, guardianships for children, time frames for pursuing claims and the importance of not signing papers without fully understanding them. In the course of this effort, the State Bar received complaints from people who said they had been solicited, in person, for the legal business by lawyers or by 'runners' working for lawyers."

Thompson told the newspaper, "N. C. State Bar regulations affirm an individual's right to choose a lawyer without having to be confronted by lawyers eager for their business in the hospital, at home or at the grave site. If this makes North Carolina lawyers 'sanctimonious yahoos' as Mr. Coale would have it, then so be it."

The decline of the image of the legal profession in the latter part of the twentieth century began in the early 1970s with the realization that virtually all of those involved in the Watergate scandal of the Nixon years – including President Richard Nixon himself – had been trained as lawyers, Nixon at Duke University's law school. And there seemed to be more Nixons around than there were Sam Ervins, the Senator from Morganton who cultivated his image as a "country lawyer" and frequently pulled a copy of the Constitution from his pocket during the televised Watergate hearings that had revealed all manner of shenanigans, many of them involving lawyers. The profession had long been the butt of jokes, but now they began to smart more than before.

The Mecklenburg Bar had long administered a system for investigating grievance claims against its members and disciplining lawyer misconduct. Mecklenburg Bar president Alton Murchison III had raised the issue of public complaints against lawyers shortly after he took office in 1989. "We do have shortcomings and an occasional 'bad apple,'" Murchison wrote in his first newsletter message to the members. "But our standards and track record of service to the community far exceed those of the general populace and are at least the equal, if not the envy, of every other profession."

Murchison continued, "It is the opinion of many leaders of the Bar that these are critical times for lawyers. The profession has changed profoundly in the twenty-five years that I have been in practice, but the changes are wrought by an increasingly complex economic and legal environment, the relentless advance of technology, the increasing appeal of specialization, the perception in the minds of users of legal services that 'bigger is somehow better,' the developing dichotomy of lawyers into either smaller, narrowly focused 'boutiques' or into mega-sized firms which compete for clients through sophisticated marketing plans and advertising – clearly legal, but upsetting to lawyers steeped in a more conservative tradition. The emergence and predominance of the hourly based fee system and the resultant demands by more and more firms for hourly quotas often deny to lawyers, especially young lawyers, the opportunity to be participants in community life or spend quality time with their families. The ensuing effects on the civility and congeniality of the Bar and the development of a 'trial-by-ordeal' mentality are problems which need to be addressed."

The county's legal community was still astir over a sensational case that had involved the namesake of one of the county's oldest legal families, a former president of the Mecklenburg Bar. In September 1984, Francis O. Clarkson Jr., the son of a Superior Court judge and grandson of a state Supreme Court justice, was convicted of embezzling more than $500,000 from clients. In the course of their duty to clients, lawyers regularly hold client funds in separate trust accounts which can be used only for the client's benefit. These accounts are subject to unannounced State Bar audits, and misuse of client funds is subject to severe disciplinary action. At the time, Clarkson's was largest case of its kind in the state's history. He served an active jail sentence and lost his law license.

Over the next twenty-five years since the Clarkson case, those disciplined by disbarment for misappropriation of client funds have included two other past presidents of the local Bar, ironically one of them Murchison. As disturbing as these incidents were, they have served to reassure the public that the bar effectively deals with misconduct among its members.

Following the Clarkson case, members of the Bar executive committee had decided against any attempt to seek funds from Bar members to reimburse some of Clarkson's victims. Later, the State Bar found a better approach, creating a fund supported by dues assessments to meet the need to reimburse the victims of lawyer malfeasance in appropriate cases.

Investigating complaints from the public or clients had been a function of the Bar since its very early days, even before the State Bar took over lawyer discipline. In 1930, the Mecklenburg Bar appropriated a portion of its dues to cover the expenses of the Bar's grievance committee. The notorious gatekeeper at the Law Building, Hundley Gover, was remembered in a memorial read following his death in 1957 for his vigorous prosecution of lawyer misconduct as chair of the Bar's grievance committee.

Beginning in 1977, the North Carolina State Bar itself had assumed the investigation of alleged violations of the Bar's code of ethics and the prosecution of offenders before the State Bar Disciplinary Hearing Commission. Once such a prosecution begins, the hearings are open to the public and accused lawyers are represented by counsel. Depending on the seriousness of the offense, the commission can issue a warning, a reprimand or censure, and it can suspend a lawyer's license to practice law for a period up to five years or, in the most egregious cases, disbar a lawyer. In the first decade of the twenty-first century, some 373 North Carolina lawyers from among the more than 20,000 members of the State Bar were suspended or disbarred.

Those who administered the disciplinary process knew what the public did not know: that many complaints about lawyers come from clients unhappy because they lost their case and occasionally even from opponents seeking to gain an advantage in litigation, and that many of these complaints are transparently without merit. They knew that the Bar actively and aggressively deals with actual professional misconduct. Following the Murchison affair, Sydnor Thompson told *The Charlotte Observer*, "While it is impossible for the Bar to prevent such defalcations altogether, it has adopted certain practices designed to ferret out ethical violations and identify high-risk practitioners." He explained that the grievance committee even included two non-lawyers, included to help ensure the public a fair hearing of complaints.

> From 2000-2010, 373 lawyers from the NC State Bar were suspended or disbarred.

The topic of lawyer misconduct remained on the Bar's agenda. In June 1995, Mecklenburg Bar President Pender McElroy, expressing a somewhat different point of view, told the members: "The time has come for us to consider full public access to our disciplinary proceedings. Perhaps the process should be open at all stages for review by members of the public. Admittedly, there is risk of unwarranted damage to a lawyer's reputation. Sensation-seeking media representatives will undoubtedly have a field day. The press will give great coverage to a grievance at the time of filing. If the lawyer is exonerated, the public will never hear about that. Nonetheless, the confidence and support of the public in our profession may very well outweigh this risk. Difficult as it is for us to do, we must acknowledge that we live in a time and in a society when secrecy and confidentiality is not always the better course."

The change in the profession's public image was troubling to 1998 Mecklenburg Bar president Judy Thompson, who asked her colleagues, "How do we explain the phenomenon which has seen perception of our profession plummet so drastically?" "We can," she continued, "blame the increasing pressures of business and competition between law firms, the unrealistic demands of clients caught up in a world of 'I win, you lose' litigation, or the media which enjoys the story of the occasional lawyer gone awry. But perhaps the real culprit is that we have allowed law to evolve from a profession to a business in our own eyes, and therefore in the eyes of the public."

Judy Thompson had indeed put her finger on a trend that continued to trouble those who understood the values on which the profession was built. From the days almost ten centuries earlier when it had emerged from the Inns of Court in London as a self-governing profession independent of the Crown with a dual duty to both client and the judicial system, the practicing bar had earned that independence and maintained its stature in the eyes of the public through responsible self-government. In a modern society focused more and more on the short-term bottom line and less and less on long-term values, the profession was beginning to wrestle within its own ranks with this phenomenon – treating the practice of law as a business instead of a profession that demanded of its members a higher standard of conduct than that of the marketplace.

INTERIOR VIEW OF SOUTH PARK MALL CIRCA 1980

CHAPTER 14

GROWTH & SPECIALIZATION

"In Charlotte, the age of the generalist is over," attorney Cart Carmichael, who had been president of the Mecklenburg Bar in 1985, observed. Talking with a writer preparing a history of his former firm, Kennedy, Covington, Lobdell & Hickman, Carmichael expressed the opinion that specialization were now essential for survival. The law had become more complex, so that, as Carmichael put it, "No matter how smart you are, you can only do so much, understand so much."

Kennedy Covington had organized into specialized teams in the early 1980s, and other large firms in Mecklenburg were doing the same. Under these new alignments, partners and associates who were knowledgeable in a particular area of the law collaborated on projects – a sort of law firm within a law firm – lunched together to discuss the progress of work for clients, and considered ways to attract new clients. More than a few among the senior members of the bar wondered aloud where in this new approach to law practice, the next generation of wise counselors, lawyers on whom clients had traditionally relied to bring a broader vision to their affairs, would come from.

In many ways, the law reflected the changing character of the Charlotte community, one that Mayor Harvey Gantt characterized as a "world-class city" with all of its complexities, diversity of interests and rising areas of new industry and commerce. The mayor's boast was premature; Charlotte had not yet reached the prominence it would achieve in the next decade as it began to emerge as a center of commerce and finance in the South and, in the late 1990s, in the nation's banking world. The city's downtown was yet to be transformed by new office towers, rehabilitated inner-city neighborhoods transformed by expensive condominiums and townhouses and large law firms serving an array of international clients. In 1996, the oldest law firm on Wall Street, Cadwalader Wickersham & Taft, opened an office in the city, moving south to be closer to homegrown banks, First Union and NationsBank, whose combined assets were by that time $886 billion and which were poised to become even larger.

UNIVERSITY OF NORTH CAROLINA AT CHARLOTTE, 1976

The city was growing in all directions, southward from SouthPark to the South Carolina line, northward towards Duke Power's newest energy center, Lake Norman, the home of the county's first nuclear power plant, northeastward around the University of North Carolina at Charlotte, and eastward towards neighboring Union County. Land once farmland was fast becoming an endless bedroom community. A new football stadium with 72,000 seats would become part of the city center, drawing ticket holders from all over the region. Fashionable shops from New York, Chicago and San Francisco would open outlets in the new upscale shopping centers.

Charlotte had long been a center of regional business, but it was banking that pushed the city into the big leagues. "Without question, . . . the most staggering economic growth in Charlotte, and one which dramatically affected the Charlotte legal market came in the banking industry," attorney Scott Syfert wrote in a 2002 paper that tracked the growth of Charlotte's law firms with a hundred or more lawyers.

Charlotte's banks had been competitors among themselves since the early part of the twentieth century. North Carolina law had allowed statewide branch banking since 1868, but no one had sought to take advantage of that singular provision, one it shared only with Oregon. In the late 1950s a group of enterprising bankers saw an opportunity. In 1958, two side-by-side one-branch banks on South Tryon Street merged, and two years later a merger with a Greensboro bank produced a new name in the banking world, North Carolina National Bank. In 1958, First Union National Bank was created from the merger of a Charlotte bank and one in Asheville. Between 1958 and the 1980s, First Union would undertake more than thirty mergers and acquisitions. In one transaction, it acquired two banks in the same North Carolina town.

PAUL J. POLKING, NCNB GENERAL COUNSEL

North Carolina National Bank was not left behind, and it and First Union fought to grow larger than Wachovia Bank and Trust Company of Winston-Salem, at the time the largest in the state. In the early 1970s, North Carolina National Bank, which along the way shortened its name to NCNB, succeeded in doing that. Before the advent of interstate banking, Wachovia and NCNB had become the largest banks between Philadelphia and Dallas.

Nothing startled the banking community more, however, than news in 1981 that NCNB had found a way to take advantage of a new Florida statute to make an end run around prohibitions against interstate banking by acquiring a commercial bank in Florida, one of the richest markets in the Southeast

In 1980, Paul J. Polking, a young lawyer recruited by NCNB from the staff of the Comptroller of the Currency, had approached the bank's CEO, Thomas Storrs, with what he believed was a way for NCNB to enter the lucrative Florida banking market. The Florida legislature had adopted a restriction that allowed only a bank already in business in Florida to acquire another Florida bank. NCNB already owned a small bank in Florida, and federal regulatory authorities proved to be in favor of interstate banking. Polking, a native of Iowa, had joined NCNB after four years in Washington, where he reviewed bank mergers and acquisitions. He was only the bank's second lawyer, joining its then general counsel, James W. Kiser, a former Charlotte city attorney. Eventually, Kiser became general counsel to the bank's holding company and Polking became the bank's general counsel.

NCNB's pioneering effort was to mark the beginning of the end of restrictions that limited banks to doing business

HUGH MCCOLL IN 1978, NCNB'S "RISING STAR"

within the boundaries of their home states, and the three large North Carolina banks, having already developed experience that enabled them to assimilate mergers, began to lead the parade. During Polking's tenure, NCNB would grow from a strong state bank to an international banking operation, whose rising young executive, Hugh L. McColl, Jr., would someday have his smiling face on a billboard announcing the bank's new office in the staid London market.

NCNB pushed the boundaries even further in 1988 when, with the encouragement of the federal regulators, it acquired an endangered First Republic Bank of Dallas, boosting the size of its assets to $55 billion and making it the tenth largest bank in the nation. The deal was made primarily with the help of a new and unique arrangement with the federal bank regulators. NCNB was allowed to keep the good loans the Dallas-based bank had made and, insulated from losses from the bad loans, to share with the FDIC the proceeds of its collection of those loans. Some later saw in this arrangement a precursor of the government's Troubled Asset Relief Program that figured prominently in the aftermath of the financial meltdown of 2008.

NCNB later merged with a Georgia bank and changed its name to NationsBank. By the 1990s, NCNB CEO Hugh McColl and First Union's Ed Crutchfield were two of the best known financial leaders in the nation. First Union grew from assets of $8.2 billion in 1985 to $254.2 billion in 2000. The acquisitions of the two big banks took them into the Northeast and, with NationsBank's merger with Bank of America in 1998, to California.

The banks' competition proved a bonanza for Charlotte's legal community. In the 1960s, as Charlotte's banks began to grow, there were only a handful of specialists, like the Blakeney firm, one of the first labor law firms in the South, the Thigpen tax firm and two patent firms that principally serviced the textile industry. At the beginning of the 1960s, only one Charlotte firm had ever handled an initial public issue of corporate stock, a practice that was otherwise traditionally confined to Wall Street, and North Carolina firms were entirely excluded from the issuance of revenue and industrial development bonds. That, however, was fast changing.

ED CRUTCHFIELD, FIRST UNION CEO

Looking back, lawyer-historian Mark Bernstein reflected that much of the growth in the local bar was being fueled by new federal legislation. "Legislation began to be enacted. OSHA [occupational safety], EEOC [employment discrimination], and other things, environmental law and all of that. It was no longer possible for a competent lawyer to service all of those needs. As a result, lawyers had to specialize. Law firms, if they were going to be all-purpose law firms, had to have specialists in those areas. In Charlotte, you had the economy growing, banking business growing, business expanding. Not only were there larger and more affluent clients that needed these services, but you had to service these clients. There was a huge functional displacement in the law and the legal profession."

MARION A. COWELL, JR.,
FIRST UNION'S GENERAL COUNSEL

There had long been an ebb and flow of lawyers in and out of local firms, with firm names changing as senior partners retired or died. Several law firms had gradually begun to become institutionally stable, preserving legacy firm names, and to grow in size. Their growth, however, had remained focused locally. On the other side of the coin, the community's established law firms, strong in civil and criminal litigation and in the corporate arena, had long made Charlotte a less than inviting place for outsiders to try to establish a beachhead.

The civil litigation explosion that had begun in the late 1960s had created an unusually strong local civil trial bar. The later escalation of criminal trial practice as Congress began to make more and more offenses federal crimes, and as the drug wars escalated in both state and federal courts, had created an equally strong local criminal trial bar. In the fifty-six years since Fred Helms became one of the first two North Carolina lawyers inducted as a Fellow of the highly selective American College of Trial Lawyers, another thirty-two local lawyers, drawn almost equally from among the civil and criminal trial bar, had been invited to its ranks. One had served as its national president.

Charlotte's growth as a business and banking center had resulted in the even greater rise of a strong collection of corporate and business lawyers who by the 1980s were regularly handling all the legal matters of major corporate clients on a par with their contemporaries in national law firms. Indeed, over time most of the growth in the bar, especially in the larger law firms, came from their growing transactional and regulatory practice. In the 1980s, North Carolina began to see a new phenomenon. As national businesses began to establish new facilities in North Carolina, some moving their corporate headquarters here, established local law firms began to realize that these new corporate citizens were continuing to go back to larger metropolitan law firms for legal services in areas such as taxation, securities issues, mergers, antitrust and major litigation. The North Carolina firms knew they had been rendering these services competently for years, holding their own against outside firms. The perceived problem was the lack of an appearance of size and full-service capability in the local firms. The middle 1980s thus saw a series of law firm expansions, both through mergers and the opening of new offices, as a number of larger North Carolina law firms expanded their reach beyond their own communities.

Moore & Van Allen was the first to expand. In 1983, it merged with Allen, Steed & Allen of Raleigh and then in 1984 with the Charlotte tax firm Thigpen & Hines. In 1986 it announced a merger with Durham's Powe, Porter & Alphin, creating a firm of 108 lawyers with a staff of 250. At the time, Winston-Salem's Womble, Carlyle, Sandridge & Rice was the state's largest firm with 117 lawyers. Eleven of the Womble Carlyle attorneys were in Charlotte, where the firm had opened an office in early in 1986. A year later, Moore & Van Allen merged with a South Carolina firm, Nexsen, Pruet, Jacobs & Pollard, becoming an interstate firm of 150 lawyers with an estimated $20 to $30 million in annual revenues.

"To keep your market share, you've got to grow."

"Most law firms in North Carolina with 20 or more lawyers have considered mergers," Raleigh lawyer J. Allen Adams told a *Charlotte Observer* reporter in 1986, at the time of the Moore & Van Allen merger with the Durham firm. "I don't see an end to the trend." William Van Allen explained, "To keep your market share, you've got to grow."

In 1986, Charlotte's Helms, Mulliss & Johnston merged with Greensboro's Smith, Moore, Smith, Schell & Hunter to form the state's second largest firm. In 1989, the newly created firm, Smith Helms Mulliss & Moore, merged with the Charlotte tax practice of Blanchfield & Moore. In 1987, Parker, Poe, Thompson, Bernstein, Gage & Preston merged with Daniels & Daniels, a small firm in the Research Triangle Park that specialized in work with emerging high-technology companies. Then in 1990, it merged with the Raleigh firm of Adams, McCullough & Beard, known for its litigation and work in legislative and public finance matters. Raleigh and Rocky Mount's Poyner & Spruill, itself the product of an earlier merger, opened a Charlotte office. Winston-Salem and Altanta's Kilpatrick Stockton merged with a Charlotte group.

Not all of these changes proved permanent. Moore & Van Allen's venture into South Carolina did not take, and the merger with the Columbia firm was reversed a year later. In 1992, the Blanchfield & Moore lawyers, having decided that they preferred to be independent of a large firm, regrouped in their own firm. Years later, in 2002, Smith Moore and Helms Mulliss parted as friends and regrouped as separate firms, with each keeping a part of the Raleigh office they had established and Helms Mulliss retaining the firm's Wilmington office. In 1992, when the Charlotte economy, like much of the nation's suffered from a recession. Kennedy, Covington, Lobdell

BANKING CHANGED CHARLOTTE'S LANDSCAPE

& Hickman, which was expanding its services from within, closed the office in suburban SouthPark that it had earlier established to handle a boom in Charlotte's real estate market.

Bank expansion also took a respite in the early 1990s, but then both NationsBank and First Union again began to roar ahead. First Union followed NCNB into Florida, eventually acquiring a larger share of its financial market than that of the competitor that had initially opened up that state to other banks. Between 1990 and 1995, First Union grew into a $132 billion bank. It later merged with Wachovia, keeping the latter's name, and then, in 2008, it was essentially acquired by San Francisco's Wells Fargo in the wake of the national banking crisis. By 1995, NationsBank's assets had grown to $182 billion, and it began looking for more opportunities in the Midwest, in 1996 acquiring Boatmen's Bankshares in St. Louis and in 1997, Barnett Banks of Florida. Upon its 1998 merger with Bank of America, it kept that bank's legendary name, but the surviving entity, the nation's largest bank in terms of assets, remained headquartered in Charlotte.

The competition between the banks helped generate new excitement in the community. A professional National Basketball Association franchise, borrowing from General Cornwallis' label for the colonial community by naming itself the Charlotte Hornets, came in 1987. After the Hornets later departed, a new team, the Charlotte Bobcats, found a home in the newly constructed Time Warner Arena. Realtor Walker Wells and lawyer R. Malloy McKeithen had been commissioned to quietly assemble the land for a stadium to assure that the community could offer a prospective National Football League expansion team a home. The community's quest was successful; in 1993, it welcomed the Carolina Panthers. From then on, the growing Charlotte skyline in the background of national television broadcasts of Panthers games helped to reinforce the image of a booming Charlotte.

Over the years, the leadership of the two major banks, at one point two of the four largest in the nation, has been a major factor in transforming uptown Charlotte into a vibrant residential and cultural center. Aided by generous contributions from the banks and other corporate sponsors, several new museums and enhanced symphony, dance and opera companies added to the city's new-found image. First Union's Ed Crutchfield observed that such advances were needed to help draw banking and other talent to Charlotte. "People in London and New York didn't want to live in a small town," he said. "They wanted pro sports, a symphony and good schools."

BANK OF AMERICA TOWER

As the footprint of the banking empires grew larger, so did the attention of law firms outside of North Carolina. It was not banking alone that raised Charlotte's profile as an attractive location for a law firm. Charlotte was becoming a regional center for international corporations. In the late 1970s, during a time of business as usual, North and South Carolina had fewer than 400 foreign-owned businesses in operation. Twenty years later, that number had reached almost 2,000. In 1999, Charlotte had 379 firms with local addresses that were considered "foreign-owned."

By the end of the 1990s, Charlotte firms had connections to law offices around the world. Parker,

Poe had an office in Frankfurt, Germany, while national law firms such as McGuireWoods, Hunton & Williams and Kilpatrick Stockton had offices in such diverse locales as Kazakhstan and London.

The influx of lawyers representing the new and expanded businesses joined the Mecklenburg Bar, adding to the Bar's steady growth, Mary Howerton recalled. In 1990, the Bar had a membership of 1,750. By 1995, it had added 325 more lawyers to its rolls. Howerton observed that these additions to the Mecklenburg Bar added a different flavor to the membership by bringing a wide variety of experiences from many different locations.

The migration of outside law firms to Charlotte was driven in part by the desire of law firms based in cities whose banks had become part of First Union or NationsBank to remain close to their former clients and continue to serve them in their new home. This was not a new phenomenon; when NCNB acquired its first Florida bank, Helms, Mulliss & Johnston had opened an office in Tampa to service that bank's lending operations there. In 1990, Cozen O'Connor of Philadelphia became the first out-of-state firm to open a Charlotte office. Hunton & Williams of Richmond, Virginia, followed in 1995 and, as previously noted, the Cadwalader firm opened its Charlotte office in 1996. Alston & Bird came from Atlanta in 1997, merging with the community's oldest patent firm. Mayer, Brown of Chicago came in 1998, merging with Blanchfield & Moore.

FIRST UNION, LATER WACHOVIA TOWER

The number of lawyers serving as in-house counsel for the banks and other large corporations such as Duke Power that were part of the Charlotte business community were also growing. Duke had long had a strong in-house legal department, one that had over the years produced several presidents of the company. The growing Belk store organization had also had an internal legal department since the post-World War II years.

Bank of America's Paul Polking and two other bank general counsel, Marion A. Cowell, Jr. of First Union and Jerone C. Herring of Winston-Salem's BB&T were featured in "The Legal Giants

That Propelled North Carolina Banks to National Prominence," a 2004 North Carolina *Banking Institute Journal* article by Lissa Broome, professor of banking law at the UNC School of Law.

Cowell, who retired from First Union in 1999, had practiced real estate law in Durham for eight years before joining the bank in 1972. He became the bank's general counsel in 1978 when Robin L. Hinson, who in his earlier career had for many years taught a bar review course that had prepared many of the lawyers of that era for the bar examination, had left the bank to enter private practice in the firm that then became Robinson, Bradshaw & Hinson. Cowell told Broome that in a merger, the bank hired outside counsel in most cases because of local connections or to gain specialized knowledge. The bank also used outside lawyers to handle litigation for the corporation, with an in-house lawyer sitting second chair to be able to assist with specialized information. In-house lawyers could handle any case for their company so long as they were members of the State Bar.

Broome wrote that at First Union, Cowell created "an environment where in house lawyers feel safe to do their jobs and deliver the needed message even if the message is not one that management wants to hear." "It is very helpful in a corporation, particularly larger corporations," Cowell said, "to have lawyers who are familiar with the corporation, who participate in board meetings and recognize the legal issues as they come up. In addition, they are responsible for employing lawyers to perform legal tasks for the corporation when they need to be done in another jurisdiction or that of going to court. So you have a person making the selection who is better able to make a judgment about the lawyer or lawyers that need to be employed to assist the corporation."

During his time at First Union, Cowell urged the bank's outside law firms to consider diversity in their firms, since diversity was an important issue to him and First Union. In doing so, he called attention to "the problems created by a population that is 30 percent nonwhite (and increasing), receiving legal representation from a lawyer population that is more than 92 percent white."

Cowell followed up on his commitment to the banking industry by helping to found the North Carolina Banking Institute at UNC School of Law, a venture headed by Professor Broome that quickly gained national stature in the world of banking law.

The number of lawyers serving as in-house counsel grew as the Charlotte business community expanded. In its 1999 Million Dollar Directory, Dun and Bradstreet listed 657 companies with facilities in Charlotte-Mecklenburg. In fact, the number of corporate lawyers had grown so large that the Mecklenburg Bar had created a separate Corporate Counsel Section. To serve this group, it offered independent CLE courses on such subjects as privacy and data protection and patents, trademarks and trade secrets. Until the creation of the section, in-house lawyers received their CLE outside the local Bar. Cowell called the creation of the section a good thing "because it probably encourages active bar membership participation."

When Steve C. Griffith, Jr. joined the Duke Power legal department in 1964, it had seven lawyers. "I don't believe there was any law firm in Charlotte that had more than eleven lawyers," he recalled. "An in-house counsel could practice law insofar as advising the corporation [was concerned], whether a member of a local bar or not. But," he noted, "all of Duke's lawyers in Charlotte were members of the Mecklenburg and State Bars. The Duke Power legal department participated in legal cases; sometimes trying them by ourselves, other times tried with local counsel, so we were not just paper-pushers or advisors to the corporation. We were active practicing lawyers. I thought we were lawyers just like everybody else in the Mecklenburg Bar."

Griffith, who retired as Duke's chief counsel in 1997 after thirty-three years with the company, was a member of the Mecklenburg Bar committee that created the Lawyers Volunteer Program in 1983. Duke Power received an award from the North Carolina Bar Association for its participation in that program.

In 2002, the five largest law firms in Mecklenburg County included three with histories that reached back more than fifty years and one, Parker, Poe, Adams & Bernstein, traced its lineage to the association of Heriot Clarkson and Charles Duls, who became partners in 1888 after Clarkson had begun a solo practice in 1884. The other four were: Kennedy, Covington, Lobdell & Hickman, formed in 1957; Moore & Van Allen, which began in 1950 as Lassiter, Moore & Van Allen, and Smith Helms Mulliss & Moore, whose antecedents were Helms & Mulliss, a partnership that began in 1939, seventeen years after Fred Helms had begun his solo law practice. Robinson, Bradshaw & Hinson had been formed in 1960 when Russell Robinson, II and J. Carlton Fleming left Moore & Van Allen to form their own firm, followed the next year by Robert W. Bradshaw, Jr. Smaller firms like Johnston, Allison & Hord and Ruff, Bond, Cobb & Wade could trace their roots back to the early 1900s.

Law firms enjoyed continued growth and generous revenues for most of the first decade of the new century. In the first decade of the twenty-first century, the names of two of the largest firms – Smith Helms and Kennedy Covington – disappeared from the roster of the Mecklenburg Bar. In the case of the first, as the practices in Greensboro and Charlotte had diverged, the two firms that had merged in 1986 parted in 2002 and the local firm became Helms Mulliss & Wicker. Then in 2008, it merged with McGuireWoods, LLP, becoming that international firm's second largest office. In

2008, Kennedy Covington became part of K&L Gates, an international firm based in Pittsburgh, a firm that then had over 2,000 lawyers with thirty-six offices on three continents. Its website was published in five languages in addition to English.

The demands on individual lawyers during those mergers and acquisitions were to keep regular clients and to attract new ones. "The impetus came when outside firms began moving in," said J. Norfleet Pruden, III of K&L Gates. "Competing with them meant you needed more people. Geographic scope also entered the picture. You needed to have offices in more than just Charlotte." W. B. (Ben) Hawfield, Jr., managing partner of Moore &Van Allen from 1992 to 2002, remembered that the expansion caused both specialists and managing partners to work harder.

An overheated economy collapsed in the summer and fall of 2008, and Charlotte banks figured prominently in both the collapse and in the subsequent measures taken to rescue the nation's financial system. The precipitous decline in the economy became painfully obvious on September 15, 2008, when the $600 billion Lehman Brothers declared bankruptcy after the federal government chose not to rescue it. But on October 13, Federal Reserve Chairman Henry Paulson announced that the government was issuing $125 billion in bailouts, including $20 billion to Bank of America and $25 billion to Wells Fargo, which now included the former First Union and Wachovia, the two of which had earlier merged in 2001, keeping the latter's name.

The fallout was heavy in Charlotte. Some outside law firms closed offices they had opened during the heady years of the late 1990s. Some of the city's largest and oldest firms laid off associates, some of whom had only a few years before seen starting salaries well in excess of $100,000. Many others postponed hiring additional lawyers, leaving many talented graduates seeking employment. In October 2008, the New York-based Dewey & LeBoeuf announced that it was closing its Charlotte office at the end of the year, leaving eleven lawyers without jobs. In November 2008, Moore & Van Allen announced it was cutting three associates. "Given the economy, we are being thoughtful about improving efficiencies whenever possible," the firm said in a statement. By September 2009, *The Business Journal of Charlotte* reported, "Recession-driven layoffs are flooding the local job market with lawyers."

Even before the banking crisis, the legal marketplace had begun to shift. Traditionally, most lawyers had practiced in small firms or alone, and this remained true in the local community even as large and growing firms began to appear as the city grew. The shift came as some lawyers began to find that the increasingly stratified structure, the emphasis on the billable hours a lawyer produced, the trend towards weeding out less profitable client relationships and the internal competition of many large law firms did not accommodate the lives they had envisioned when they chose law as a profession. In the early years of the decade, these lawyers were starting to leave large firms to open small offices of their own, often locating in the suburbs, where they were closer to their individual clients. In most cases the partings were cordial. In 2007, one large local firm invited all its alumni to a highly successful reunion evening that drew former members from as far away as California. More than a few of the newer firms thrived on referrals from the firms they left.

One of the profession's traditions is passing from generation to generation training in both the practice of law and in the values on which the profession must operate. The late Joseph A. Ball of California, one of the lions of the twentieth century legal profession, once said: "Teach the young; that is all you can leave behind." Many of the smaller firms that now proliferate in the local bar trace their professional roots and owe their professional training to the city's larger, older firms.

"Teach the young; that is all you can leave behind."
—Joseph A. Ball

Typical of these new boutique firms, Nicole Gardner and Renee Hughes left 300-lawyer Moore & Van Allen to form their own firm in March 2008. "We are a two-woman law firm with a male paralegal," Gardner explained. "On the professional side they [Moore & Van Allen] had really decided that they did not want to do traditional employment law work, that being non-litigation work. Renee and I are both trained as and enjoy being traditional employment law lawyers . . . ."

Moore & Van Allen had asked Gardner to move many of her clients out of the firm, and so she decided to take those clients with her and form a new firm. "They were very, very gracious when we left and they send us work all the time," Gardner said. "They actually gave us a going-away party, and it was a very amicable departure and we've maintained relationships with the people over there," Hughes said. "They're really a class act."

Hughes, who chaired the Bar's solo and small firm section in 2011, and Gardner enjoyed the advantages of a small firm. Both liked the "back to the future" feeling of one-on-one lawyer-client relationships. "Having personal relationships with clients is meaningful," Gardner said. "I really enjoy my clients and I think they enjoy me. It has some of the hallmarks of a profession of old in a different way."

Gardner and Hughes noted that the trend toward large firms spinning off lawyers into boutique firms had been growing. "There are a lot of people making similar choices," Gardner said.

Historic smokestacks come tumbling down in Kannapolis to make way for David Murdock's $1 billion biotechnology research campus, giving rise to the Bar's "Project Pillowtex"

CHAPTER 15

One Era Ends; Another Begins

In 2002, Mary Howerton announced she was retiring as Executive Director of the Mecklenburg Bar to pursue a doctorate in counseling. Since her arrival in 1984, the membership had more than tripled to 3,421. The staff had grown from Howerton and part-time employee Nadine Keating to a dozen, each with a specialized job. New programs had enhanced the Bar's reputation in the community and provided service and training to its members. There was a revived effort to renew the collegiality within its ranks. The one thing that remained unchanged was that the Bar offices were again barely adequate to handle its growth.

Upon Howerton's retirement, Congressman Mel Watt, who had worked with her when he was Bar president, told *The Charlotte Observer*, "Mary cares about lawyers, their professionalism and their contributions to this community. She's done an outstanding job."

"I strongly believe in the concept of teamwork," Howerton told the *Observer*. "Together, we have built programs which have touched not only lawyers, but the public at large. That is my legacy."

At her retirement dinner on May 17, 2003, Ray Farris, the president who had hired Howerton in 1984, said, "Mary brought out the best in us, staff and lawyers. She managed to keep conflicts to a minimum and developed Bar programs without the usual fits and starts."

In her years as Executive Director, Howerton had not only presided over the explosive expansion of the Bar membership, but she had also supervised the opening of the Bar's first permanent headquarters, introduced technology to the office, initiated Law and Society Lectures and helped establish funding for the Mecklenburg Bar Foundation. Her record of accomplishments and innovation was such that before retiring from her job to complete work on a doctoral degree, she had been slated to be nominated as president of the National Association of Bar Executives, on whose board she had served for several years.

Applauding Howerton's success at her retirement dinner in 2003 were many members who were relative newcomers to the community. During the 1990s, new lawyers who became members of the Bar added to its rolls in only ten years as many members as there had been in the entire bar when she had taken the job. Some of the old timers present could recall when a "large" law firm had five, six, or even seven lawyers practicing together. Now the large firms counted associates by the score. Traditionalists treasured memories of the law as a profession, but in the eyes of many the law had become big business. Advertising for legal services, now called "marketing," seemed to be everywhere, from billboards to television. Word-of-mouth referrals seemed as quaint as a secretary taking dictation.

Word-of-mouth referrals seemed as quaint as a secretary taking dictation.

Of all the transformative changes, perhaps technology had reshaped the profession more profoundly, and certainly more rapidly, than anything that had come before. "There were Xerox machines and automatic typing," recalled Hugh Campbell, Jr. from his early days in the 1960s. "When I came here, we were still using stenographers: 'Mrs. Sullivan, come in and take a letter.' The first copy machine looked like Jello; put piece of paper down, had some gelatin in a tray, it would make an image of it. My father had a wire recorder. The first one was a great big machine with a big microphone. You would dictate into that. Then they had plastic tapes, then cassette tapes."

Past President Ayscue recalls that when he became secretary of the Bar in 1964, he made the mistake of having his secretary put the membership roll on his firm's new "word processor," an MTST. "It took me three years to get rid of the job," he laughingly remembers. "I finally talked Jim Crews into taking the office by promising that my secretary could continue to keep the roll. She probably did that until Mary Howerton came along and took us into modernity."

Beginning in the 1980s, changes had come rapidly, even to such bastions of tradition as the state's Supreme Court, where until the late 1970s, secretaries were still using carbon paper to produce nine copies of drafts of decisions. The big change for the court was the acquisition of a copying machine. Law firms began to acquire desktop computers to produce the piles of documents that were the products of their work and, as a consequence, Campbell notes, "Lawyers are wordier now." By 1990, Moore & Van Allen was consuming 350,000 pages of paper each month.

"Service in lawsuits was almost always by U.S. Mail," recalled Jon Buchan, Bar president in 2004. He began practicing law in the late 1970s. "You learned of appellate court decisions in your cases," he recalled, "a few days after the fact by opening the morning mail with the Raleigh return address. Young lawyers – not paralegals – went to the courthouse to file their own pleadings, giving them a chance to stop and chat with the clerk of court or the courthouse staff, valuable allies to have over time."

The emergence of the Internet brought instant communication with clients, the courts and with colleagues. Documents laden with boiler-plate copy could be accessed immediately and names, dates, and other particulars inserted to suit the needs of the client. Law libraries became nearly obsolete, with reference services available through a few keystrokes on a computer keyboard. Where real estate attorneys once haunted the office of the Register of Deeds, the digitalization of deeds and other property records now allowed lawyers to conduct title searches from the comfort of their desks.

In time, as law firms grew and merged, and with offices spread not only around the country, but around the globe, a lawyer in Charlotte could get an opinion on a matter from a colleague in Tokyo. In his paper on the large Charlotte firms, Scott Syfert observed, "Client information could now be down-loaded from secure web sites; multiple attorneys could electronically access one document at the same time. The destruction of distance, coupled with high-speed copiers and laser printers, enabled law firms to produce staggering amounts of paper in short periods of time. The once relaxed and genteel atmosphere of the firms began to give way to the cold efficiency and speed of the corporation," Syfert concluded, "Law was becoming a business and required the systems and mechanisms to run like one."

Tradition did not limit innovation. According to *The Charlotte Observer,* Womble, Carlyle, Sandridge & Rice, mounted the first law firm webpage in 1995. The firm used it to handle e-mail and as a place to post information that was of particular interest to clients involved in technology.

Howerton recalled that the first computers at the Mecklenburg Bar offices arrived in about 1986. "We were still located in the old Law Building, and about the same time we got our first fax machine. The original computers provided us with a new means of communication; originally we had only interoffice email." In about 1988 or 1989, Howerton recalled, the Mecklenburg Bar was connected to the Web, receiving e-mail from members as well as from others outside the Bar. "Later, about 1993 or 1994, members could respond to events through e-mail," she said. "It sure made our lives busier. However, we could respond more quickly to members' requests, rather than relying on phone or fax."

A little more than a decade later, the use of technology had allowed lawyers to leap many obstacles in getting a new practice started. Charlotte lawyer Margaret A. (Maggie) Shankle, a 1999 graduate of Campbell Law School, began using every possible advantage, especially social networking websites such as Facebook. "Several clients have found me on Facebook and added the firm as a 'friend'," she reported in the February 2009 *Mecklenburg Bar News*. "Also, various other business professionals have located me through this method. I am amazed by how many people are on Facebook, especially how many attorneys have a presence there. People are addicted to it." The adoption of technology was essential, she said. "Most sole practitioners who are plaintiff's lawyers are behind in embracing technology."

The advance of technology had its drawbacks. Lawyers once congregated in the soda shop at the Law Building or after the weekly civil calendar call to share stories, courthouse gossip, and not infrequently to deal with one another face to face about their pending engagements. Electronic media greatly reduced casual encounters such as these. Lawyers specializing in real estate and zoning matters no longer saw as much of one another as they did when searching a title required a visit to the registry of deeds, where they might spend hours in the company of other lawyers. This continuing separation of fellow members of the Bar disturbed Howerton as she approached retirement. In 1998, she created the Lawyers Lunch Ladder, Coffee Connections, and Lawyer Links to provide opportunities for more personal contact of the members.

Howerton's successor, Nancy Roberson, expanded Howerton's efforts. A native of Charlotte, Roberson came to the job on June 16, 2003 after serving as senior vice president for external affairs at Thompson Children's Home in Charlotte. A *summa cum laude* graduate of the University of North Carolina at Chapel Hill, Roberson earned a master's degree in counseling there in 1982 and a master's degree in vocational evaluation from East Carolina University in 1984. Before coming to the Bar, she had also worked as major gifts officer and assistant director of the Annual Fund at Duke University and as assistant dean for external relations at the UNC School of Law. She and her husband David and their three children lived in her family house on her grandparents' farm in Lincoln County, across the Catawba River.

NANCY ROBERSON

"Frank Emory, [the Bar's second African American president, elected in 2002] was very persuasive and convinced me that this position would be a good fit, and he was right," Roberson recalled. "One of the first things I realized was that I had some huge shoes to fill in succeeding Mary Howerton. She had a long, successful tenure, and the Bar was well poised for the future."

Numerous projects had been put on hold during the search process for Howerton's successor, and Roberson says many Bar members were eager to launch additional projects and explore ideas for other innovative initiatives. At the same time, the Bar Center was in dire need of maintenance. Plans had already been made for plumbing repairs, rewiring, and replacing rotting wood when, during Roberson's first month at the Bar, the sewage backed up into the basement. The aging Bar Center's increasing maintenance needs and the need for new staff to serve the Bar's steadily growing membership and to provide new programs made it clear that that it was even more urgent to find a more suitable headquarters building.

By 2010, the Bar had reached 4,400 members and CLE class participation increased accordingly. The Bar Center, which could hold only 40 comfortably, was hardpressed to accommodate the rise in attendance. Though annual CLE revenues were in excess of $500,000, they were offset by the high cost of securing meeting space at hotels. Offering some CLE courses over the Bar's website, allowing lawyers to participate from their offices, provided a partial solution.

The staff was operating in less than 6,000 square feet, but needed more than three times that for offices and programs. The Bar's board began considering a new headquarters of 20,000 square feet plus parking space. Roberson, also serving as the executive director of the Mecklenburg Bar Foundation, explained that the MBF owns the building that the MCB leases. "The Foundation is separate from the MCB, but vitally important to the MCB," she noted. "The Foundation, a non-profit, is a legitimate way to raise money and to give that money back to the community, particularly for needs that have a legal nexus. The Bar can do a lot as a mandatory Bar, but we can't raise money and provide a tax deduction [to the donors] and give it back to the community. The Bar can provide legal services, but it can't be the charitable arm that the Foundation is.

Thanks to the generosity of the Bar members, the Bar Foundation Fund drive grew from $30,000 a year in 2002 to more than $300,000 by 2010. This was not, however, enough to offset the cost of a future Bar Center. In 2010, to help fund this project, the Bar dues increased for the first time in a decade. Though members voted to accept the increase, the move was not popular with all members, especially the unemployed and public interest lawyers. The Foundation created a fund to help offset some of these lawyers' professional expenditures.

After eight-plus years in her job, Roberson was pleased with the Bar's progress. "I certainly believe we are innovative and progressive," she said. "We have more than 70 committees, sections, subcommittees, boards and divisions. All of them are doing something relevant on behalf of the Bar and giving back to the community. We have a talented membership. The great majority of our attorneys are not only highly ethi-

MECKLENBURG COUNTY'S EIGHTH COURTHOUSE, ON EAST FOURTH AND MCDOWELL STREETS

cal, but also civic minded, and they place a high importance on their *pro bono* work."

CHIEF JUSTICE SARAH PARKER

Roberson kept up with developments at other local bars by attending national meetings. In 2011 she said, "I just completed five years on the national programming committee, and as I complete my year as programming committee chair, I have accepted an officer position on the National Association of Bar Executives. I think that's largely a reflection of the fact that the Mecklenburg County Bar compares favorably with other Bars. We are recognized as trend setters, and are known both for our progressive programs and for our dedicated volunteers."

Growth continued to be the major challenge for the Mecklenburg County Bar. Perhaps the most visible evidence of that growth and the expectation that growth would continue to be the norm, was the building in 2007 of the county's eighth courthouse, located at the corner of East Fourth and McDowell Streets. While the building was still in the design stage, the architect took the decision-makers to Boston and showed them two courthouses, one built of marble, and one of modern construction methods. He wanted to avoid the problems that Harry Wolf encountered thirty years earlier. He pointed out that a courthouse built of marble and stone would stand for a century. The other would have to be repainted and repaired every few years. The long-term cost favored the former, though the up-front cost would be significantly greater. The County Commission chose the hundred-year alternative, whose initial cost was $148 million.

The towering nine-story building at the northwest corner of Fourth and McDowell streets featured a four-story porch above the entrance. Architect Michael McKinney of Boston called it a "modern interpretation of the traditional porch of a courthouse." Inside the triangular shaped lobby hung a spectacular mobile sculpture of constantly changing images of 3,200 faces, created to reflect the diversity of the county's population. Historic quotes chosen by the state's poet laureate, Fred Chappell, were chiseled in the building's exterior marble. Inside are courtrooms equipped with the latest technology. There is even an attended playroom for children whose parents must bring them to court.

Chief Justice Sarah Parker's dedicatory address quoted extensively from a short story by North Carolina native Thomas Wolfe, reflecting on the county courthouse as the historic center of the life of a community.

Two developments have accompanied growth and provided additional challenges for the Bar in serving all its members. In 1958, not a single lawyer in the county was listed as practicing outside Charlotte. The 2011 Bar membership rolls listed almost 250 lawyers whose offices were in five communities that had grown up in the county: Davidson, Huntersville, Mint Hill, Matthews and Pineville. Many other members had offices within the Charlotte city limits in places that in 1958 were still farmland or were remote from the city's center.

The Bar has enjoyed the reputation of responding quickly to its members' needs. The Bar's diversity program won a national award for its innovative efforts, including a mentoring program for young associates who are interested in learning more about what it takes to become a partner. Roberson said that while the Bar has succeeded at minority recruitment, it also realizes the importance of retention.

Reflecting the growing diversity in race, gender and sexual orientation among the Bar's members, by 2011, a number of "affinity" lawyer organizations with organized local groups that focused on the particular interests of their members had emerged. Independent of the Mecklenburg County Bar itself, they included the long-standing John Sinclair Leary, Sr. Association of Black Lawyers, the Mecklenburg County Hispanic Latino Lawyers Bar, founded in 2008 and the Mecklenburg County Asian Pacific American Bar Association, founded in 2010. In addition, a Lesbian Gay Bisexual Transexual (LGBT) lawyers group was organizing in 2011.

In 2008, the Bar's Special Committee on Diversity created the Julius L. Chambers Diversity Champion Award. The Award, named after its first recipient, celebrates exemplary advocates for the cause of diversity and equal opportunity in the Charlotte-Mecklenburg community. It is presented annually at the McMillan Fellowship Dinner. In its first four years, recipients of the award in addition to Chambers have been George V. Hanna, III, Judge Clifton Johnson and James Ferguson. The Diversity Committee created a summer clerkship program for first-year law students, placing students from diverse backgrounds in corporate law departments and law firms to give then an introduction to Charlotte as a place to live and work.

In 2011, the Mecklenburg County Bar was awarded the American Bar Association's Partnership Award, recognizing its Diversity Day and Lunch With a Lawyer programs. That award salutes bar association projects that seek to increase the participation and advancement of lawyers of color as well as other underrepresented constituents.

In late 2010, one of the leaders in creating the Diversity Committee and the Lunch With A Lawyer program, Superior Court Judge Albert Diaz, was confirmed as the first Latino member of the United States Court of Appeals for the Fourth Circuit.

Among other successes, the Bar's Volunteer Lawyer Program won the ABA's 2004

PRO BONO LEGAL SERVICES WERE OFFERED TO FAMILIES AFFECTED BY THE CLOSING OF THE KANNAPOLIS PILLOWTEX PLANT

Harrison Tweed Award for preserving and increasing access to legal services for the poor. Although the program had been around since 1983, VLP received the award primarily for two new efforts: Pro Bono for Nonprofits and Project PillowTex. The Pro Bono project was the first of its kind in North Carolina. During its first year, it assisted twenty charitable organizations and recruited one hundred lawyers who provided more than 209 hours of legal services, valued at nearly $60,000. Project PillowTex contributed *pro bono* legal services to families affected by the 2000 closing of the PillowTex plant in nearby Kannapolis. It was a collaborative effort with Legal Services of Southern Piedmont and Legal Aid of North Carolina, the latter an organization created to deal with matters that LSSP cannot address because of increasing congressional limitations on the types of cases that legal services organizations can handle using federal funds.

Since the creation of LSSP in the 1960s in partnership with the local Bar, it and the later-created Legal Aid of North Carolina have been the beneficiaries of many thousands of hours and days of *pro bono* services from local Bar members, and local lawyers have also been generous with their dollars to support these programs.

SARAH DARBY AT WORK AT THE LAWYER REFERAL SERVICE DESK

Another of the Bar's early public service programs, the Lawyer Referral Service, is still a viable part of the Bar's agenda. Not long before the centennial of the Bar's founding, the telephone at Sarah Darby's Lawyer Referral Service (LRS) desk in the Bar headquarters rang an average of 45 times per day, evidence that the service was the most visible sign to the public that the Bar existed. The calls seeking legal help ranged from the mundane to the tragic. Someone was evicted, someone was facing a DUI, a man wanted to sue his veterinarian because his dog died. But then a woman called whose husband left her and two young children without any money, not even enough to pay the telephone bill. She was calling from a pay phone. The calls from people in need were not that different from those lawyers had been responding to for generations. Darby patiently explained how the service worked, and if the caller could not afford an initial consultation, she would be referred to the Lawyers Volunteer Program.

"I remember the first time I cried at this job," said Darby, who had been at her post four years. "A woman had been married a long time and she had cancer and her husband just up and left her without any money. She really needed help from a lawyer." Most of the time Darby had no idea how a case was resolved, but there were exceptions.

In 2008, when a man named Mir Mukarram Ali Khan called from Saudi Arabia. He was seeking joint custody of his only son who was living in Charlotte. Darby referred Khan to longtime LRS panel member Steve Ockerman at Wishart Norris Henninger & Pittman. Ten months after Khan's first call to LRS, he walked into Bar headquarters to thank Darby and the LRS staff. Khan emphasized his gratitude in a letter for referring him to "an excellent lawyer who gives a professional and personal touch to his cases. I have just spent my first weekend with my son after seven long years. We had the most wonderful moments."

LRS was not always as successful. In the early 2000s it failed to break even, then lost money. The Bar's executive committee considered shutting it down, but asked the ABA's Program of Assistance and Review to evaluate and recommend changes, which it did in 2002. "It is important to remember that the LRS is often the Bar Association's most publicly visible program," the review stated. "For example, there are not many activities sponsored by the Mecklenburg County Bar that attract almost 7,000 phone calls from the public. An effective lawyer referral program reflects positively on the sponsoring bar association and enhances the reputation of the profession as a whole."

Roberson reflected that providing services to the members and the community is much more important than winning ABA awards. "When we are doing that, we are fulfilling a significant part of our mission. Our Bar members encourage us to take risks and to be creative. This is critical in the changing environment that we face today."

The programs offered by the Bar and the Bar Foundation have continued to grow and to change with the needs of the community. For example, the Coffee Connections program and the Linking Lawyers mentoring programs were developed as a result of the post-2008 economic conditions. These programs were created for all Bar members, including those who were unemployed or in transition and looking for support.

A new strategic plan, a major accomplishment of the 2009 presidency of John W. Lassiter, resulted in the Lawyers as Volunteers program, which includes *pro bono* projects and volunteer opportunities within the Bar and the community. Other events include the Luncheon Series, an informal monthly networking lunch with a local speaker, several diversity projects, and a draft certification process for the Indigent Defense Service Representatives. The Bar has fostered a closer connection to the judiciary, with programs that include informal lunches and formal dinners honoring our state and federal judges. A Juvenile Section and an Immigration and Nationality Section have been added as well.

Roberson observed, "The Bar's mission statement, that we are 'to serve the public and the bar members in improving and preserving the administration of justice and

TODD A. BROWN
2010-11 MCB PRESIDENT

assist the North Carolina State Bar as described by statutory requirements,' is still valid today. I hope we will continue to recognize the privileges and the nobility of the legal profession as we strive 'to promote the highest standards of professionalism, competence and ethical behavior among our members.'"

To reinforce these traditional values, in 2004 the Mecklenburg Bar created the Ayscue Professionalism Award to recognize a current or former member who exemplifies professionalism. Named after the first recipient, it has since honored Julius Chambers, Russell Robinson, II, Joseph Grier, Jr., Chief Justice Sarah Parker, Ray Farris and long-time District Attorney Peter S. Gilchrist, III, and at the time of publication, Kenneth Schorr and Ted Filette, who have devoted their professional careers to the local Legal Service offices.

Despite economic challenges that faced the country and the legal profession, "A look forward offers encouragement," Bar President A. Todd Brown wrote in the first issue of the *Mecklenburg Bar News* for 2011. Brown was especially optimistic about the Bar's ongoing and nationally recognized efforts to promote ethnic diversity within the profession. "It is beyond serious dispute that a diverse legal profession promotes the public's trust in the rule of law, and that a diversity of perspectives leads to better questions, analyses and solutions." As the Bar moved toward the year 2050, he wrote, "It should remain in the vanguard of leaders who will shape the new landscape."

ROBERT C. DORTCH, JR.
2011-12 MCB PRESIDENT

Reflecting on the magnitude of the office he had just assumed, Brown's 2011-2012 successor, Robert C. Dortch, Jr., observed in his first president's column in the Bar newsletter, "We are very fortunate to belong to a strong and respected bar. We can always make it better." Clearly a major item on his agenda, as the Mecklenburg County Bar approached its second century, would be to find a new home – a new Bar Center – to house the Bar's ever-increasing programs that serve both its members and the community.

Epilogue

Inevitably, the history of any organization tends to focus on those who have been its leaders. Theirs are the names reflected in the organization's documents – minutes, meeting notes, files. Theirs are the names that most often appear in its publications and in the public media. Their stories are the most accessible.

In an organization of professionals, however, particularly an organization of lawyers, whose role in society traditionally goes far beyond simply serving their clients, its leaders are only a part of the story. And its leaders themselves often have roles in the profession, in their communities and in the wider world that go far beyond their service to their local bar organization.

Any meaningful attempt to describe the larger role of lawyers who have been a part of the Charlotte-Mecklenburg legal community would in itself require a separate volume. Indeed, there are many lawyers about whom an entire book could well be written. On the other hand, total omission of some mention of this aspect of lawyers' lives would leave a history of the local Bar unbalanced and incomplete.

The local bar has produced seven Justices of the North Carolina Supreme Court, including two Chief Justices, eight Judges of the North Carolina Court of Appeals, at least six Federal District Judges, three Judges of the Fourth Circuit Court of Appeals, including the nation's longest-serving Chief Judge, one Judge of the District of Columbia Court of Appeals and one of the two United States judges at the Nuremberg war crimes trials. It has provided eighteen presidents of North Carolina Bar Association, including its first president, and ten presidents of the North Carolina State Bar. Several local lawyers have served as president of other statewide lawyers organizations. Two have been the North Carolinas State Delegate in the ABA House of Delegates and three have served on the ABA Board of Governors. Two have served as presidents of the American College of Trust and Estate Counsel and one as president of the American College of Trial Lawyers.

In the political arena, the local bar has produced two Governors, two United States Senators and two members of the United States House of Representatives, including one of the first two African American members of that body from North Carolina since the nineteenth century. At the state level, three have served in the North Carolina Senate and one in the North Carolina House of Representatives. Several have served as the state's Attorney General. On the local scene, since 1900, nine members of the Bar have served as mayors of Charlotte (including current mayor Anthony Foxx), two have chaired the Board of County Commissioners, two have served on the post-*Swann* era Board of Education and several have served on the City Council and the Board of County Commissioners.

Few, if any, local charitable, religious or educational organizations have not at some time been led by lawyers. Several have served on boards of trustees or boards of governors of North Carolina institutions of higher education; several have chaired those boards. Several have led national fraternal and religious organizations. Hundreds have served their country in the armed services, including those who have seen active duty in the 2000s in Afghanistan and Iraq, one of whom gave up his seat on the bench to do so.

Two local lawyers have been singularly honored for undertaking the unpopular *pro bono* representation in habeas corpus proceedings of detainees at the United States Naval Station at Guantanamo after the United States Supreme Court found them to be protected by the Geneva Conventions and entitled to hearings to determine the legality of their detention.

Members of the local Bar have been the recipients of innumerable state and national awards, including the Chief Justice's Professionalism Award, the North Carolina Bar Association's John J. Parker, I. Beverly Lake Public Service and Citizen Lawyer Awards and the American Inns of Court Professionalism Award.

Those who made up the local bar from the late eighteenth century through the first three-quarters of the twentieth century would hardly recognize the Mecklenburg County Bar of today. They might find an echo of their own collegial dinner meetings in the performances of the Mecklenburg Bar Revue, a group of lawyers and judges whose performances at local and state bar meetings – and even once at the staid Cosmopolitan Club in Washington, D.C. – poke fun at lawyers, the bar and the community. But they would see a state court system that now has eight local Superior Court judges, nineteen District Court judges and state court personnel whose listings require five full pages in the current Bar membership directory. They would see four local federal district judges, two federal magistrate judges and two bankruptcy judges with a full complement of staff that long ago overflowed from the Federal Courthouse into nearby office buildings. They would see a Bar that now has six seats on the Council of the North Carolina State Bar and a seat in the American Bar Association's House of Delegates.

They would also see a very different set of lawyers, reflected in a front-page newspaper photo of an African American lawyer-mayor emerging from a presidential conference in the White House, in a North Carolina Supreme Court, a majority of whose members are female, presided over by a woman lawyer from Charlotte, in the investiture of a local state court judge as the first Latino judge to sit on the Fourth Circuit Court of Appeals and in the appointment as a federal bankruptcy judge of the first woman to sit as a full-time judge in the local federal court. All of this would have been inconceivable to those of an earlier day.

One would hope, however, that beneath the surface, the lawyers of an earlier day would still see in the lawyers practicing in this vastly changed community the values on which they built their own careers over those many years. After the death of revered Federal District Judge Brent McKnight, the North Carolina Bar Association created the H. Brent McKnight, Jr. Renaissance Lawyer Award. That four of the first five lawyers to be honored with that award were members of the Mecklenburg County Bar speaks strongly to that hope.

And finally, as a link to the distant past, the oldest remaining habitation left standing in Mecklenburg County is the stone house of Hezekiah Alexander, the colonial landowner who brought his kinsman, Waightstill Avery, to that 1769 crossroads village to become its first lawyer.

ROCK HOUSE, HOME OF HEZEKIAH ALEXANDER,
OLDEST REMAINING HOMESITE IN MECKLENBURG COUNTY

AUTHORS' ACKNOWLEDGMENTS

The genesis of this history was the appointment in 2008 of a committee by President Robert Stephens. The work progressed under co-chairmen Mark Bernstein and Ray Farris who gathered material and accepted studies done by a number of members who undertook to focus on particular periods and developments in the history of the legal profession in Mecklenburg County and in the Mecklenburg County Bar, from its formation in 1912 to the present. The writers are indebted to the work of members of the Mecklenburg Bar who took assignments from the committee and gathered both factual and anecdotal material that became a part of this history. Especially useful was material gathered by Deborah Nance on African American lawyers in Mecklenburg County and Scott Syfert's thorough study of the growth and development of large law firms in the last half of the twentieth century. Richard Boner wrote about the Mecklenburg Bar between the Civil War and the early years of the twentieth century while David H. Henderson recounted the World War II years.

The writers also drew upon the privately published memoirs of Fred B. Helms, Ben Horack and other books, such as Sydnor Thompson's *Sydnor Knows The Answer*, Richard E. Thigpen's *90 Years Into The Twentieth Century* and *The History of Kennedy Covington Lobdell & Hickman*. Other general histories helped complete the picture. Especially useful for the early days of the region were D. A. Tompkins's *History of Mecklenburg County* and *The City of Charlotte, from 1740 to 1903* (Observer Printing House, 1903); J. B. Alexander's *History of Mecklenburg County* (Observer Publishing House, 1902); and attorney Julia Alexander's *Charlotte in Pictures and Prose*. A visitor's look at Mecklenburg, Charlotte, and the courts in the mid-nineteenth century was found in the *Autobiography of Rear Admiral Charles Wilkes, U.S. Navy, 1798-1977* (Naval History Division, 1978). Janette Thomas Greenwood's *Bittersweet Legacy: The Black and White 'Better Classes' in Charlotte, 1850-1910* (UNC Press 1994) helped illustrate the lives of early African American lawyers in Charlotte during Reconstruction and the early years of the twentieth century.

Background on the growth and development of Charlotte and Mecklenburg was found in Mary Kratt's *Charlotte, North Carolina: A Brief History* (The History Press, 2009) and *Hornet's Nest, The Story of Charlotte and Mecklenburg County* (McNally of Charlotte 1961) by LeGette Blythe and Charles R. Brockmann. A record of the participation of members of the Mecklenburg Bar in the N. C. Bar Association was found in *Seeking Liberty and Justice, A History of the North Carolina Bar Association 1899-1999*.

We have many other persons to thank for their generous support during the research for this history. We especially want to give appreciation to: Mary Howerton, Nancy Roberson and her competent staff, David Erdman for photos and Rick Rothacker for his book, *Banktown*, about the banking crisis of 2008. The authors also thank the other members of the history committee: E. Osborne Ayscue Jr., Robert P. Johnston, Luther T. Moore, Deborah A. Nance, E. Fitzgerald Parnell III, Claire J. Rauscher, Chase B. Saunders.

COMMITTEE ACKNOWLEDGMENTS

A number of people have been involved in compiling the Mecklenburg County Bar Association History. While it is not possible to recognize all of them, we express special acknowledgement and appreciation to those who made important contributions and helped complete the Bar's history in time for our one hundred-year celebration.

We are indebted to Nancy Roberson, Executive Director of the Bar and the Bar Foundation, and her staff with special recognition to Leah Campbell and Rhea Kelley who worked conscientiously with our committee, providing valuable logistical support. Our fellow Bar History Committee members (E. Osborne Ayscue, Jr., Robert P. Johnston, Luther T. Moore, Deborah A. Nance, E. Fitzgerald Pamell, III, Claire J. Rauscher, and Chase B. Saunders) attended numerous meetings, most early in the morning, and all contributed meaningfully.

The financial underwriting by both the Mecklenburg County Bar Association and the Mecklenburg County Bar Foundation, which has now been reimbursed, was critical in producing this history. For their support and encouragement, we are grateful to Bar Presidents Robert C. Stephens, John W. Lassiter, Patrick E. Kelly, and A. Todd Brown, and Bar Foundation Presidents James R. Bryant III, Claire J. Rauscher, and DeWitt F. "Mac" McCarley, who headed these organizations while we were working on the project. The leadership of the law firms and individual lawyers who contributed to the costs of the project, especially during the depths of the recession, allowed us to proceed.

"OZZIE" AYSCUE
EDITOR-IN-CHIEF

Last, but certainly not least, we express our deep gratitude to E. Osborne ("Ozzie") Ayscue, Jr. who undertook the daunting task of serving as our Editor-in-Chief. Ozzie has been a voluntary Bar historian for many years, preserving articles about lawyers and their work, as well as the work of multiple Bar entities. He has conscientiously kept track of our Bar's programs and the contributions of individual members. As a result, he provided a unique and invaluable insight to our authors and to our Committee. When editing the manuscript, he endured with patience and grace the many comments from the Committee members on both form and content and made only those corrections which contributed to the process. More importantly, Ozzie gave context to growth of the Charlotte region and how contributions by lawyers and the Bar made this transformation more orderly and responsible.

Mark R. Bernstein
Ray S. Farris
Co-Chairs, Mecklenburg County Bar History Committee

MECKLENBURG COUNTY BAR PRESIDENTS

1912-13 C. H. Duls
1913-14 Thomas G. Guthrie
1914-15 Johnson D. McCall
1915-16 Frank R. McNinch
1916-17 J. W. Keerans
1917-18 F. M. Redd
1918-19 Plummer Stewart
1919-20 John M. Robinson
1920-21 Hon. Cameron Morrison
1921-22 Hon. John A. McRae
1922-23 Hon. C. H. Gover
1923-24 Hon. Carol D. Taliferro
1924-25 C. W. Tillett, Jr.
1925-26 Carrie L. McLean
1926-27 James L. DeLaney
1927-28 James A. Lockhart
1928-29 Hamilton C. Jones
1929-30 H. N. Pharr
1930-31 P. C. Whitlock
1931-32 J. Frank Flowers
1932-33 T. L. Kirkpatrick
1933-34 J. Laurence Jones
1934-35 D. B. Smith
1935-36 F. O. Clarkson
1936-37 R. Marion Ross
1937-38 E. T. Cansler, Sr.
1938-39 Fred C. Hunter
1939-40 D. E. Henderson
1940-41 Frank A. McCleneghan
1941-42 W. C. Davis
1942-43 Henry C. Dockery
1943-44 C. A. Cochran
1944-45 James A. Bell
1945-46 Jake F. Newell
1946-47 T. A. Adams
1947-48 William T. Covington
1948-49 J. Spencer Bell
1949-50 W. B. McGuire
1950-51 B. Irvin Boyle
1951-52 Guy T. Carswell
1952-53 Hon. Hugh B. Campbell
1953-54 H. I. McDougle
1954-55 Warren C. Stack
1955-56 J. W. Alexander, Jr.
1956-57 Joseph W. Grier, Jr.
1957-58 Hon. James B. McMillan
1958-59 Hunter Jones
1959-60 Hugh L. Lobdell
1960-61 David J. Craig, Jr.
1961-62 Fred H. Hasty
1962-63 John S. Cansler
1963-64 Lewis B. Carpenter
1964-65 Charles E. Knox
1965-66 Richard M. Welling
1966-67 James E. Walker
1967-68 Benjamin S. Horack
1968-69 David H. Henderson
1969-70 Francis I. Parker
1970-71 Russell M. Robinson, II
1971-72 J. J. Wade, Jr.
1972-73 James O. Cobb, Jr.
1973-74 Lloyd C. Caudle
1974-75 Larry J. Dagenhart
1975-76 John G. Golding
1976-77 Alvin A. London
1977-78 S. Dean Hamrick
1978-79 William E. Poe
1979-80 Robert W. King, Jr.
1980-81 E. Osborne Ayscue, Jr.
1981-82 Francis O. Clarkson, Jr.
1982-83 Hamlin L. Wade
1983-84 Francis M. Pinckney, Jr.
1984-85 Ray S. Farris
1985-86 R. Cartwright Carmichael, Jr.
1986-87 Robert C. Sink
1987-88 Lloyd F. Baucom
1988-89 Melvin L. Watt
1989-90 Alton G. Murchison, III
1990-91 C. Sydnor Thompson
1991-92 Catherine E. Thompson
1992-93 Edgar Love III
1993-94 A. Ward McKeithen
1994-95 Pender R. McElroy
1995-96 Mark R. Bernstein
1996-97 William M. Claytor
1997-98 Judy D. Thompson
1998-99 David B. Hamilton
1999-00 Nancy Black Norelli
2000-01 Mark W. Merritt
2001-02 Robert E. Henderson
2002-03 Frank E. Emory, Jr.
2003-04 George V. Hanna III
2004-05 Jonathan E. Buchan Jr.
2005-06 Hon. Shirley L. Fulton
2006-07 Anthony T. Lathrop
2007-08 Robert C. Stephens
2008-09 John Lassiter
2009-10 Patrick Kelly
2010-11 A. Todd Brown
2011-12 Robert C. Dortch, Jr.

MECKLENBURG BAR FOUNDATION PRESIDENTS

1986-91 Francis I. Parker
1991-96 Hon. Robert P. Johnston
1996-97 C. Ralph Kinsey
1997-2000 George V. Hanna III
2000-02 John W. Gresham
2002-04 Robert C. Stephens
2004-06 Marion A. Cowell, Jr.
2006-08 James R. Bryant III
2008-10 Claire J. Rauscher
2010-11 DeWitt F. (Mac) McCarley
2011-12 Richard M. Thigpen

JUDGES OF FEDERAL CIRCUIT COURTS OF APPEAL

John J. Parker, Chief Judge, Fourth Circuit
J. Spencer Bell, Fourth Circuit
Albert Diaz, Fourth Circuit
David B. Sentelle, Chief Judge, District of Columbia Circuit

JUSTICES OF THE NORTH CAROLINA SUPREME COURT

William H. Bobbitt, Chief Justice
Armistead Burwell, Associate Justice
W. P. Bynum, Associate Justice
Heriot Clarkson, Associate Justice
Francis Iredell Parker, Associate Justice
Sarah E. Parker, Chief Justice
Platt D. Walker, Associate Justice

JUDGES OF THE NORTH CAROLINA COURT OF APPEALS

Hugh B. Campbell, Sr.
Hugh B. Campbell, Jr.
James H. Carson, Jr.
James C. Fuller, Jr.
William E. Graham, Jr.
Clifton E. Johnston
Eric L. Levinson
Sarah E. Parker
C. Sydnor Thompson

GOVERNORS OF NORTH CAROLINA

Cameron A. Morrison
Zebulon Baird Vance

UNITED STATES SENATE

Cameron A. Morrison
Zebulon Baird Vance

UNITED STATES HOUSE OF REPRESENTATIVES

Joseph W. Ervin
Melvin L. Watt

UNITED STATES DISTRICT JUDGES

Robert J. Conrad, Jr.
David E. Henderson
H. Brent McKnight, Jr.
James Bryan McMillan
Robert D. Potter
David B. Sentelle
Frank D. Whitney

MAYORS OF CHARLOTTE

E. M. Currie
Anthony R. Foxx
Thomas W. Hawkins
Thomas LeRoy Kirkpatrick
H. Edward Knox
Johnson D. McCall
Frank R. McNinch
F. Marion Redd
Richard A. Vinroot

GIFTS

LAW FIRM CONTRIBUTORS

PLATINUM

Alston & Bird LLP
Hunton & Williams
James, McElroy & Diehl, P.A.
K & L Gates
McGuireWoods LLP
Moore & Van Allen PLLC
Parker Poe Adams & Bernstein LLP
Robinson, Bradshaw & Hinson, P.A.
Womble Carlyle Sandridge & Rice, LLP

GOLD

Johnston, Allison & Hord, P.A.
Poyner & Spruill, LLP

SILVER

Hamilton Stephens Steele & Martin, PLLC
Hedrick Gardner Kincheloe & Garofalo, L.L.P.
Horack Talley Pharr & Lowndes, P.A.
King & Spalding LLP
Nelson Mullins Riley & Scarborough, LLP
Nexsen Pruet, PLLC
Shumaker, Loop & Kendrick, LLP

BRONZE

Adams Intellectual Property Law
Baucom, Claytor, Benton, Morgan & Wood, P.A.
Culp Elliott & Carpenter, P.L.L.C.
Ferguson, Stein, Chambers, Gresham & Sumter, P.A.
Ruff, Bond, Cobb, Wade & Bethune, L.L.P.
The Law Offices of Swindell & Jones
Wells Daisley Rabon, P.A.
Wishart Norris Henninger & Pittman, P.A.

INDIVIDUAL CONTRIBUTORS

E. Osborne Ayscue Jr.
Mark R. Bernstein
Jonathan E. Buchan Jr.
James O. Cobb Jr.
Marion A. Cowell Jr.
Ray S. Farris Jr.
S. Dean Hamrick
A. Myles Haynes
Josephine H. Hicks
Steve C. Griffith Jr.
Hon. Robert P. Johnston
Anthony T. Lathrop
Pender R. McElroy
A. Ward McKeithen
Luther T. Moore
Deborah A. Nance
Nancy Black Norelli
Russell M. Robinson II
Chase B. Saunders
C. Sydnor Thompson
Catherine E. Thompson
Judy D. Thompson
Hamlin L. Wade

MEMORIALS

Hon. William H. Abernathy
Anonymous

J. W. Alexander Jr.
John O. Pollard

Lelia M. Alexander
Robert C. Hord

John T. Allred
Louise L. Allred

Howard B. Arbuckle Jr.
Corinne A. Allen
Howard B. Arbuckle III

Allen A. Bailey
Tia G. Hartley

Brock Barkley
Anonymous

A. Marshall Basinger II
Mark R. Bernstein
Jane & Gaston Gage

Charles Vincent Bell
Deborah A. Nance

Hon. J. Spencer Bell
Anonymous

H. A. (Jake) Berry Jr.
W. Scott Cooper
Ashley L. Hogewood Jr.

Whiteford S. Blakeney
John O. Pollard

Margaret Marie Bledsoe
Louis A. Bledsoe Jr.
Suzanne & Louis Bledsoe III
Cassandra Harris Tydings

Chief Justice William H. Bobbitt Sr.
Anonymous

William Haywood Bobbitt Jr.
Members of McGuireWoods LLP

William H. Booe
Anonymous

Ruffin Paige Boulding
Deborah A. Nance

Jesse Simpson Bowser
Deborah A. Nance

B. Irvin Boyle
Robert C. Hord

Ray W. Bradley Jr.
Horack Talley Pharr & Lowndes, P.A.

James N. Brennan IV
Donald P. Ubell
Joan M. Waldron

Charles W. Bundy
Anonymous

Armistead Burwell
Armistead Burwell Jr.

James J. Caldwell
Nelson M. Casstevens Jr.

Hon. Hugh Brown Campbell
Leah & Thomas Campbell

John Scott Cansler
Thomas Ashe Lockhart
W. Thomas Ray

Hon. Daphene Ledford Cantrell
Joseph L. Ledford
Jill Ledford Cheek

R. Cartwright Carmichael Jr.
John H. Carmichael
Alice Carmichael Richey

Lewis B. Carpenter
Anonymous

Guy T. Carswell
Carl Horn III

Lloyd C. Caudle
L. Cameron Caudle Jr.
Caudle & Spears, P.A.

Robert Gordon Chambers
Members of McGuireWoods LLP

Gary D. Chamblee
Womble Carlyle Sandridge & Rice, LLP

Stuart B. Childs
E. Osborne Ayscue Jr.

Walter Clark Jr.
Thomas Ashe Lockhart

Hon. Francis O. Clarkson
C. Sydnor Thompson

Justice Heriot Clarkson
Mark R. Bernstein

Claude A. Cochran
H. Morrison Johnston

George C. Covington
Jonathan A. Barrett

William T. Covington Jr.
J. Donnell Lassiter

David J. Craig Jr.
Anonymous

James B. Craighill
Mrs. James B. Craighill

James P. Crews
Mary A. Crews

Hon. E. McArthur Currie
Penelope Alexander Currie
Bonnie Gilbert Currie

Robert D. Dearborn
George V. Hanna, III

Ernest S. Delaney Jr.
Ernest S. Delaney III

Hon. Charles Duls
Mark R. Bernstein
C. Sydnor Thompson

Paul R. Ervin Sr.
Paul R. Ervin Jr.

Joseph John Estwanik IV
His Loving Parents,
Family & Friends
Christopher S. Walker

Francis H. Fairley
Anonymous

Ray S. Farris Sr.
Ray S. Farris Jr.

Henry E. Fisher
Anonymous

Elbert Ellsworth Foster
Beverley Foster Liles
George Randolph Foster

Claude Q. Freeman Jr.
Robinson, Bradshaw & Hinson, P.A.

Hon. Willard Gatling
Claudia Belk

Robert Davis Glass
Deborah A. Nance

Arthur Goodman Jr.
Goodman, Carr, Laughrun, Levine &
Greene, P.A.

C. Hundley Gover
Anonymous

John L. Green Jr.
Luther T. Moore
Paul B. Wyche Jr.

Joseph W. Grier Jr.
James Y. Preston

Joseph M. Griffin
N. Deane Brunson

Hon. Kenneth A. Griffin
Anonymous

Hon. William T. Grist
Anonymous

Thomas Guthrie
Ray S. Farris Jr.

Henry Lee Harkey
Philip D. Lambeth
Henry A. Harkey
Averill C. Harkey
Patricia W. Nystrom

Leon Peter Harris
Deborah A. Nance

Hon. Fred H. Hasty
John H. Hasty

Philip R. Hedrick
Mel J. Garofalo

Fred B. Helms
Members of McGuireWoods LLP

Charles J. Henderson
The Henderson Family

David E. (Zeke) Henderson
The Henderson Family

David H. Henderson
The Henderson Family

Harry C. Hewson
Anonymous

Marcus T. Hickman
Eugene C. Pridgen

John Darwin Hicks
E. Osborne Ayscue Jr.

Robin L. Hinson
Robinson, Bradshaw &
Hinson, P.A.
Weaver, Bennett & Bland, P.A.

Carl Horn Jr.
Carl Horn III

Hon. Clifton E. Johnson
John S. Leary Association
of Black Attorneys
Hon. Kimberly Best-Staton
Hon. Charlotte D. Brown
Hon. Donald R. Cureton Jr.
Hon. Karen Eady-Williams
Hon. Yvonne Mims Evans
Hon. Linwood O. Foust
Hon. Tyyawdi M. Hands
Hon. Donnie Hoover
Hon. Rickye McKoy-Mitchell
Hon. Regan A. Miller
Hon. Calvin E. Murphy

John W. Johnston
Members of McGuireWoods LLP

Hunter M. Jones
Anonymous

Hon. Julia Virginia Jones
Jonathan E. Buchan Jr.

James Foy Justice
R. Michael Eve Jr.
David L. Edwards
Justice, Eve & Edwards, P.A.

Lisa T. Kelly
G. Miller Jordan

Frank H. Kennedy
Clarence W. (Ace) Walker

John P. Kennedy Jr.
C. Sydnor Thompson

Joseph B. Kennedy
Womble Carlyle Sandridge & Rice, LLP

Jack M. Knight
Robinson, Bradshaw & Hinson, P.A.

Charles E. Knox
Allen C. Brotherton
Sherry & James Champion
Lisa G. Godfrey
Edward & Frances Knox
Sandra L. Knox
Peter McArdle
Laura C. Manfreda
Knox, Brotherton, Knox & Godfrey

Thomas G. Lane Jr.
Anonymous

Robert H. Lassiter
Robert W. King

John Sinclair Leary Sr.
Deborah A. Nance

James Buren Ledford
Joseph L. Ledford
Jill Ledford Cheek

Lawrence Glen Ledford
Joseph L. Ledford
Jill Ledford Cheek

Solomon Levine
Goodman, Carr, Laughrun, Levine & Greene, P.A.

Hugh L. Lobdell
C. Richard Rayburn Jr.
Charles V. Tompkins Jr.

James A. Lockhart Jr.
Thomas Ashe Lockhart

Alvin A. London
Nancy E. Walker

Edgar Love III
Penelope D. Love

Ernest W. Machen Jr.
Members of McGuireWoods LLP

Frank A. McClenaghan
James W. Allison

David M. McConnell
Luther T. Moore
Paul B. Wyche Jr.

Susan I. McCrory
Robinson, Bradshaw & Hinson, P.A.

Herbert Irwin McDougle
Benjamin S. Horack

Hon. H. Brent McKnight
Claire J. Rauscher
The Whelpley Family

Hon. James Bryan McMillan
E. Osborne Ayscue Jr.

John A. McRae Jr.
Ralph H. Dougherty
Jameson P. Wells

Neil M. Miller
Robinson, Bradshaw & Hinson, P.A.

Nick J. Miller
George N. Miller
Weaver, Bennett & Bland, P.A.

F. Thomas Miller Jr.
J. Darrell Shealy

James O. Moore
His Partners

William F. Mulliss
Members of McGuireWoods LLP

Douglas P. Munson
Culp Elliott & Carpenter, P.L.L.C.

Walter Brewer Nivens
Deborah A. Nance

Leon Olive
Lee Olive

G. Bruce Park
Theo X. Nixon

Francis I. Parker
John J. Parker III

John J. Parker
John J. Parker III

Past Presidents of the Mecklenburg County Bar and Mecklenburg Bar Foundation
Nancy M. Roberson

Thomas R. Payne
Anonymous

Robert E. Perry Jr.
Former Members of Perry Patrick Farmer & Michaux

Henry Neal Pharr
Henry N. Pharr II
Henry N. Pharr III

Neal Yates Pharr
Henry N. Pharr II
Henry N. Pharr III

F. Grainger Pierce
L. Cameron Caudle Jr.

John G. Plumides
Plumides Law Office, P. C.

William E. Poe
W. Edward Poe Jr.

Hon. Robert D. Potter
Robert D. Potter Jr.
Mary Potter Summa
Anne Potter Gleason

Marvin Lee Ritch
Anonymous

John Mosley Robinson
Russell M. Robinson II

Thomas C. Ruff
Hamlin L. Wade

John Thomas Sanders
Deborah A. Nance

Robert G. Sanders
Frances G. Sanders

Hon. William H. Scarborough
His Colleagues

John Schuber Jr.
Patricia Schuber Terrell

John Small
Anonymous

Ross J. Smyth
J. Norfleet Pruden III

Hon. Frank W. Snepp Jr.
Horack Talley Pharr & Lowndes, P.A.

Warren C. Stack
Richard D. Stephens

Plummer Stewart
Anonymous

Hon. J. Edward Stukes
His Colleagues

Carol D. Taliaferro
William P. Farthing Jr.

Richard E. Thigpen
Richard E. Thigpen Jr.
Richard M. Thigpen

William K. Van Allen
His Partners

James E. (Bill) Walker
Nancy E. Walker

Platt D. Walker
Anonymous

William B. Webb
Will Webb

Maurice A. Weinstein
R. A. Bigger Jr.

Paul C. Whitlock
Anonymous

C. Nicks Williams
United States Attorney's Office
Western District of North Carolina

Henry Hall Wilson III
Jonathan E. Buchan Jr.

William L. Woolard
Anonymous

Thomas Henry Wyche
Deborah A. Nance

John B. Yorke
Members of McGuireWoods LLP

HONORARIUMS

Mark R. Bernstein
Foundation for Judicial Reform

Hon. Hugh Brown Campbell Jr.
Leah & Thomas Campbell

Ray S. Farris Jr.
J. Neil Robinson

Past Presidents of the Mecklenburg County Bar and Mecklenburg Bar Foundation
Nancy M. Roberson

Leroy Robinson
Luther T. Moore
Paul B. Wyche Jr.

ADDITIONAL ACKNOWLEDGMENTS & PERMISSIONS

Page *ii*: Courtouse Orb © Kurt Rindoks; Page *iv-v*: Courthouse Elevation by Louis Asbury, courtesy of UNC-Charlotte, Special Collections; Page *vi-vii*: 1897 Courthouse, Front Entrance © Kurt Rindoks; Page *viii-ix*: "A Compleat Map of North Carolina" courtesy of North Carolina Collection, University of North Carolina Library at Chapel Hill; Page *x*: Statue of Hezekiah Alexander © Leslie Rindoks; Page *xii*: Uptown Charlotte © Kurt Rindoks; Page *xiii*: Waightstill Avery plaque courtesy of David Erdman; Page *xiv*: 1911 Map of Mecklenburg County courtesy of North Carolina Collection, University of North Carolina Library at Chapel Hill; Page 4: Portrait of Heriot Clarkson courtesy of Parker Poe Adams & Bernstein LLP; ; Page 6-7: Fourth Courthouse courtesy of David Erdman; Page 8: "Captain Jack" © Kurt Rindoks; Page 9: First Court Marker by E. Osborne Ayscue, Jr.; Page 10: Andrew Jackson portrait courtesy of Library of Congress, Washington D.C.; Page 11: William Richardson Davie, http://www.northcarolinahistory.org/commentary/115/entry; Page 10: Replica of first Mecklenburg County Courthouse courtesy of David Erdman; Page 15: Hornet's Nest Plaque © Kurt Rindoks; Page 16: detail from 1911 Map of Mecklenburg County courtesy of North Carolina Collection, University of North Carolina Library at Chapel Hill; Page 17: Great Seal of the Confederacy courtesy of Armed Forces History Division National Museum of American History; Page 18: Signers Monument © Kurt Rindoks;Page 20: Zebulon Baird Vance courtesy of North Carolina Collection, University of North Carolina Library at Chapel Hill Page 21: 1869 Rules of the Bar of Charlotte courtesy of the Mecklenburg County Bar; Page 26: Charles Duls courtesy of Parker Poe Adams & Bernstein LLP; Page 34: 1921 Rules of the Bar courtesy of the Mecklenburg County Bar; Page 37: Governor Cameron Morrison and daughter http://ncpedia.org/biography/governors/morrison; Page 42-43: Fifth County Courthouse courtesy of UNC-Charlotte, Special Collections; Page 45: New Law Building courtesy of UNC-Charlotte, Special Collections; Page 48: Ella May Wiggins courtesy of Victor Wiggins; Page 51: Gastonia Strike Pin courtesy of North Carolina Collection, University of North Carolina Library at Chapel Hill; Page 55 Judge John J. Parker courtesy of John Parker; Page 57: Smith Building courtesy of Charly Mann; Page 64: Stuart B. Childs and Jet courtesy of Neil Corbett; Page 66: NurembergTrials judges Francis Biddle and John Johnston Parker courtesy of the Harvard Law School Library, Harvard University, Cambridge, Mass.; Page 67: Plummer Stewart papers courtesy of Duke University Archives; Page 70: Carol D. Taliaferro courtesy of Parker Poe Adams & Bernstein LLP; Page 72: Spencer Bell senior class portrait courtesy of Duke University Archives; Page 81: Bonnie Brae Pettioners courtesy of James Alsop, Mecklenburg County Park & Recreation Department; Page 85: Julius Chambers courtesy of UNC School of Law; Page 88: David Simpson and John Wilson courtesy of Legal Services of Southern Piedmont; Page 95: Legal Service Offices by Leslie Rindoks; Page 96: Bill Walker courtesy of Legal Services of Southern Piedmont; Page 99: James McMillan courtesy of the Mecklenburg County Bar; Page 106: Exterior Julian Chambers office courtesy Ferguson Stein Chambers; Page 106: Interior Julian Chambers office courtesy Ferguson Stein Chambers; Page 109: Supreme Court by Lawrence Weslowksi; Page 111: Correspondence from Judge McMillan to Bill Poe courtesy of E. Osborne Ayscue, Jr.; Page 114: George Daly courtesy of George Daly; Page 120: County's Sixth Courthouse © Kurt Rindoks; Page 121: Judge Clifton Johnson courtesy of Clifton Johnson, Jr.; Page 123: Charlotte School of Law © Paul Purser; Page 126: East Boulevard Bar Center courtesy of the Mecklenburg County Bar; Page 128: Ray Farris courtesy of Ray Farris; Page 129: Mary Howerton courtesy of Mary Howerton; Page 130: E. Osborne Ayscue, Jr. courtesy of E. Osborne Ayscue, Jr.; Page 131: LueAnn Whitten courtesy of the Mecklenburg County Bar; Page 137: Leslie Winner courtesy of Leslie Winner; Page 138: MCB Queen's Road office courtesy of the Mecklenburg County Bar; Page 141: Terence Roche courtesy of Legal Services of Southern Piedmont; Page 142: John "Buddy" Wester courtesy of John Wester; Page 144: Past presidents courtesy of the Mecklenburg County Bar; Page 146: Nancy Norelli courtesy of the Mecklenburg County Bar; Page 147: Catherine Thompson courtesy of the Mecklenburg County Bar; Page 148 Judge Shirley Fulton courtesy of the Mecklenburg County Bar; Page 151: Mel Watt courtesy of the Mecklenburg County Bar; Page 159: Sydnor Thompson courtesy of Parker Poe Adams & Bernstein LLP; Page 173: Skyline Pre-dawn © Paul Purser; Page 174: Bank of America Tower © Paul Purser; Page 175: Wachovia Tower © Paul Purser; Page 184: Nancy Roberson courtesy of the Mecklenburg County Bar; Page 186: Mecklenburg County's Eighth Courthouse © Kurt Rindoks; Page 187: Chief Justice Sarah Parker courtesy of David Erdman; Page 190: Sarah Darby at Work courtesy of the Mecklenburg County Bar; Page 192: Todd A. Brown courtesy of the Mecklenburg County Bar; Page 192: Robert C. Dortch, Jr. courtesy of the Mecklenburg County Bar; Page 193: Window to the Future © Kurt Rindoks; Page 194: Rock House © Kurt Rindoks; Page 199: E. Osborne Ayscue, Jr. courtesy of E. Osborne Ayscue, Jr.; Page 210: Pediment © Kurt Rindoks.

COURTESY OF THE CHARLOTTE OBSERVER

Page 35: Julia M. Alexander
Page 78: John Sinclair Leary, Sr.
Page 79: Thomas H. Wyche
Page 82-83: Black Attorneys
Page 90: Thomas Lockhart
Page 91: November 19, 1966 Headline
Page 98: Benjamin Horack
Page 102: CMS Busing Protestors
Page 104: Joseph Grier
Page 108: William Poe
Page 115: Billy Graham and President Nixon, 1971
Page 122: Charlotte Douglas Municipal Airport, 1975
Page 140: Ted Fillette
Page 149: Mayor Harvey Gantt, 1983
Page 156: Habitat for Humanity Volunteers, 1991
Page 159: Eulada Watt, 1982
Page 161: Padlocked Fire Door, Imperial Food Products Plant
Page 169: Paul Polking
Page 169: Hugh McCall, 1978
Page 170: Ed Crutchfield
Page 171: Marion A. Cowell, Jr.
Page 180: Tumbling Smokestacks in Kannapolis
Page 189: PillowTex Worker Receives Counsel

COURTESY OF NORTH CAROLINA ARCHIVES

Page 46: Loray Mill Trial
Page 49: National Guardsmen at Loray Mill
Page 60: WASPS at Camp Davis
Page 62: Army Mess Hall
Page 80: "We Reserve the Right" sign
Page 112 "Just a Cup of Coffee"

COURTESY OF THE ROBINSON-SPANGLER CAROLINA ROOM

PUBLIC LIBRARY OF CHARLOTTE & MECKLENBURG COUNTY

Page 3: Platt D. Walker
Page 5: Post Office, U.S. Mint and Shipp Monument
Page 13: County's Third Courthouse
Page 23: Temporary Location of First City Hall
Page 24: New City Hall, 1891
Page 28: President Woodrow Wilson visits Charlotte, May, 1916
Page 30: Mayor Thomas LeRoy Kirkpatrick, 1916
Page 31: President and First Lady Wilson, 1916
Page 32: Colonel Macomb and staff at Camp Green, 1919
Page 42: Redd Law Office, 1925
Page 52-53: Belk Brothers Department Store, 1910
Page 59: Charlotte Detectives, 1933
Page 65: Federal Reserve Bank, 1945
Page 74: Shopper at the Square, 1955
Page 76: Second Ward Class of 1927
Page 124: Uptown Charlotte, 1961
Page 166: SouthPark, circa 1980
Page 168: University of North Carolina-Charlotte, 1976

ABOUT THE AUTHORS

Marion Arthur Ellis is a Durham-based writer who has authored or co-authored a number of books, including a 50-year history of the American College of Trial Lawyers, a history of NationsBank (now Bank of America) and biographies of Terry Sanford, Frank Kenan, Irwin Belk and Dean Colvard. A former newspaper writer, he was a member of *The Charlotte Observer* team which won the 1981 Pulitzer Prize for Public Service. A graduate of the University of Missouri Journalism School, he also attended UNC-Chapel Hill on a Ford Foundation fellowship.

Howard E. Covington Jr. of Greensboro, N.C., is a former journalist who has written more than twenty works of history and biography. Earlier collaborations with Marion A. Ellis include *The Story of NationsBank* (1993), a biography of former governor and U. S. senator Terry Sanford published in 1999, and *The North Carolina Century* (2002), a collection of biographical sketches of twentieth-century North Carolinians for the Levine Museum of the New South in Charlotte. Mr. Covington's latest book is *The Good Government Man*, a biography of Albert Coates, the founder of the Institute of Government at the University of North Carolina at Chapel Hill.